The Great War in the Heart of Dixie

The Great War in the Heart of Dixie

Alabama During World War I

Edited by
Martin T. Olliff

THE UNIVERSITY OF ALABAMA PRESS
Tuscaloosa

Manufactured in the United States of America

Typeface: ACaslon

∞

The paper on which this book is printed meets the minimum requirements of American National Standard for Information Sciences-Permanence of Paper for Printed Library Materials, ANSI Z39.48-1984.

Library of Congress Cataloging-in-Publication Data

The Great War in the heart of Dixie : Alabama during World War I / edited by Martin T. Olliff.

p. cm.

Includes bibliographical references and index.

ISBN 978-0-8173-1616-7 (cloth : alk. paper) — ISBN 978-0-8173-5492-3 (pbk. : alk. paper) — ISBN 978-0-8173-8058-8 (electronic : alk. paper) 1. World War, 1914–1918—Alabama. 2. Alabama—History—1819–1950. I. Olliff, Martin T.

D769.85.A2G74 2008

940.3′761—dc22

2008003195

Contents

Acknowledgments vii

1. Introduction: Alabama, April 1917 1
Martin T. Olliff

2. Military Participation at Home and Abroad, 1917–1918 24
Ruth Smith Truss

3. "Tenting Tonight on the Old Camp Grounds": Alabama's Military Bases in World War I 41
Wesley Phillips Newton

4. Alabama's Black Baptist Leaders, the Progressive Era, and World War I 66
Wilson Fallin, Jr.

5. A Call to Arms for African Americans during the Age of Jim Crow: Black Alabamians' Response to the U.S. Declaration of War in 1917 81
David Alsobrook

6. From the Cotton Field to the Great Waterway: African Americans and the Muscle Shoals Project during World War I 101
Victoria E. Ott

7. Mobile in World War I 121
Michael V. R. Thomason

8. The Alabama Council of Defense, 1917–1918 152
Dowe Littleton

9. "Can All We Can, and Can the Kaiser, Too": The Montgomery Cooperative Canning Club 169
Martin T. Olliff

10. World War I: Catalyst for Social Change in Alabama 185
Robert Saunders, Jr.

11. Memorializing World War I in Alabama 201
Robert J. Jakeman

Notes 221

Contributors 261

Index 265

Acknowledgments

Books are collaborative projects; even a single author relies on research assistance, editorial guidance, institutional backing, and support—including an occasional swift kick—from friends and loved ones. By its very nature as a compilation, this work has required the energies and expertise of many more people than if it had been a single-author monograph.

I begin by thanking the authors who have contributed chapters—that herd of cats without whom this volume would not have been possible—for their patience, perseverance, hard work, and expertise. Whatever parts of this work the critics praise belongs to them; whatever flaws the critics find belong to me.

Personally, I thank the former Troy State University—Dothan Faculty Council for the initial funds and inspiration that turned a small personal research project into this book; the editorial staff, unknown manuscript referees, advisory committee, and the University of Alabama Press for guiding this project to completion; and those institutions that have given permission to use their images—the University of South Alabama Archives, the Alabama Department of Archives and History (ADAH), the Archives at the Birmingham Public Library, the Florence-Lauderdale Public Library, the Eufaula Athenaeum, the Museum of Mobile, the Alabama Federation of Women's Clubs, and the Archives of Wiregrass History and Culture. I also thank the *Southern Historian,* the graduate student journal produced at the University of Alabama, for permission to use a modified version of Victoria Ott's previously published article.

The authors and I thank all those who helped us individually and as a group. First are our families, from whom we stole time to research, think, and write. Then there are various mentors and manuscript readers: Leah

Rawls Atkins of Birmingham, Allen W. Jones of Auburn, Timothy Walch of the Herbert Hoover Presidential Library, Ed Bridges of ADAH, Robert J. Norrell of the University of Tennessee Department of History, and Janice Poplau of Birmingham-Southern College. Next we thank the reference geniuses Jim Baggett and Yvonne Crumpler of the Birmingham Public Library; Debbie Pendleton, Norwood Kerr, Frazine Taylor, Cynthia Luckie, Meredith McLemore, and the staff of ADAH; Spencer Howard of the Hoover Presidential Library; Lee Freeman, head of the Local History and Genealogy Department at the Florence-Lauderdale Public Library; Tollef Tollefsen, Jr., of Mobile; Carol Ellis and her staff at the University of South Alabama Archives; and the librarians at the University of Montevallo. Last, and proverbially not least, we thank the University of South Alabama for providing a semester sabbatical to Michael Thomason to pursue his research.

Finally, we thank the now-anonymous computer programmers who devised word processing, image scanning, e-mail, and, for me at least, Spell Check.

The Great War in the Heart of Dixie

1
Introduction
Alabama, April 1917

Martin T. Olliff

On April 2, 1917, President Woodrow Wilson asked Congress to declare war against Germany. He specifically wanted to "take immediate steps not only to put the country in a more thorough state of defense but also to exert all its power and employ all its resources to bring the Government of the German Empire to terms and end the war."[1] Four days later Congress committed the United States to "total war."

Mobilization—the first on such a scale since the Civil War—strained the country's economic, social, and political institutions. The sudden change from a peacetime to a wartime economy led to inflation, hoarding, profiteering, and labor problems. At the national level, America's rail transportation system provides an immediate and tangible example of mobilization-caused economic dislocation. Rail transport was vital to America's mobilization as well as to the ability of the Allies to continue fighting. The railroad was also the largest industry in the United States and had long dominated the industrial economy. In 1917 the United States had 375,000 miles of track, over which 66,000 locomotives pulled 55,000 passengers and 2,500,000 freight cars.[2]

Even before the outbreak of war in April, the rail system bogged down. The lines had not modernized their facilities, had been fighting a rate war with shipping interests, and had lost workers to higher-paid manufacturing employment. In 1916 the British and French dramatically increased their orders for war materiel but were not able to supply enough ships to move it from the United States' eastern ports. Rail managers could neither unload the trains on arrival nor, because of railroad policies that required cars to be filled for return legs, move the empty cars that began to amass at the ports. To complicate matters, the Departments of War and the Navy competed with one another over priority freight and personnel shipments throughout 1917, further tying up rail lines and rolling stock. At the height of the crisis, newspapers reported between 148,000 and 180,000 freight cars short of their destinations. Walter Hines, the director-general of railroads from 1919 to 1920, reported that in May 1917, the worst month of the crisis, 164,000 cars sat idled on the tracks.[3] This situation created a transportation shortage as far away as St. Louis, Chicago, and even Alabama. At a hearing of the Railway Commission of the Council of National Defense in May, Birmingham magnate Henry DeBardeleben claimed that Alabama's economy would suffer if the traffic jam was not cleared quickly.[4] Even so, it was only when the voluntary Railroad War Board utterly failed to ameliorate the crisis that President Wilson federalized the lines in late December. Wilson's secretary of the treasury and son-in-law, William McAdoo, headed the U.S. Railroad Administration and ultimately unsnarled the lines through incentives and command. Although no other sector of the economy reacted to mobilization quite so poorly, the war gave noticeable jolts to them all.

Fighting the war in Europe required coordinating resources on an unprecedented scale and preparing the citizenry for great sacrifice. The federated political system of the United States had almost no experience in accommodating the demands of such a war. Congress took the first tentative steps toward erecting a nationwide mobilization infrastructure in 1916 when it dragooned the secretaries of the Departments of War, Labor, the Navy, Commerce, Agriculture, and the Interior into forming the Council of National Defense (CND) to coordinate war industries. But the CND lacked the political stature to challenge Americans' dearly held notions of limited federal power, nor did it have the muscle to order compliance with its directives from Washington, D.C., as evidenced by its inability to deal with the rail traffic jam in 1917. With little power, the CND set about doing what it could. It replicated itself at the local level, building a hierarchy of state, county, and community branches peopled with local business leaders; then it created a gendered counterpart—the Women's Committee of the Council of National Defense. The declaration of war in 1917 allowed President Wilson to consolidate at least some power at the national level for the duration. He created an entire system of Washington-based bureaucracies that paralleled the CND: the War Industry Board, the War Finance Board, the National War Labor Board, the U.S. Food Administration, the U.S. Fuel Administration, the U.S. Railroad Administration, and the U.S. Shipping Board. Led by, and for the most part staffed by, government and industry volunteers called "dollar-a-year-men" (and women), these bureaus subdivided into task-specific units. The state-level affiliates of the CND coordinated local actions of some of these bureaus, and others worked directly with farmers, citizens, manufacturers, shippers, and labor unions.[5]

Many scholars have examined how the nation as a whole prosecuted the war, but few have considered how Alabama responded.[6] Did the state follow the federal government's lead in organizing its resources, or did Alabamians concoct their own solutions to unique problems they faced? How did the state's cultural institutions and government react to the sudden changes that mobilization produced? How did its economy and way of life cope? What, if any, were the war's long-term consequences in Alabama? How did women, blacks, and poor whites, all without the franchise, support the war to make the world safe for a democracy in which they could not participate? The chapters in this book address these questions and form, the authors hope, a basis for further investigation of the people and institutions of Alabama during this important but understudied era.

These chapters illustrate how Alabamians responded to the war within the limits on their action set by preexisting paradigms, some imposed from without, others from within. How Alabama's militia, renamed the National Guard by the National Defense Act of 1916, organized for domestic and foreign duty fell within the model established by the U.S. Army. That model served the national purpose of prosecuting the war, and local custom had little impact if it deviated from the service's professional culture. The nationally focused needs of the military, coupled with the internal political machinations of Congress, led the army to build training camps and airfields in the state. Here, too, the culture of the military took precedence over local customs in building and operating the reservations. But in many areas—organizing local citizens, coping with dramatic economic changes, carving out public space for women and blacks to act, defining the role of government, and serving memory and identity—Alabamians responded to the Great War bounded by the cultural, social, economic, and political arrangements they themselves had created as of April 1917. These arrangements set the parameters within which Alabama's institutions tried to solve the problems created by nineteen months of war.

Alabama's Cultural "Arrangements"

Alabamians built a culture of inequality in the half-century between the Civil War and World War I. Nowhere was this more apparent than in race relations, where white supremacy became an obsession enforced by white cultural hegemony, law, and, when those failed, vigilantism. Throughout the New South era, white Alabamians struggled with the end of slavery and sought to restrict the social place of free African Americans. Racial attitudes hardened as whites saw their own social status and economic position threatened by the presence of free blacks, even after a new generation of politicians legalized inequality and segregation in the 1890s. Between 1882 and 1930, mobs, mostly whites, vented their anger in a wave of lynchings. Of Alabama's 300 lynching victims in those troubled years, 262 were blacks murdered by white mobs sending the message that white citizens would enforce inequality even outside the law.[7]

Political "redemption" of the state from Republican rule by Democratic victories in 1874 squelched whatever public voice black Alabamians had exercised during Reconstruction, and the constitution of 1875 ensured that the state would do as little as it could to reempower them. For two generations these Redeemers and their successors—called Bourbons by their enemies and Conservative Democrats by themselves—centralized social, economic, and political power in the state legislature dominated by the "Big Mules," a coalition of Black Belt planters and Birmingham industrialists who shared a desire for "low taxes . . . minimal education required by farm laborers and factory workers, no effective labor unions, a small electorate, and racial segregation."[8] Until 1901, the Bourbons kept political power by vote fraud and the shrill rhetoric of white supremacy that drove a wedge between poor whites and blacks. After 1901 the revised constitution made vote fraud and demagoguery unnecessary. It simply disfranchised black voters outright and began disfranchising poor white farmers and workers. It also made white supremacy the law of the land at the polls, in public conveyances, and at the marriage altar.[9]

It is unnecessary to construct a long litany of Bourbon abuse and misrule. The hobbling of public education shows how the state maintained racial inequality. The ambitious—even liberal—but ineffective public education law of 1854 had whetted Alabamians' appetite for state-supported schools. After the Civil War, Reconstruction legislatures tried but failed to create an effective school system for both whites and blacks. The Bourbons who succeeded them, rightly claiming mismanagement and public impoverishment, reduced state fiscal support for public education while restricting localities from levying school taxes. The Bourbons continued to impose governmental parsimony and low taxes even during the relatively prosperous 1880s, ensuring that schools fell further behind in adequate funding. Although educational revenues grew between 1868 and 1891, the total number of schools almost doubled, and per-student expenditures for both races fell from $1.47 to $1.27. Black schools, always abysmally underfunded, were hamstrung even more after the 1891 school law allowed local officials to distribute state funds according to their own judgment. In 1888 officials allocated 38 percent of state school funds to black schools that served 42 percent of Alabama's students. By 1908 the legislature gave black schools only 12 percent of the state's total school funds while requiring them to educate 44 percent of the state's total student population.[10]

Some Alabamians disparaged book learning when doing so served their purposes. Planters who used black laborers and sharecroppers complained that educating blacks ruined them as field hands, and only four of ten black children attended any state school in 1910. Others scorned education when it was hard to come by or was inadequate to advance them in life. Poor whites kept their own children out of school in droves. Average attendance of the school-aged population in the period 1869–1890 varied from 13.4 to 34.8 percent. The 1910 census reported 51.4 percent of school-aged children attended class, though that proportion dropped sharply after age fourteen. Correspondingly, illiteracy rates were astounding. The 1910 census documents that almost one-quarter of voting-age white males were illiterate.[11] Ten years later, Alabama's 16.1 percent overall illiteracy rate made it the fourth least literate population after Louisiana, South Carolina, and Mississippi. Trailing Alabama, but still with illiteracy rates above 10 percent in 1920, were New Mexico, Georgia, Arizona, North Carolina, Virginia, and Tennessee.[12]

The Political Economy of Agriculture

Alabama's economy both reinforced and mirrored its culture of inequality. Farming prevailed throughout the state, even near urban areas, setting the boundaries within which Alabama's other institutions could act. Plantation-sized land holdings worked by freed tenants rather than gangs of slaves predominated in the Black Belt while yeoman farmers in the Wiregrass and Tennessee River valley rented or sharecropped to replace their lost land or to supplement their small holdings. King Cotton had resumed its reign, planted across the state despite an overall decline in price between Reconstruction and the Great War. Cotton prices teased farmers in that half century, starting out rather high immediately after the Civil War, declining until they revived in the late 1890s, and then resuming a steady drift downward. By 1914, in fact, the price of cotton had fallen to 7.35 cents per pound, significantly lower than its nominal 1869 price of 16.5 cents per pound. The 1914 harvest brought less than the 12.2 cents per pound it might have commanded if only corrected for deflation.[13] These economic arrangements—rebuilding of plantations in the Black Belt, inadequate small holdings in the northern and southern tiers, and dependence on continually less-valuable cotton—exacerbated poverty, powerlessness, and racism for the majority of Alabamians. The state's economic structure kept black farmers under the thumb of a powerful elite in the Black Belt and kept white farmers too poor and divided to become a successful countervailing force against the elite "Big Mule" political coalition that emerged in the state.[14]

The cotton monoculture not only wreaked havoc on its market price but also set the stage for radical changes in the state's agricultural mix as time passed. By World War I, cotton cultivation was wearing out the land even in the fecund Black Belt; farmers were able to make the 1914 crop only by record use of costly fertilizer. Furthermore, overcultivation opened the door to the ravages of the Mexican boll weevil after 1910. The weevils spread rapidly from the initial infestation in Mobile County across the southern half of the state, laying waste to the cotton in their path. Farmers had resisted pleas to vary their crops and even responded to the plunge in cotton prices by planting more, but the weevils and war finally drove many to diversify. Melon farms, strawberry fields, and truck farms sprang up in the state's southwestern counties and in the Sand Mountain area of North Alabama. For example, in Baldwin and Mobile counties between 1909 and 1919, sweet potato production rose by 68 percent, pecan harvest by 300 percent, and orange yields by an astounding 3600 percent. The Wiregrass counties of southeast Alabama made their storied switch from cotton to peanut cultivation on land cleared by timbering and made arable by commercial fertilizers.[15]

Wiregrass peanuts, a million acres of which grew in 1918, were not a direct consumer product until Tuskegee Institute's George Washington Carver's experimental successes of the 1930s. Farmers fed "goober peas" to livestock, the market for which grew because of the war. Between 1914 and 1918, cattle production in Alabama increased by 57.5 percent, and hog production rose 145 percent, with most of the increase occurring in areas hit hardest by the weevil.[16]

By the time the boll weevil pressured farmers to diversify, the state had taken its first steps to modernize farming. The federal Morrill Act of 1862 and its extension in 1890 provided land grants by which the states could fund college instruction in agriculture and mechanics as well as the traditional liberal arts. Alabama split these funds—at least those that were not lost to mismanagement—between the white Alabama Polytechnic Institute (API) at Auburn and the black Alabama A&M College in Normal. The federal Hatch Act of 1887 funded agricultural experiment stations and basic research. By combining Hatch Act funds with a small tax on commercial fertilizer and, after 1907, direct appropriations, the Alabama legislature created experiment stations under the auspices of API.[17]

Agricultural research began to pay off by 1900 when, as historian A. B. Moore notes, "a number of trained agriculturalists had been developed, a considerable percentage of farmers had been led to improve their methods and a scientific agriculture was clearly taking root."[18] The state's racially segregated land-grant colleges, its Department of Agriculture, and the experiment stations developed an assortment of flyers, pamphlets, and news articles, the articles for use by the rapidly expanding network of weekly newspapers.[19] But most farmers did not trust new methods or were unable to get or understand the research. To the colleges, the solution seemed obvious—explain the research to the farmers in practical and understandable ways and encourage farm families to apply their new knowledge. Implementing this required more time and more federal money.

Each summer between 1890 and 1915, the white agricultural faculty at API and the black faculty at Tuskegee Institute held weeklong on-campus training institutes, gave local lectures, conducted demonstrations, and addressed agricultural fairs. In 1908, J. J. Doster of the University of Alabama suggested that faculty inaugurate "extension work" through boys' corn clubs and girls' tomato-canning clubs. The Alabama legislature appropriated money to start such clubs and to hire the state's first full-time county demonstration agents three years later. The Smith-Lever Act of 1914 gave federal money to expand this state program, and the Smith-Hughes Act of 1917 provided vocational and home economics teachers for rural schools. With the rudiments of federal-state cooperation providing enough money for support, county and home demonstration agents became the leading edge of Progressive Era reform and uplift in rural Alabama.[20]

Economic insecurity and debt kept most of Alabama's rural population from practicing "book farming" and, in fact, forced many to continue planting cotton regardless of price, soil depletion, or weevil infestations. The structure of farm indebtedness in Alabama was a relic from the capital-poor Reconstruction era that bound tenant farmers tightly to tradition, buried them in poverty, and made them afraid of change. By 1910 mortgage indebtedness amounted to almost one-third the value of farmlands. But an even larger problem was short-term loans for supplies and seed, the infamous crop-lien system. Lenders—banks, landowners, and furnishing merchants—demanded that tenants plant cotton, the state's principal cash crop. Even after the Federal Reserve Act of 1913 made capital more available and the national government created land banks in 1916, the crop-lien system stifled crop diversification throughout Alabama and the South.[21]

Crop lien was only the financial mechanism of farm tenancy. Tenancy as a generational institution first emerged in the turmoil of Reconstruction as a way to control the agricultural labor pool of newly freed blacks. For their part, these former slaves defined freedom in terms familiar to Jeffersonians and Jacksonians: they detested the old gang system of slave labor and wanted to avoid close supervision by farming their own lands as much as possible. Without capital to buy farms, many freedmen, and ultimately many former Confederates, had to accept the compromise of sharecropping or cash tenancy. Of Alabama's reported 262,901 farms in 1910, owners operated 39.5 percent, and tenants worked 60.2 percent. This arrangement fell heaviest on African Americans, who operated 60 percent of tenant farms by 1910 though they made up only 51.4 percent of Alabama's rural population.[22] Poor whites fell prey to this arrangement when they failed to acquire enough money to purchase land during the long depression of the late nineteenth century. They operated 40 percent of tenant farms by 1910, and though they tended to be better off than their black neighbors, white tenants were unable to change significantly their crops or methods.[23]

Industrialism

Agriculture dominated the economy, but Alabama's New South boosters promoted industry to supplement it. Extractive industries such as timber harvesting and mining (coal, iron ore, and limestone in particular) complemented the manufacturing of cotton textiles, pig iron, cast-iron pipe, rail cars, and a few consumer durables.

Timber harvesting, lumbering, and turpentine distilling thrived from Mobile to Dothan and provided off-season work and cash incomes for local farmers. It was such a dynamic part of the South Alabama economy that Marie Bankhead Owen's 1938 textbook, *Alabama: A Social and Economic History of the State,* called the region the "Timber Belt." The lumber and timber industries employed almost one-third of all Alabama industrial workers and made up 54 percent of the state's total business concerns in 1909. Turpentine and rosin manufacturers added another 5 percent to both totals. The nation's voracious appetite for lumber denuded the pine forests south of Montgomery. Annual production exceeded one billion board feet and opened vast tracts of land to cotton, peanuts, and livestock husbandry.[24]

The cotton textile manufacturing industry offered an alternative to farm life for many white workers as well as profits for mill owners. Between 1880 and 1909, local investors and New England textile companies drawn to Alabama's expansive cotton fields, emerging rail and water transport system, and nonunionized white workforce had erected forty-five new mills, making textiles the state's second industry in value of goods produced. Advances in steam engine technology allowed textile mills to concentrate in existing towns, particularly Huntsville, Anniston, Opelika, and a complex of mill villages in Chambers County. After 1895, investors erected mills in more rural areas—Talladega, Walker, Wilcox, and Houston counties. Together these mills employed more than thirteen thousand workers by 1900, a number that remained the same nine years later.[25]

But it was the coal and iron industry of the southern Appalachian foothills that led Alabama to become the most industrialized Deep South state by the eve of the Great War. Deposits of coal, iron, and limestone in unusual proximity had excited New South boosters and launched a burgeoning pig iron industry from Tuscaloosa through Calhoun counties. Industrial booms and busts followed in close succession after 1880 as entrepreneurs raced to open mines, furnaces, railroads, and the dozens of businesses required to make useful goods from pig iron and to support the workforce. Many of these businesses failed in the panics of 1893 and 1907, but others were scooped up by giant holding companies such as Tennessee Coal and Iron (TCI) and, later, U.S. Steel. By 1909 Alabama's furnaces, foundries, machine shops, railroad shops, and coke ovens employed one-quarter of the state's industrial workers and accounted for 43 percent of the gross value of all industrial products made in the state.[26]

Industry begat towns and cities throughout post-Reconstruction Alabama just as trade and local government had in an earlier era. The 1910 census lists 270 incorporated places in the state. Twenty-six had more than 2,500 residents, making them cities according to Census Bureau definition. Alabama boasted seven cities with populations over ten thousand by World War I of which only three—Mobile, Montgomery, and Selma—had long antebellum roots. Three others—Gadsden, Bessemer, and Anniston—were as much products of industry as were the iron pigs they cast, the railcars they made, and the cloth they wove.[27]

The seventh city, Birmingham, was Alabama's industrial and urban hub. It sprang from the dreams of mineral wealth and the outright chicanery of postbellum boosters, incorporating in December 1871, with a population slightly above nine hundred. Alabama's industrial boom of the 1880s turned the hamlet into an industrial giant—called the "Magic City," "Pittsburgh of the South," or, because of its reputation as the murder capital of the world, "Bad Birmingham." By 1890 it boasted more than 26,000 residents, and by 1910, partly as a result of annexations that occurred four months before the census, its population crested 133,000.[28]

Rapid industrialization put tremendous strain on Alabama's rural, racially segregated culture by introducing an urban, class-based dynamic that had to be accommodated. Industrial workers were fresh off the farm, even after World War I, and they brought their rural traditions and worldviews with them. In town they ran headlong into a reality sculpted by industrial capitalism. Racial politics stirred the mix. Cotton mill workers were almost universally white, but coal and iron workers tended to be black, particularly in the low-skilled jobs. Birmingham's founders had dreamed that their new city would become a "Negro Eden," making cheap iron based on low labor costs, but most employers there wanted to hire white workers. Industrial leaders tried many ways to entice skilled white workers to the city—except pay satisfactory wages. In 1882, for example, they considered building a textile factory to employ white workers' wives and children, thereby offering a larger total family wage than was available in most other iron-making centers. Their plans fell through. After 1900, Birmingham's industrial managers changed tactics; they specifically advertised for white workers throughout the eastern United States and Europe. Though employers offered racial fealty as a bulwark against the strife of class consciousness that was emerging in other mining and iron regions, white immigration did not meet their labor needs. So bowing to necessity, mine and furnace operators hired blacks, at least for the lowest-skill, lowest-wage work. As white workers continued to avoid Birmingham's mines and mills, a few blacks advanced slowly and unevenly into semiskilled and skilled jobs before the war.[29]

Between 1890 and 1908, the imperatives of industrial capitalism led some workers to challenge white supremacist ideology in the Birmingham district, but most white workers supported the racial caste system. Skilled white workers organized craft unions and affiliated with the American Federation of Labor (AFL). The AFL tried to build parallel unions to prevent industrialists from using blacks as strikebreakers, but this tactic succeeded only marginally. Company owners exploited the unions' own segregated organization to drive a wedge between workers. Spurred by their own racism and supported by the rampant Jim Crowism that infected almost the entire white population of the state, white ironworkers did their best to bar blacks from skilled jobs until the demand for labor after 1914 forced companies to train African American workers. When the AFL resumed organizing Birmingham's foundries during the war, skilled black workers considered the union itself a threat to their improving economic status.[30]

The United Mine Workers (UMW) and its successor, the United Mine Workers of Alabama, tried a different strategy in the coalfields and ore mines. The UMW organized in January 1890, and that April the Miners' Trade Council of Birmingham joined it as District 20—representing black as well as white locals. Henry DeBardeleben and other mine operators sorely tested the union's commitment to racial cooperation in that year's strike by importing black strikebreakers. Defeated, the union languished until October 1893, when workers organized the biracial United Mine Workers of Alabama. This bold experiment survived in the face of the brutal 1894 strike, increasing racial tensions, and cyclic economic calamity until the disastrous strike of 1908 broke the UMW of Alabama and gave the coal operators unrivaled control over the industry. Only in 1917 did the national UMW attempt another organizing drive in the Birmingham district. Like the AFL's attempts to organize anew, the UMW drive petered out after the 1920 strike.[31]

Besides employing racial animosity to break the unions, employers attacked with outright suppression, welfare capitalism, and convict labor. To squash the coal strikes of 1894 and 1908, for example, mine owners persuaded Governors Thomas Goode Jones and B. B. Comer, respectively, to call out the state militia. During respites from the intermittent warfare of strikes, industrialists continued pressuring the unions. In 1901 they organized the Alabama Coal Operators Association to impose the open shop, and in 1903 they won an antiboycott law that effectively criminalized the unions' most effective strike tactic.[32]

The employers' ruthlessness drove some of their highly skilled workers to northern mines and factories prior to the Great War, leaving behind a large pool of untrained laborers whose inexperience ate away at company profits. To combat the emigration of skilled workers and the inefficiency of their replacements, U.S. Steel brought in George Crawford in 1908 to manage its TCI subsidiary and implement a new company welfare system. Crawford's program differed greatly from that of other Birmingham bosses. He wanted to entice workers to greater effectiveness rather than crush them beneath the company's power. Crawford surveyed working conditions in TCI's mines and factories as well as living conditions in its villages. He hired professionals to implement reforms, employed teachers for company-subsidized schools, and engaged social workers to improve housing and recreation. Crawford's welfare capitalism and improvements in the national economy reduced TCI's labor turnover rate from 400 percent in 1912 to 13.3 percent in 1929. Regardless of this success, the only other major employer in Birmingham to implement any kind of welfare capitalism was John Eagan's American Cast Iron Pipe Company (ACIPCO). In 1921, well after World War I, this company shared its profits with workers and provided pensions, medical services, insurance, housing, cooperative stores, a bank, and recreational facilities.[33]

Welfare capitalism worked for TCI, but most coal and iron operators filled mine jobs through the horrendous convict lease system. Convict lease began in 1846 when the state legislature privatized the prison. Drs. Meriwether Moore and Fleming Jordan leased the prison in 1852 and installed its first industry—a ropewalk and bag-making factory—using prisoners as labor. In 1858, Dr. Ambrose Burrows bought the lease and even opened a store in Montgomery to sell prisoner-made shoes, sashes and doors, blankets, and blinds. The leasing of individual prisoners to businesses began in 1875 as Alabama struggled with a debt crisis. By the following year, the state cleared a profit of at least $11,000, thereby ensuring the system's continuation.[34]

Virtually enslaved and in almost limitless supply, convict laborers provided not only a large pool of labor but also an effective counterforce to unionization. Coal mines received the most prisoners and the most attention from unsuccessful reformers, but convicts also worked in the lumber and naval stores industries, marble quarries, gravel pits, and plantations. Regardless of multiple safety and fiscal scandals as well as a long series of investigations, Alabama halted convict leasing only in 1928, the last state in the nation to do so. Convict lease was a constant reminder to workers that powerful white entities would use even the legal mechanism of the state to secure their positions within the state's overall culture of inequality.[35]

Progressivism in Alabama

Alabama's preexisting social and economic order was resilient in the face of industrialization, but a new force arose in the 1900s to challenge it, albeit weakly. In the countryside, agricultural extension agents proselytized farmers and tenants in favor of uplift, scientific farming, prosperity, and reform with encouraging results. In the cities, industrialization added a small but active body of managers to the nascent middle class composed of merchants and professional men—lawyers, physicians, ministers, and occasionally teachers. This middle class challenged traditional social structures in an attempt to find a place for itself and gave birth to the Progressive movement for which the era immediately preceding World War I is named. Progressivism in Alabama was weaker than its northern counterparts and just as fragmented into sometimes-contradictory factions, but Progressives generally sought to uplift the weak and poor, rein in the worst excesses of the powerful, reduce some kinds of social inequity, encourage good government as an agent of human welfare, promote the benefits of expertise, and generally remake society to conform with their own morality and ethos.[36]

Progressivism in Alabama and across the South expressed itself in three interconnected ways—through attempts to impose social control, drives to make government efficient, and humanitarianism. Though it was part of the nationwide reform impulse, southern Progressivism had deep roots in its native soil. Historian Dewey Grantham notes that the Progressive movement was more indigenous than Radical Reconstruction and "less disruptive and more successful" than Populism, for southern Progressives proposed only a few assaults on industrial prerogatives and filtered their goals through the region's peculiar single-party political institutions and racial obsession.[37]

Progressives believed in good government, meaning the exercise of "responsible citizenship" by powerful businesses, government officials, the general electorate as a body, and private individuals. To them, laws and regulations were the most effective means of promoting this ideal. The story of railroad regulation in Alabama illustrates how Progressives used legislation to control rapacious businesses while the story of the disfranchisement of African American voters in the 1901 constitution documents their support of the racial caste system in the name of good government.

Progressives also believed that government should play a role in protecting the weak against the strong. In Alabama, regulating railroad freight and passenger rates became a talisman of Alabama's political progressivism between the 1880s and the Great War. The Railroad Commission Act of 1881 created a three-member board with the right to recommend rates but without enforcement power. The commission weakened even from that, particularly in 1885 when commission chair Henry Shorter refused to consider rate regulation, then in 1890 when Louisville and Nashville attorney Thomas Goode Jones became governor, and finally in 1898 when the United States Supreme Court ruled that intrastate rate regulations were illegal.[38]

Advocates of railroad regulation became stronger as the commission itself weakened. In 1890 cotton farmer, Anniston merchant, and Birmingham textile magnate Braxton Bragg Comer joined the movement to give real power to the Alabama Railroad Commission. By 1903 Comer led the most important regulatory pressure group and in that year succeeded in making the commission elective. He rode that success and his election as the commission's chair to the governorship in 1906. Comer's first legislature (1907) passed nineteen of his twenty regulatory bills—empowering the Railroad Commission, setting freight and passenger rates, and punishing any railroad that appealed to the federal courts. The railroads sued, and the legal warfare lasted another six years. In 1913 the state won, but seven months passed before Governor Emmet O'Neal and the railroads reached a workable compromise on rates and appeals.[39]

The battle for railroad regulation opened the door for the Progressives' larger regulatory agenda. Believing that plutocracy threatened good government because politicians were corruptible, Comer's Progressive 1907 legislature forbade state and local officials from taking free railroad passes, defined corrupt solicitation in an antilobbying law, and restrained corporations from partisan political participation. The legislature also took aim at the venality inherent in the way most local officials were paid. City and county officials paid themselves from the fees and fines they levied. The 1897 *Code of Alabama,* for example, lists thirty-nine distinct fees for circuit and city court clerks, including ten cents for filing any papers, fifteen cents per one hundred words to make copies, and thirty cents for entering judgments. Probate judges received sixty-eight fees in addition to a small salary, and justices of the peace and sheriffs received a salary plus the proceeds of thirty-four fees. Citizens widely assumed that these officials worked the system to their own advantage. The 1907 legislature converted much of the fee system to payment by salary and required officials who collected fees to turn all proceeds over to the county or city general fund.[40]

Demonstrating the limits of Alabama's prewar political progressivism, the 1907 legislature and its successors failed to attack other systemic problems in government or to regulate corporations beyond setting railroad rates. The Progressives' abbreviated political clout was a product of their uneasy partnership with the Big Mule coalition, which they needed to gain power and which they sealed by disfranchising black voters in the constitution of 1901. By that time, according to Sheldon Hackney's chronicle of this sad episode, Black Belt whites had grown "tired of the burden of controlling the Negro vote" and feared the "real Negro power" that the Populist revolt of the 1890s had exposed. They demanded government action. Progressives, for their part, rejected the "organized electoral fraud" by which planters controlled the black vote and wanted a formal way to purge the electorate of this corrupting paternalism. Frank S. White, whom Hackney called the "organizational genius of Alabama Progressivism," summed up the Progressives' goal: black voters were "disfranchised years ago by fraud and the purpose now [of the constitutional convention of 1901] was to do it by constitutional enactment." So Progressives, in exchange for Black Belt support for Progressive candidates, gave Black Belt politicians enough votes in the constitutional convention to strip blacks of their political voice.[41]

Progressive reforms addressed more than good government, railroad regulation, and responsible citizenship. Progressives had great sympathy for the plight of the poor and weak within the boundaries set by the color line. White Progressives wanted to uplift whites; black Progressives wanted to uplift blacks. Alabama's women Progressives, who otherwise had minimal access to public policy discussions, found their voice in conducting humanitarian campaigns. They focused on issues that appeared to be extensions of their private, long-established, caregiving roles: cultural enhancement, education, aid to the poor, improved working conditions for women, restriction of child labor, reform of the penal system for women and juveniles, and, after 1910, Prohibition. Of course many—though not all—Alabama women Progressives sought the right to vote as a tool to gain greater leverage in the public world.[42]

Although we remember many individuals who were active in the Progressive Era, most reform efforts were the work of organizations. Men founded professional societies and chambers of commerce in the late nineteenth century, but their individual access to political power forestalled the same rush to organize that affected Alabama's middle-class women after 1890.

The Alabama Federation of Women's Clubs and the Alabama Federation of Colored Women's Clubs were the archetypal organizations for Progressive women not only in their statewide and local affiliates' agendas but also in their institutional trajectories. In the late 1880s and early 1890s, elite white women in the most prominent Alabama cities created study and literary clubs for social support and intellectual stimulation. In 1895, six of these clubs from Birmingham, Montgomery, Selma, Tuscaloosa, and Decatur allied into the Alabama Federation of Women's Clubs (AFWC), the fourth such state organization in the nation, primarily for the purpose of cultural exchange. Later, these clubs and the federation itself added Progressive reform to their literary and cultural programs. The number of local clubs grew apace; by 1915 the AFWC claimed 153 affiliated clubs and 4,250 individual members.[43]

Black women formed their own organizations at the local, state, and national level. As they did in the highly visible white clubs, middle-class women led the black clubs; but unlike the white clubs, most of the black clubs' general members were working, poor, and rural women. Montgomery's Ten Times One Is Ten Club formed in 1890, and five years later Margaret Murray Washington, wife of Booker T. Washington, organized the important Tuskegee Woman's Club. In 1899 Washington served as founding president of the Alabama Federation of Colored Women's Clubs and in 1914 took the reins of the National Association of Colored Women.[44]

From their inception, African American women's clubs actively supplied much-needed social services to their communities. Washington's Tuskegee club, for example, improved neighborhood and home life among the hundreds of destitute and uneducated tenants and convict laborers on the Russell plantation in Macon County. The club taught Sunday school, held sewing classes, organized a plantation mother's club, and led both a boys' club and men's reading club. Members built a plantation school and maintained its teachers until the state absorbed it in 1907 and then later took over Tuskegee Institute's night school, where they taught 103 reading classes. Providing for industrial education as well, the club taught cookery classes to women who would use their education to improve their own families or gain employment as domestic help for white families. No uplift work was too trivial for the Tuskegee Women's Club. Its members regularly cleaned, decorated, and provided reading materials for Tuskegee's segregated railroad depot waiting rooms.[45]

The Alabama Federation of Colored Women's Clubs had an active agenda, too. It created a boys' reformatory at Mt. Meigs in 1907 and supported it until 1912, when it transferred ownership to the state. The federation campaigned for years to build and fund a Girls' Rescue Home, a Progressive dream it realized only in 1921. In the intervening years the federation and its affiliates established kindergartens, worked to extend the school year for black children, sought to separate youthful offenders from adult criminals in jails, campaigned for literacy, and established the Big Sister movement.[46]

White women's clubs also created programs to ameliorate the plight of the poor and helpless. In keeping with the Progressives' ethos of responsible citizenship, white women's clubs advocated school reform and improvement and waged long campaigns for compulsory attendance, literacy, manual training, home economics training, and kindergarten. Lura Harris Craighead, president and chronicler of the AFWC, founded the Alabama School Improvement movement in 1905 as a project of the federation. The movement spread rapidly because of its interest in "the betterment of their [communities'] schools and bringing together the home and school." By 1907 the movement became an independent association with three hundred to five hundred local chapters. An accurate count was impossible because chapters organized so rapidly.[47]

Supporters of school improvement believed they were making great strides forward. In 1915 state voters adopted a constitutional amendment allowing counties to levy local school taxes, and the legislature made women eligible to serve on school boards, passed a compulsory attendance law, and opened the way to create county boards of education run by full-time, professionally qualified superintendents. But this was not enough. The wartime draft revealed embarrassingly high rates of illiteracy among young men, and in 1918 Hastings H. Hart of the Russell Sage Foundation reported that Alabama trailed every other state in financial support for its schools. Education reformers were shocked and mortified to learn just how little they had actually accomplished.[48]

Club women were much more successful in their campaign to establish a statewide Boys' Industrial School as an alternative to incarcerating juvenile delinquents with hardened criminals. Elizabeth Johnston, wife of Governor Joseph Johnston, built such a school in Birmingham's East Lake area in 1900, and Judge N. B. Feagin, who almost single-handedly created Alabama's first juvenile justice system, provided its first nine inmates. When the school's population overstrained its resources, local clubs took up the campaign for county-level institutions. Local clubs maintained their crusades even during the war. In one instance of success, the women's clubs of Montgomery succeeded in gaining county support for their local Boys' Industrial School during the spring of 1918, thus illustrating the common characteristic of women-led reforms in Alabama—state and local reforms mirrored one another in substance as well as method.[49]

Substantial numbers of club women realized that reform required access to political power that came only with suffrage. After failing to gain the vote in the 1901 constitution, the women's suffrage movement languished until statewide prohibition failed in 1910. Seeing that women's political action was necessary to secure Progressive reforms, the movement organized the Birmingham Equal Suffrage Association and the statewide Alabama Equal Suffrage Association. Local literary and service clubs split over the issue in the state suffrage campaign of 1915 and the national campaign of 1916–19, leading prominent women such as Marie Bankhead Owen of Montgomery to organize their own group, the Southern Women's Anti-Ratification League. Alabama hardly participated in the wartime suffrage campaign because its legislature met quadrennially. Alabama women were unable to push suffrage through the 1915 session, the last before the Great War, and when it met again in 1919, the legislature refused to act on the Nineteenth Amendment to the U.S. Constitution. Alabama accepted women's suffrage as a fait accompli after other states ratified it in 1920.[50]

So this was the economic, social, and political landscape of Alabama in April 1917. Widespread poverty, illiteracy, tenancy, and debt stalked farmers, while low wages, racism, paternalism, and the battle against unions oppressed industrial workers. The Big Mules found themselves in hock to the world they had created and were stung by not only the resentment of the poor but also the disdain of the rising middle class. But beneath all that was a spark of reform, part of the greater Progressive movement that inspired the ambitions of that rising middle class, particularly women. This spark quickened toward 1917 as reformers fought for social order, business regulation, good government, uplift, succor for the poor and weak, and their own hegemony.

The Chapters in the Book

The urge to "pitch in" to the war effort turned that spark of Progressivism into a flame of organizational activity on the one hand and startled reaction to change on the other. The war intensified trends that were present in Alabama's multifaceted and frequently contradictory culture. Though some of those trends fizzled out with the return of peace, others continued into the 1920s and beyond. Prosecuting the war demonstrated the efficacy of a number of distinctly modern lines of thought. It showed that racially divided cities could come together in pursuit of common goals and that women could improve their communities by public action. It showed that federal largess could expand the local and state economy. It showed that forward-looking government, providing at least some services for the people themselves, improved life in the state. The Great War, then, was a pivot on which Alabama turned, with limited success, from a nineteenth-century culture fixated on the Civil War and Reconstruction and the elite-dominated economy and society of the New South toward a twentieth century of increased governmental activity, technology-driven economic growth, and social space for women and African Americans to pursue their interests. The chapters that follow examine how Alabamians responded to the pressures and changes brought on by the Great War, but with a single caveat: singly and collectively, they are not the final word on any of the points raised. Their authors merely want to initiate a discussion; so much of this era remains unexplored that they can only point the way. Nevertheless, their work is important because the era itself is important. As political economist Marc Allen Eisner writes, the great change in political development in the twentieth century was inaugurated not by the New Deal but in the effort of Americans to manage the home front in World War I. These chapters extend Eisner's observations to Alabama and to events beyond politics.[51]

Military historian Ruth Smith Truss makes a close study of how Alabama's four militia regiments mobilized for war. She follows each regiment as they guarded transportation infrastructure at the beginning of the war, their conversion into National Guard units, their training for modern warfare, their subsequent incorporation into the American Expeditionary Force, and their actions while in France. One regiment, the old 4th Alabama Infantry, became the 167th Regiment of the 42nd (Rainbow) Division, and men of the other regiments joined it or the 31st (Dixie) Division. The 167th acquitted itself well in combat between February and November 1918. Its Alabama men received fifty-four medals—including one congressional Medal of Honor—and commanders cited 167 men of the regiment for their performance.

Military mobilization was impossible without semipermanent installations to house and train soldiers. Wesley P. Newton, best known for his work on Charles Lindbergh and on Montgomery during World War II, examines Montgomery's Camp Sheridan and Taylor Field and Anniston's

Camp McClellan. He describes their physical plants, different missions, and postwar fates and traces the local and national political maneuvering that surrounded each facility's inception and growth. Newton also discusses how the local and "Yankee" troops stationed at each camp interacted with townspeople as well as how the town governments coped with the influx of soldiers and workers that doubled the cities' populations and areas.

Wilson Fallin, Jr., opens an important conversation about the persistence of racial inequality in Alabama. Shunned by the politically powerful, Alabama's African Americans formed a vibrant, segregated culture with the church at its center. Naturally, church leaders held important positions of power and respect in the segregated communities. Their opinions about, and responses to, the Great War significantly affected overall efforts to mobilize the home front. Because of their denominational preponderance in the state, black Baptist leaders were especially important. They believed in the promise of American democracy and called on the African American community to support the war effort fervently. They also insisted that the U.S. government reward such support with the return of civil rights. Fallin concludes that the actual beginnings of the civil rights movement of the twentieth century began with these calls for full citizenship.

David Alsobrook looks at three interlocking trends in race relations in wartime Alabama—the fear and suspicion of the white community concerning its black neighbors, the activities of both religious and secular black leaders to ameliorate that dangerous suspicion, and the reactions of the black community itself to mobilization and the war. Whites irrationally feared the black community at the beginning of the mobilization emergency. Paradoxically, many whites prepared for black insurrection fomented by German agents while they simultaneously bewailed the exodus of African Americans in the so-called Great Migration. On the other hand, many African Americans, though heavily conflicted about their lives and opportunities in the South, demonstrated their commitment to home and hearth by constantly pledging loyalty and fully participating in rallies, Liberty Loan drives, and conscription. Paralleling Fallin's chapter about religious leaders, Alsobrook examines the rising expectations of black troops about the prospects of attaining equality when they returned from Europe. He notes that those hopes were dashed quickly, subordinating blacks once again to white cultural hegemony. According to Alsobrook, "white public officials, civic boosters, and journalists" in the

1920s interpreted for their own benefit the experience of blacks during the war. He calls on historians to correct that inauthentic interpretation with concentrated research in the underused papers of prominent black leaders, as well as the records of the National Association for the Advancement of Colored People (NAACP) and federal agencies.

Much of white Alabama's racial animosity is aggravated by competition with blacks for limited economic resources. Perversely, this continues even in flush times. The war-related industrial boom created economic opportunities for rural and underemployed urban labor. Two related federal projects—the massive nitrate plants at Muscle Shoals and the construction of the Wilson Dam on the Tennessee River—provided good jobs for Alabamians. But Jim Crow worked on these projects and lived in the close-by towns of Florence, Sheffield, and Tuscumbia. Victoria E. Ott examines the discrimination at work and in town that black laborers hoped they had left behind as well as how their segregated community supported their efforts to gain respect. Like Fallin, Ott locates the origins of the twentieth-century civil rights movement in the response of World War I black workers to the crippling legalized inequality they could not overcome even after good wages lifted them from abject poverty.

Cities throughout the state were hotbeds of patriotic activity and economic growth during the war's nineteen months, but none had so much to gain from war-driven infrastructural improvements as Mobile. Michael V. R. Thomason chronicles the critical growth of Mobile's waterfront as city and state projects expanded its port and revived the shipping power it had lost to New Orleans. He discusses the temporary growth of the shipbuilding industry upriver from town and how the city was barely able to accommodate the rapid influx of workers these ventures brought with them. Thomason also examines how the city's racially segregated communities paralleled one another in supporting the war effort, as well as how rapid postwar deindustrialization left the city with many half-finished projects and few prospects for their immediate completion.

Governments and private associations at the federal, state, and local levels worked in tandem to support the war effort. President Woodrow Wilson tried to "keep our boys out of war," but in 1916 agreed to a nationwide "Preparedness Campaign." Congress reorganized the army and expanded the navy, and the president created a council of advisors—the Council of National Defense—to coordinate mobilization if necessary. Dowe Littleton tells the story of the council's state affiliate, the Alabama Council of Defense, created by gubernatorial decree in April 1917.

Launched between quadrennial legislative sessions, the Alabama council spent its first year trying to construct itself and raise operating funds, without much success. Only with its June 1918 reorganization did it begin to function effectively, and then only in cajoling farmers into planting foodstuffs, raising Liberty Loans, and spreading patriotic propaganda. Nevertheless, in a state with little tradition of coordinated effort, Littleton makes it clear that the Alabama Council of Defense became something of a model for interaction between government and the private sector.

Martin T. Olliff focuses his study not on governmental actions at the state or even city level, but on the response of Montgomery's women's clubs to the need, as they saw it, to preserve the bounty of victory gardens in order to keep escalating food prices from leading to hunger. Elite white women formed the Montgomery Cooperative Canning Club, sold stock, erected a factory, and preserved and sold thousands of cans of fruits and vegetables. These women used the emergency of war to transcend their socially assigned place in life, even though they had no greater ambition than to do something helpful for their neighbors. When other projects and opportunities for service, such as assistance to the soldiers at Camp Sheridan or work in conjunction with national organizations such as the Red Cross presented themselves, club women allowed the cannery to languish, and it closed with a whimper as they took on other challenges.

What long-term impact did this short war and its frantic home-front activities have on the lethargic institutions of Alabama? Robert Saunders, Jr., examines the state's public health system to argue that reformers made substantive gains only after army physicians rejected large numbers of Alabama draftees because of preventable diseases such as pellagra and hookworm. Alabamians had reveled in the Old South myth of military might—"one Reb can whip ten Yankees"—and were mortified when so many did not measure up to the minimum standard. In consequence, the public changed its view of the role of government, rejecting the hard-core laissez faire of the nineteenth century in favor of the state government taking greater responsibility for public health and education. This ushered in more than twelve years of Progressive reform. Saunders posits that had it not been for the state's experiences during the war, the people of Alabama would have settled for a continuation of the political and social status quo. In that regard, World War I provided a true watershed in Alabama history—second only to World War II—in ushering in long-lasting and substantive improvements.

Finally, how did Alabamians, who even today pride themselves on stubbornly holding on to their memories, remember and honor their sacrifices in this short war? Robert J. Jakeman analyzes the efforts of Thomas McAdory Owen and his widow, Marie Bankhead Owen, to construct the War Memorial Building that served as both a commemoration of the doughboys and the headquarters of the Alabama Department of Archives and History (ADAH). Thomas Owen, ADAH founding director, conceived the idea for the War Memorial shortly after the armistice, but his sudden death in 1920 delayed the project for a generation. His widow, the politically connected Marie Bankhead Owen, succeeded him as ADAH director, but accomplished her husband's vision only after she obtained Works Progress Administration funds in the 1930s. Alabama's War Memorial Building was as much a monument to Owen's memory as to the memory of the soldiers who served in the war. Ironically, its dedication in 1940 occurred on the eve of the United States' entry into the next world war. That war changed Alabama once again.

2
Military Participation at Home and Abroad, 1917–1918

Ruth Smith Truss

When the United States entered World War I, Alabama's standing military organization, the National Guard, became the core of training and recruiting efforts in the state. Although they were only a minority (about 5 percent) of the total number from Alabama who eventually served in World War I, these Guardsmen alone retained cohesiveness and unit identity as Alabamians. They generally acquitted themselves well during the World War I years, in service both at home on guard duty and overseas on the battlefields of Europe.

Alabama's National Guard, as most states' guard units, had been on Mexican border duty for several months in 1916 and early 1917 as part of the United States' attempt to deal with the problems associated with Francisco "Pancho" Villa. In April 1917 these Guardsmen remained on active duty but anticipated returning to their civilian lives soon. However, at 3:45 p.m. on April 6, the Eastern Department of the U.S. War Department notified officials at the Alabama National Guard's mobilization camp in Montgomery that a state of war existed with Germany. Military commanders then cancelled demobilization orders and retained the National Guard troops in service.[1]

On May 18 the War Department notified Alabama adjutant general G. J. Hubbard that guard units were to recruit to "maximum strength," provide as much training as possible, and complete medical examinations and vaccinations.[2] In response, National Guard recruiters covered every section of the state. They placed posters in post offices, giving information on the organizations that needed men and whom to contact.[3] In Mobile the First Infantry Regiment held a mass meeting in Bienville Square every evening "to stimulate recruiting." The regimental commander, Colonel

F. M. Maddox, hoped that many recruits could be secured if Guardsmen attended these meetings and suggested to civilians that "the recruiting office [was] just across the street."[4] Once he had "thoroughly worked" and "practically combed" all of the Mobile area for recruits, Maddox sent recruiting parties into the southern and western Alabama counties of Washington, Choctaw, Sumter, and Pickens. The Second and Fourth Infantry regiments likewise worked in other areas of the state to recruit the men needed to bring their units to war strength.[5]

Medical officers examined the recruits for physical fitness to regular army standards. The rejection rate was generally 25 to 30 percent. For example, from April 1 to June 15, doctors examined 841 men at the mobilization camp. Of these, 572 (68.01 percent) qualified while 269 (31.98 percent) failed. The most common reasons the doctors gave for rejecting these recruits were being underweight or having venereal diseases (gonorrhea and syphilis), "bad teeth," tuberculosis, or heart diseases.[6]

Once accepted, recruits received the required series of vaccinations and began their training. The First Infantry had three levels of "recruit companies"—recruit, junior, and senior—through which the new men progressed on the basis of their work over the course of three to four weeks of training. The training schedule for the morning hours usually included forty-five minutes each of physical drills, school of the soldier (during which the men learned their duties as individual soldiers), foot movements of bayonet exercises, and instruction in rifle use—target sighting, elevation, and windage—as well as thirty minutes in rifle nomenclature class. Afternoon lectures for the first six days covered such topics as personal hygiene and venereal diseases, military courtesy, the Articles of War, army rations and pay, and care of equipment and assemblage of a pack. The second week's lecture topics covered camp sanitation, army regulations, care of feet, esprit de corps, and the infantry in war. After the second week the men practiced guard duty, receiving instructions on walking their posts and performing interior and exterior guard duty, and learning the general and specific orders of a sentinel posted for guard duty. When they made sufficient progress, recruits received assignments to established companies. Usually, company commanders ordered an additional two weeks' special instructions for these new men.[7]

While recruiting efforts went on, the War Department ordered most veteran Alabama Guardsmen to begin guard duty at specified locations around the state. Military and civil officials worked to establish acceptable guidelines for such duty and to deal with requests for assistance that came from every part of the state. The initial duty of the Alabama National Guard was to protect structures essential to transportation in the state, such as bridges, locks, and tunnels. The emphasis was on protection of property rather than on safety of individuals. The War Department instructed Guardsmen to repress and deal "sternly" with acts of violence "inspired by disloyalty or sedition," including opening fire on anyone attempting to damage property under their protection.[8]

Designation of guards for a structure depended on the structure's importance in ensuring the smooth flow of traffic in Alabama. National Guard commanders consulted officials from railroads and other public utilities on the distribution of troops. Consequently, the majority of the men guarded railroad bridges such as those that crossed the Perdido River between Alabama and Florida and the Chattahoochee River between southeastern Alabama and Georgia. Troops also guarded several of the larger plants of the Alabama Power Company in the northern region of the state, particularly those in Birmingham, Gadsden, and Anniston.[9] Montgomery's Camp Sheridan continued as the central headquarters for the Alabama National Guard during the period of guard duty.

Only in an emergency would the Eastern Department allow troops to guard private factories such as munitions plants; in such a situation Guardsmen would be used as a reserve if a concerted attack on the plants occurred. Troops were not to serve as watchmen—providing security guards was a responsibility of the plant itself.[10] Department policy notwithstanding, National Guard commanders received many requests to furnish guards for various factories and public utilities. The mayor of Birmingham asked for a guard at the water filtering plant. One company argued that its plants and warehouses containing 267,000 bales of cotton were an "invaluable" government resource and thus eligible for guards. Requests for troops also came from a munitions plant, the port city of Mobile, the duPont magazines around the state, the Pratt Cotton Mills in Prattville, and the Troy acid plant and water works.[11]

The federal government honored some of these requests for troop protection of private property, but in return imposed certain requirements. In April the commander of Camp Sheridan, Brigadier General Robert Eugene Steiner, wrote to the mayor of the central Alabama town of Clanton, the sheriff of Chilton County, and an official of the Alabama Power Company asking for their help to stop the sale of alcohol to men guarding Alabama Power Company property near Clanton. The commander noted that such sales were "detrimental" and likely to provoke trouble between the troops and citizens. The vice president of Alabama Power replied that he and local authorities were trying to stop liquor sales and that they hoped to succeed eventually.[12]

The government also made several requests of railroad companies, the largest benefactors of troop protection of private property, which generally cooperated. Railroads provided Alabama National Guard officers with transportation passes when travel was necessary to their duties and established telephone communications in some areas so detachment commanders could communicate promptly with their headquarters.[13]

If the railroads complied too slowly with military requests or refused to do so, National Guard commanders complained directly to railroad executives or regular army officers. For example, the government required railroads to distribute supplies and water at the points under guard.[14] Occasionally, conductors refused to stop the trains. At such times, the railroad crews simply threw supplies from the moving train, often resulting in damage to packages. Disregard for the soldiers and the prearranged stops sometimes had more serious consequences. Major T. C. Locke, adjutant for the commander of the state's mobilization camp, complained to the Western of Alabama Railway when train No. 2 had "refused to stop at a bridge," forcing Guardsmen to carry a sick comrade two miles to the next station to place him on a train to be taken for treatment. Reminding the Western's passenger agent that troops benefited the railroad, the major noted that in emergencies it was "absolutely necessary" that trains stop at the prearranged points. In some cases, a refusal to stop could "mean the loss of a man."[15]

Between April 7 and May 15, 1917, Alabama had 2,971 of its 3,500 Guardsmen on duty around the state. The remaining men were assigned to Camp Sheridan—the mobilization camp in Montgomery—to train new recruits, maintain headquarters, care for the animals, and perform other duties as necessary.[16] The First, Second, and cavalry regiments stayed on duty approximately three months—April, May, June, and the first days of July. The Fourth Infantry was out only two months, from April 7 to June 7.

With some exceptions Alabama's four regiments divided the state among themselves. The First Infantry guarded the wharves, dry docks, and shipping facilities of Mobile as well as the railroad bridges over the Tombigbee and Cahaba rivers in the western and southern regions of the state. Troops who rotated out of duty in the hinterlands or who were assigned to stations in Mobile itself quartered at the First Infantry's headquarters on the grounds of Mobile's Gulf Coast Fair Association. When not standing guard the troops drilled. This regimen operated effectively. On April 19 the federal inspector reviewed the First Infantry, reporting that Colonel Maddox had placed no unnecessary guards and had guarded all places of importance in the area. His opinion was that Maddox and the First Infantry troops deserved praise for "prompt and efficient performance." Nevertheless, troopers did not always execute their duties rigidly. Troops stationed at bridges over rivers took fishing poles with them, although their commander insisted that men fished only during their off-duty hours, and a guard in Bay Minette severed a communications wire while shooting at what he thought was an alligator.[17]

But guard duty was a serious and potentially dangerous occupation. On May 18 a train hit and killed Private John Creel while he was on the Louisville and Nashville Railroad bridge over the Dog River. A board of inquiry determined that the accident happened "in the line of duty."[18] At 12:30 a.m. on May 19, Private Ellis DeWinter fired twice at an unidentified man who attempted to enter the grounds of the Mobile and Ohio Railroad Shops at Whistler, Alabama. The private fired after the man refused an order to halt, but apparently he missed. The man disappeared.[19] Unfortunately for Henry J. Mathews, Corporal C. C. Windham was a better shot; Windham killed Mathews on the Mobile and Ohio docks. Mathews, a black man, had also failed to halt as ordered.[20] The First Infantry obviously intended to obey its orders from the War Department to fire on any person acting suspiciously.

The First Infantry troops also performed duties unrelated to guarding transportation facilities in the state, duties not mentioned by the War Department. On May 11 the captain with Company B in Bay Minette was asked to retrieve a French poodle named Rags, which a private had taken from the owner. The captain reported to Colonel Maddox on May 24 that the "French Poodle Dog was returned to its mistress on May 22nd 1917." With both patriotism and a sense of humor, the captain noted: "Owing to the Nationality of the Dog I directed that exceptional care be taken in perfecting its safe delivery."[21]

Maddox issued strict orders to the troops quartered at the city fairgrounds to respect and protect the Gulf Coast Fair Association's property. He also forbade the soldiers to enter private homes or grounds around the camp. The custodian of the fairgrounds and buildings praised the good behavior of the troops during their three months in Mobile. He and his family lived on the grounds and had a vegetable garden in the yard, including a watermelon patch. According to this custodian, no soldier had been the "slightest" inconvenience to his family.[22] Presumably, the custodian was satisfied that the soldiers had resisted the lure of the melons.

Others were not so happy with the First Infantry. Several reports of disorder by soldiers at Monroe Park in Mobile appeared in a state newspaper. The Mobile police chief notified First Infantry Headquarters that he would "arrest every man in uniform" to curb the disorders, of which he had five complaints. Maddox's superior suggested that these episodes be kept out of the newspapers if possible and to take prompt disciplinary action if it was warranted.[23]

Another complaint concerned soldiers from the detachment at Flomaton who were drunk and disorderly in the lunchroom of the railroad station.[24] The assistant superintendent of the Louisville and Nashville Railroad Company also complained to Maddox of First Infantry troops riding trains when unauthorized to do so. The L and N night yardmaster at Mobile reported that thirty-five soldiers tried to board a train in Mobile, but the railroad official refused them at the gate. One soldier "[went] round back way and got on." When the flagman asked for his ticket, the soldier touched his gun and said, "Here it is." The yardmaster also complained that at night he had trouble with soldiers at the depot. Some were drunk and "lying around" while others walked "around with their knives open." He feared trouble unless the situation was remedied. The superintendent asked Maddox to prevent a recurrence, but he also requested that the colonel not punish the men because they "had been in the habit of riding as they pleased," adding that railroad officials were, "no doubt, somewhat to blame" for the incident.[25]

Maddox himself complained about his officers in Mobile. Some officers attended formation at reveille and then returned to their quarters to sleep. The commander noted that these officers had been in the military "long enough to know" that such action was improper. The problem, he decided, was that the officers spent too much time in town at night. Maddox then ordered all officers to be in camp by taps, unless specifically permitted otherwise; henceforth, permission from his headquarters was required to leave camp.[26]

The necessity for Maddox's order reflected that the city of Mobile provided a variety of distractions and amusements for the men, the majority of whom lived in the area. Some entertainment encouraged a martial spirit among the soldiers and civilians. The Mobile League of American Pen Women held a "Patriotic Song Festival" and invited the First Infantry troops to attend. The Empire Theatre featured "Womanhood," a "special moving picture," with a patriotic theme.[27] All in all, the First Infantry had plenty of entertainment opportunities to help the men enjoy themselves during their guard duty in south Alabama.

The Second Infantry stood duty in Birmingham and north Alabama, though two of its companies guarded bridges in Memphis, Tennessee, and its supply company remained in Montgomery.[28] One company guarded Camp McClellan in Anniston in northeastern Alabama. As construction of Camp McClellan progressed, the guard increased to battalion strength. Other companies guarded bridges belonging to the Frisco Railroad at Jasper and Cordova, north of Birmingham, and one squad protected the New River Steel Railway bridge northwest of Carbon Hill. The federal inspector wrote that the manner in which the Alabama troops performed guard duty "agreeably surprised" him.[29] He found officers and men interested, "zealous," and "efficient" in their work. The Second's commander maintained military élan through physical conditioning drills, and he ordered all company commanders to provide other drills and instructional classes as needed.[30]

The inspector particularly praised the "excellent" work of the troops of Companies A and D who guarded the Harahan's and Frisco's Mississippi River bridges in Memphis. Major Carl H. Seals, commanding this detachment, gave his men strict instructions. Only soldiers on duty had permission to be on the bridges. Any other person on the bridge had to have a written pass from the Rock Island Railroad officials countersigned by Major Seals. Hoboes on trains were to be arrested and turned over to civil authorities. Sentinels were cautioned not to converse with anyone except in the line of duty and were to prevent loitering by anyone crossing the bridges. Seals ordered the troops to direct "particular attention" to the bridge piers. The object of the guard was to prevent damage, and anyone who damaged or attempted to damage the bridges should be shot instantly. In late April the mobilization camp commander heard a rumor that a box containing dynamite was found under the Harahan bridge and wrote to Seals asking whether the rumor was true and, if so, why Seals's men had not found the dynamite. Seals replied that the rumor was unfounded and that his men were "strictly on the job." He added that they, too, heard "of a great many things happening that never happen." A few days later Seals reported that dynamite had been found under a small trestle within the city limits of Memphis, outside of his jurisdiction. He suggested that that incident probably accounted for the rumor.[31]

Twice in late April 1917, Seals's men fired on persons on or near the bridges. On April 22, about 9:00 p.m., someone approached the southwestern end of the Frisco bridge trestle and did not stop when ordered to do so. Two sentinels "fired one shot each at the object and it disappeared." Seals reported that his investigation suggested that the object, fifty to seventy yards away, was a man. Seals closed the matter. At 10:00 p.m. on April 25, sentinels again fired shots at "parties" near the bridge. The parties "hastily withdrew."[32]

In June, Seals reported another problem with a man wanting to cross the river. He came first to the Harahan bridge and then to the Frisco bridge, insisting that he "would cross and that no one could stop him." One sentinel pointed his gun at the man, who then threatened the sentinel with an iron rod. A second sentinel knocked the man to the ground with the butt of his rifle, fracturing the man's arm. A third soldier helped the others hold the man to deliver him to the local civil authorities. Wrote Seals: "The man is evidently crazy."[33]

Though they obeyed well when on duty, Second Infantry troops, like those of the First, caused their commander problems by riding trains to visit Birmingham and other points without permission. Soldiers apparently believed that because they guarded the railroad, they were entitled to rides whenever their off-duty time allowed. Birmingham, like Mobile, offered attractions that few soldiers wanted to resist. The regimental commander posted a provost guard in Birmingham to enforce his order against such activity.[34]

The Fourth Infantry performed its assigned guard duty in eastern Alabama. Several guards protected the Western of Alabama Railway's bridges at Line Creek and Cubahatchie Creek near Tysonville and at Euphaubee Creek near Chehaw and the Central of Georgia's bridge over the Tallapoosa River.[35] On April 18 a detachment from Company M had "quite a little battle" at the Tallapoosa River bridge. At 8:15 p.m. the sentinel challenged someone standing approximately thirty yards from the bridge. The person ran into the woods, and the sentinel and a corporal who was inspecting the guard each fired one shot at the man. Fifteen minutes later, two or more persons appeared in the same area. When challenged, they ran in the same direction as the first man. Two sentries fired six shots. At 9:00 p.m. the same people again appeared near the bridge and refused to halt on order by a sentry. Again the soldier fired. The "unknown persons" ran approximately fifty yards into the woods and fired four shots at the sentries. The soldiers then fired nine shots, and the persons escaped by motorboat. The soldiers were unhurt and so, apparently, were the "unknown persons." The captain of Company M strengthened the guard and cautioned his men to remain alert at all times because the bridge was vital as a direct line for shipping coal to the coast.[36]

The cavalry guarded bridges over the Warrior River and Big Sandy Creek near Tuscaloosa and other railroad property near Gadsden and Anniston, including the tunnel at Tumlin's Gap. Like their fellow Guardsmen, sentinels at these posts had difficulties with accidents and intruders. On April 17 Private John T. Martin accidentally shot Private John C. Austin in the side. The two men were cleaning their pistols when Martin's gun discharged. Austin, the victim, insisted that the incident was "purely accidental" and that Martin was more upset about it than he was. Austin traveled to St. Luke's Hospital in Anniston for treatment, although the wound was not serious.[37]

Private Avner Jones, on duty at the Tombigbee River bridge near Epps, was less fortunate. On May 22, between 11:00 p.m. and midnight, Jones was killed by a passing train. A board of inquiry decided that Jones was on his post and was sober and that his death occurred in the line of duty. The train that passed over the bridge while Jones was on duty was unscheduled. According to the testimony of a railroad employee, the engineer did not blow the whistle while on the bridge, only when on the trestle. Two Guardsmen who relieved Jones at midnight found his body, which had been decapitated. His head was eighty-five yards up the tracks.[38]

On April 21, at 2:20 a.m., sentinels at the Warrior River bridge exchanged shots with four men who, according to railroad officials, were tramps trying to steal a ride. No one was injured in the incident.[39] Two days later, on the Big Sandy Creek bridge near Tuscaloosa, Private Fred Campbell shot and killed John White, a black employee of Vrendenburg Saw Mill Company. Two sentinels were on post, Campbell and Private Marion Roberts, and both men gave similar accounts of the incident. According to Roberts, Campbell called three or four times to White to halt, but White continued coming onto the bridge. Campbell said, "Stop, I don't mean any foolishness." The two guards began firing, and White walked another two or three feet toward them, then jumped off the track and "started under the bridge." Roberts and Campbell each fired again, and the soldiers saw White fall. The squad commander investigated the shooting and reported that White lay near the end of the bridge. He judged from the bullet's path that the victim faced "almost directly towards the sentinels at the time he was shot."[40]

Complying with War Department regulations, the commander immediately arrested the two sentinels so that the military could retain control of the case. The men understood that the confinement was not a punishment; rather, they were commended for carrying out their orders. Their commander reported that the two privates had acted within the scope of their orders. The Tuscaloosa County coroner examined the body and attached no blame to the sentinels. On the coroner's advice, cavalrymen buried White's body and marked the gravesite. The two privates were soon released from confinement and restored to duty.[41]

Difficulty exists with any attempt to draw conclusions from the shooting incidents. Most of those on whom soldiers fired were never identified. The two men killed were both African Americans. In the case of Mathews in Mobile, no time of day was noted. In the case of White, the time was 2:20 a.m., too dark for soldiers to identify race—indeed, in other cases, the soldiers were not certain that the "object" on which they fired was even a person. The sources fail to indicate why White was on a railroad bridge at 2:20 a.m. Even less information is available for the case of Mathews.[42]

Guard duty lasted only a few weeks. On June 7 the Fourth Infantry received orders to begin the return march to Camp Sheridan. The First and Second Infantry and the First Cavalry regiments followed a month later. All units, except the two companies in Memphis, marched to Montgomery. Depending on where they had been stationed, the men marched as few as 4 miles to as many as 238 miles. Most groups averaged ten to sixteen miles per day.[43]

When the men returned to Camp Sheridan, Brigadier General Steiner took charge of the state's troops.[44] The inhabitants of Montgomery immediately involved themselves with the soldiers in camp. The Montgomery Library Association invited the men to "make the library their headquarters" while in town and to borrow books for use in camp. The Alabama School Teachers Association asked for sixteen men to act as escorts for their members who planned a tour of the capitol and grounds. The City of Montgomery asked for a volunteer to dress as Paul Revere at a patriotic meeting and parade. A Second Infantry lieutenant volunteered to be the "dashing" Revere, complete with "suitable costume." The committee asked the Fourth Infantry band to provide music and invited all officers "to ride at the head of the column" with the governor, the mayor, and the speakers in automobiles provided for the event.[45]

Steiner concerned himself with all aspects of camp life. He worked with the civilian contractors and public utilities to improve Camp Sheridan's conditions, including drainage, electricity, and construction of mess halls.[46] The camp had only poor streetcar services into the city—one hour or longer for a round trip. Some officers had private automobiles, but the mainstays of transportation were horses, mules, and wagons. By May 18 the camp had 2,598 men in the three infantry regiments alone. The cavalry regiments and the medical corps, which consisted of one ambulance company, four sanitation companies, one field hospital, and one camp hospital, added to that number, as did recruitment. By July more than four thousand troops were in camp. In June the camp bakery's average daily output was 950 pounds of bread. One regimental hospital required a minimum of 160 pounds of ice per day. And the camp had approximately sixteen hundred horses and mules to stable and feed.[47]

The camp commander focused attention on the officers. Steiner required them to attend all formations with their men and to sleep within the camp limits. Quoting a maxim of Napoleon's—"If you expect to get any results out of your Army you will have to Bivouac with it"—Steiner made it clear that he expected both professional attitudes and actions from his officers toward their service. He encouraged conservation of food, noting that the shortages would "soon become serious in this Country" and that the War Department would eventually implement its own orders to curb waste. By acting immediately, Alabama's troops would avoid trouble later.[48]

Steiner also wanted his men to dress neatly. He complained to commanders about enlisted men who went about camp and the city with unbuttoned shirts and rolled sleeves and threatened disciplinary action. Soon afterward he required all officers and enlisted men to wear their uniforms whether on or off duty. Enlisted men, in fact, could not have civilian clothes in their possession.[49] Before leaving the camp on a pass, enlisted men reported to an officer or noncommissioned officer for inspection of appearance. The Southeastern Department required "strictest compliance" by officers to the regulations on military appearance, correct uniform, careful saluting, and proper conduct in public as an example to enlisted men. The officers were to insist on the prescribed salute in every case where a salute was required. Any offender would be corrected, if possible; if not able to correct at the time of the improper conduct, the officer was to report the man to his commanding officer.[50]

Guardsmen also received specific instructions regarding their conduct outside camp. Some men called taxis to transport them to town; others rode in private automobiles. Steiner soon issued an order forbidding men to "ride on the outside of automobiles." After receiving complaints that some men carried their guns into town and used them "carelessly," Steiner commanded the men to leave in the camp all firearms and ammunition.[51] He also prohibited troops from "visiting houses of prostitution," noting that such action cast a "slur on the uniform." The military police, identified by a blue band with "MP" worn on the upper left arm, worked with civil authorities to maintain order among the soldiers. The military police enforced curfews, arrested drunk or disorderly soldiers, and reported to civil authorities establishments that sold liquor to men in uniform.[52]

Steiner did not confine his concerns to the men. With sixteen hundred horses and mules in camp, regulations for the use and care of these animals were also necessary. Mounted orderlies and sanitation officers had permission to ride at a "slow trot"; all other troops riding or driving horses and mules were to do so only at a walk.[53] Accidents among the men handling the animals and, in the summer months, overheating of the animals were primary concerns.[54]

As always, sanitation was vitally important. Inspections at the camps where troops were on guard duty revealed generally satisfactory sanitary conditions.[55] But in the Montgomery camp the number of soldiers strained the facilities. The bathhouses of the Fourth Infantry and First Cavalry regiments were "positively filthy" because of the inadequacy of the facilities. In the cavalry fourteen hundred men shared one bathhouse. Both the infantry and cavalry bathhouses were "entirely inadequate," with improper drainage and poor locations. Both regimental commanders requested permission to build new bathhouses.[56] Inspectors discovered that the major sanitation problem was laxity in the care of latrines. This lack of attention and the presence of more than sixteen hundred animals meant that a large number of flies were about the camp, especially in the mess halls. The First Infantry's regimental surgeon blamed the numerous cases of intestinal problems on the presence of flies in mess areas, and Steiner urged all commanders to take the steps necessary to improve sanitary conditions.[57]

Medical officers were responsible for the health of the men. They treated men for hookworm infection and dental problems and tested new sources of water at the camp and at guard posts.[58] Medical officers were concerned especially about such infectious diseases as measles and about updating vaccinations for typhoid and paratyphoid fevers. The threat of malarial infection also caused concern for those men on guard duty near wet areas such as rivers, swamps, and creeks. To combat the threat, the medical officers prescribed 7.5 grains of quinine twice a week.[59]

In five months, April 1 to September 1, medical corps personnel at the mobilization camp handled 184 cases of measles, 152 of malaria, 55 of mumps, 22 of pneumonia, 2 of typhoid, 1 of small pox, and 577 of venereal and all other diseases. The measles cases were not newly contracted but remained from border duty. Few of the malaria cases were certain diagnoses, but initial symptoms suggested malaria, so doctors treated them as such. Yet the sick rate of the camp was less than 1 percent. Two deaths occurred from sickness contracted outside camp but no deaths from illness contracted within the camp.[60] The army wanted healthy soldiers, but as one captain reminded his medical personnel in May 1917, among the most important duties of medical officers was "to return soldiers to duty as quickly as possible."[61]

Steiner, too, worked diligently to keep his men as healthy as possible. In his opinion the major health detriment facing Alabama soldiers stemmed from the "two evils, prostitution and liquor."[62] In May Steiner sent to all commanders a memorandum concerning prostitution, liquor, venereal disease, and an army's energy. He quoted from an article he had read and directed that the information be distributed among the Guardsmen. According to the article, venereal disease was "the greatest sap of the efficiency" of the armies in Europe. The brothels followed the saloons. Thus, "as a military measure" the article recommended "prohibition first of the saloon and next of the brothel." The officers knew where the houses of prostitution were located and prohibited soldiers from visiting such establishments. Steiner ordered his officers to report frequently on their efforts to address the "evils of liquor and prostitution." In June, while still in Mobile, the First Infantry's regimental surgeon recommended the establishment of a separate camp to care for the men diagnosed with venereal diseases. Likewise, a separate ward housed venereal cases in the Montgomery camp. Officers did make an effort in Montgomery to close the houses of prostitution. A medical officer from Camp Sheridan "reported that there 'were enough prostitutes in town to serve a city of 400,000.' He explained, 'All have been ordered to leave by Monday, November 12, 1917. The majority have left already.'" But closing the known houses of prostitution in prohibited districts would "not completely eliminate prostitution." Rather, "the prostitute would simply continue her activities in hotels, rooming houses, and apartments."[63] Thus, the efficacy of Steiner's orders is not readily apparent.

Once the soldiers returned to Camp Sheridan, training became their primary duty. The morning hours were filled with exercises and various drills by squad, platoon, company, and battalion. The afternoon hours were devoted to lectures, practical work, inspections, various schools for commissioned and noncommissioned officers, duties related to sanitation, and the occasional review. Men heard lectures on military courtesy and discipline, tent housekeeping and property accounts, camp sanitation and personal hygiene, courts-martial, patrols and outpost work, and map reading and sketching. The "practical work" consisted of performing the techniques learned from the morning drill work—such as practice on the firing range using the information gained from the sighting, aiming, and trigger squeeze drills and practice with signals discussed in the semaphore signaling drills. Most Saturday mornings were spent cleaning equipment, policing the area, and preparing for the inspection later that morning. Some commissioned and noncommissioned officers attended planning sessions for the next week's work for two hours on Saturdays. Except for those men kept on such necessary duties as guard or kitchen details, the men had Saturday afternoons and Sundays as a "holiday." Church services were held at the Young Men's Christian Association tent on Sundays for those men who wished to attend.[64]

Training during this period included practice marches for all elements of the guard—infantry, cavalry, ambulance and hospital corps, and supply units. These marches, lasting from one to nine days, gave the troops practice in bivouacking and in methods of supply in the field. Rations for men, forage and feed for horses and mules, camp sanitation, selection of camp grounds, cooking, camp discipline—all parts of a military camp—were integrated on these marches. Rest periods provided commanding officers with time for lectures and practical demonstrations. Commanders also had to judge how best to attend to illnesses and injuries of both men and animals.[65]

In early August 1917 the Alabama National Guard, a total of 5,025 officers and men, was mustered into federal service at Camp Sheridan. The War Department chose the Fourth Alabama Infantry Regiment to become the 167th Infantry, Forty-second Division, which was one of the first American divisions sent overseas. Many Guardsmen from the other Alabama infantry and cavalry regiments joined the Fourth as the regiment recruited to war strength, bringing the total to 3,677.[66] The remaining officers and men of the First and Second Alabama Infantry regiments were assigned to the Thirty-first Division. This division, composed of National Guard units from Alabama, Georgia, and Florida, went to Camp Joseph Wheeler near Macon, Georgia, to begin training for the war. Unlike the Forty-second, the Thirty-first (Dixie Division) spent most of the war at Camp Wheeler. Sections of the Alabama National Guard moved to Camp Wheeler in late August, and by September the men were settled at their new quarters.[67]

The former Alabama National Guardsmen began once again the routine of camp life. At Camp Wheeler, officers prepared the Thirty-first for war. Officers and men drilled, marched, attended schools and lectures, and dug trenches—in general, trained extensively in anticipation of going abroad. The division arrived in Brest, France, in late October 1918, just weeks before the armistice. It served as a depot division whose members filled individual vacancies in other organizations. Thus, members of the Thirty-first saw little or no combat, but they retained the knowledge and experience of their training at Camp Wheeler.

The Fourth Alabama, which became the newly organized 167th Infantry Regiment of the 42nd Division, did see combat. On August 1, 1917, the War Department organized the Forty-second, called the Rainbow Division, from National Guard units representing twenty-seven states and the District of Columbia. Alabama's 167th was one of four infantry regiments in the Forty-second. The other three came from New York, Ohio, and Iowa.[68]

During most of August the Fourth Alabama busily transferred enlisted men; completed paperwork; requisitioned clothing, equipment, animals, and vehicles to prepare for overseas service; and allowed some final visits home.[69] Medical personnel examined the officers of the Fourth Alabama Infantry and found all but one physically qualified.[70] The regiment shipped 101 mules and 44 horses to Newport News, Virginia, the embarkation point for the animals' journey to France.[71] Also during this preparation period a few men attempted to obtain discharges by claiming that they were the sole support of their families. Such claims had to be verified. If verification came, the man received discharge papers. But several such applications from privates were disapproved. The commander of Company G disapproved one request, noting that when the man enlisted on May 30, 1917, "he stated that no one was dependent upon him." The captain wrote that "the thought of the trenches in France" was the soldier's true reason for seeking discharge.[72] But most men were willing and even eager to go overseas. John H. Gardiner, who left the cavalry to join an infantry regiment, claimed no special bravery or patriotism for his actions. He remembered that in 1917 joining the service was "the thing to do." Thus, he left his horse, Buck, and the cavalry for an opportunity to "see some action."[73] The last days of August presented the final opportunity for visiting families and hometowns. Men received forty-eight-hour passes. Of his pass, one Alabama soldier wrote: "I took mine on August 19th, making a whirlwind trip to Albany and Jackson for a few hours each with homefolks and my sweetheart."[74]

On August 15, 1917, the War Department officially designated the Fourth Alabama Infantry as the 167th Infantry, Eighty-fourth Brigade, Forty-second Division. On August 28 and 29 the 167th, under Colonel William P. Screws, a former regular army inspector and current commander of the Fourth Alabama, entrained from Camp Sheridan in Montgomery for Camp Albert L. Mills in Garden City, Long Island, New York.[75] At Camp Mills the 167th joined other National Guard units, and the Forty-second Division came together for the first time.

The Alabamians of the Forty-second Division proceeded to Britain and then France, where they amassed an impressive combat record. The 167th participated in the Champagne-Marne defensive, the Aisne-Marne offensive, the St. Mihiel offensive, and the Meuse-Argonne offensives. Battle participation lasted from February to November 1918.[76] The Forty-second Division was the first American division to "take over a complete divisional sector of front line trenches." It "held a sector longer than any other American division," and the 167th Infantry established a record time of service on the front line without relief—110 days. The 167th's most notable battlefield service came in July 1918, when it participated in the attack on the Château-Thierry salient during the Aisne-Marne offensive. The regiment encountered especially difficult resistance at La Croix Rouge Farm. The 167th took the farm and surrounding town from the Germans and played a key role later the same month in crossing the Ourcq River. During the Croix Rouge Farm fight the 167th lost ten lieutenants and two captains killed and all but one field officer wounded. Forty-second Division Headquarters cited the 167th for overcoming the strongpoints of both La Croix Rouge and La Croix Blanche farms, for forcing the German retreat "through sheer aggressiveness," for "valiantly" holding its positions, and for its "willingness to go forward to the attack when called upon."[77]

Several members of the 167th received medals and awards in recognition of their service during the war. Corporal Sidney E. Manning of Flomaton, Alabama, and Private Thomas O. Neibour of Sugar City, Idaho, received the Congressional Medal of Honor. Thirty-six men received the Distinguished Service Cross, thirteen the Croix de Guerre, one the Croix de Guerre with Palm and Military Medal, one the Order of Leopold, one the Order of the Crown, and one the Military Medal. In addition to these awards, Major General Charles T. Menoher, commander of the Forty-second Division, cited seventy-seven soldiers of the 167th for their performances, and the 167th's regimental commander, Colonel Screws, cited ninety.[78]

Approximately ninety-five thousand Alabamians served in World War I, the great majority inducted through the selective service. Of that total, 6,262 died. Still, only the five thousand or so men of the Alabama National Guard had any state unit identity. Many of the Guardsmen had been in active military service since 1916. Some remained in Germany into 1919 as part of the occupation forces. As the era of the Great War drew to a close, Alabamians demonstrated their pride in and gratitude for the service of these men. The troops returned to their home state to an outpouring of welcome, honor, and celebration. Major cities and lesser ones—Huntsville, Gadsden, Anniston, Albany, Decatur, Birmingham, Montgomery, Mobile, and others—held parades. During four days in May 1919, the troop trains moved through the state. Montgomery held an all-day celebration on May 12.[79] These sons of Alabama had acquitted themselves well, receiving both individual and unit citations for service well rendered. The men had earned the enthusiastic homecoming they received from the citizens of their state.

3
"Tenting Tonight on the Old Camp Grounds"
Alabama's Military Bases in World War I

Wesley Phillips Newton

In the "Great War," as Americans called it, the U.S. Army built a number of mobilization and training bases in Alabama. These bases represented the most significant federal military presence in the state since Reconstruction, and although many white Alabamans thought poorly of that era, municipal officials and congressmen vied to secure these bases to enhance both local prestige and local economies. This chapter discusses the motivations for and circumstances surrounding the establishment of these bases in Alabama during World War I. Furthermore, the chapter examines the politics of each base's creation, the social and governmental interaction between base and adjacent city, the economic impact of each base on its neighborhood, and the overall military contribution of each base to the war effort. Finally, it recounts the postwar fates of the bases.

In the war period between 1914 and 1917, when the United States was keeping its neutral stance, Alabama had no large camps or cantonments for military units. The only bases of the United States armed forces in Alabama before 1917 were Fort Morgan and Fort Gaines, two army coastal artillery forts that guarded each side of the narrow entrance to Mobile Bay. They dated back to the Civil War era. The state had a militia brigade (National Guard after 1916) composed of four undermanned regiments—the First Infantry headquartered in Mobile and the Second Infantry, Fourth Infantry, and First Cavalry headquartered in Montgomery. Their companies and the artillery batteries were scattered in various towns and cities. Alabama's Third Infantry Regiment, headquartered in Birmingham, was inactivated earlier in the twentieth century.

In June 1916, the War Department established a mobilization camp for these guard units at Vandiver Park, site of the Montgomery County fairgrounds and racetrack and home to the annual Alabama state fair. Guardsmen traditionally spent only a few weeks each year on active duty, but in October 1916, Alabama's four regiments mobilized for service against the Mexican revolutionary leader Francisco "Pancho" Villa. In March 1917, after seeing virtually no action along the Mexican border, they reassembled at Vandiver Park, where regimental commanders were given orders to demobilize.[1]

On April 3, 1917, without providing a reason, the War Department cancelled those orders. Principally because the German government had resumed its strategy of unrestricted submarine warfare early in 1917, on April 6, 1917, the United States declared war on Germany. That same day commanders of the four Alabama regiments were notified. Elements of these units quickly deployed across the state to protect essential components of its transportation and infrastructure system, with the emphasis on railroads and utilities. Troops established posts at bridges, locks, tunnels, wharves, power plants, and other locations. A small force remained at the mobilization camp.[2]

The Fourth Infantry Regiment returned to Vandiver Park early in June; the other regiments marched back to Montgomery in July. The troops drilled and awaited further orders. Brigadier General Robert E. Steiner, a Montgomery lawyer and commander of the Alabama National Guard brigade, took command of the mobilization camp.[3]

In May 1917, Montgomery city officials sought consideration from the War Department for the city to become the site of an army training camp. Their cause was aided by the fact that Alabama's capital city was in the district of U.S. representative Stanley Dent, Jr., chairman of the House Committee on Military Affairs. Major General Leonard Wood, commanding the War Department's southeastern regional headquarters in Charleston, South Carolina, recommended to the War Department that the mobilization camp and surrounding acreage become a large base named Camp Sheridan in honor of Phil Sheridan, former Union cavalry general and longtime soldier in the West. On July 5, Mayor W. T. Robertson, as authorized by his city commission, announced that Montgomery had leased two thousand acres of land in Montgomery County north of the city for use by the government. Vandiver Park formed the core of the camp, the boundaries of which were Pickett Springs—a popular resort for picnics and other social gatherings—on the north, Jackson Ferry Road on the west, the tracks of the Central of Georgia Railway on the south, and the forests and fields that were four miles east of the park. The acreage included land owned by the Forbes, Vandiver, and Carter families as well as two banks and a railroad company.[4]

The local daily newspaper, the *Montgomery Advertiser*, noted that once the camp was under construction and the personnel of an entire infantry division began to assemble, there would be "immense sums to be spent here." The prospect of this money stifled the criticism over the War Department's naming the camp after the famed Union army cavalry leader. The reality of this financial bonanza for the city was underscored when Majors J. A. Reynolds and John M. Bingham of the Ohio National Guard came to Montgomery on July 17. They informed city officials that the Ohio National Guard's federalized Thirty-seventh "Buckeye" Division—thirty thousand troops in all, both white and a few black—would be based at Camp Sheridan. This number was startling. In 1917 Montgomery's population was only forty thousand. The presence of "Yankees" in the former capital of the Confederacy was startling, too. The War Department assigned them to Alabama because Ohio and other northern states had too many National Guard units to house and train and because the weather was better in Alabama than in the north.[5]

While the plans for Camp Sheridan took shape, the city's business and municipal leaders prepared for the swelling military presence in its midst. Even before details were known about the Thirty-seventh Division's arrival, city leaders organized a number of committees to deal with, as the *Advertiser* reported, "the thousands of soldiers who are coming for training at the big cantonment" and the families who would follow some of them to Montgomery. A central committee of five, appointed by the board of directors of the local chamber of commerce, selected members for seven committees to deal with various issues that might arise with the arrival of so many visitors. Committees included such groups as the Committee on the Control of Vice and Enforcement of Prohibition Law, the Committee on the Comfort of Soldiers and Visitors, and the Committee on Health and Sanitation. The forty-nine members of the committees were, the *Advertiser* proclaimed, "representative and responsible citizens," but they included no women and no blacks. The welfare of black soldiers was not much of a concern to the all-white, all-male committees.[6]

The Committee on the Comfort of Soldiers and Visitors soon met, joined by members of Montgomery's Real Estate Exchange. The principal topic of discussion was housing for the incoming civilians following the troops who were soon to arrive. The *Advertiser* reported that "the number of soldiers coming will be so great as to double the white population of the city." These newcomers would include families of the soldiers and others, some of whom would be "attracted to the city for business purposes," and they would "fill every vacant house in every respectable neighborhood in the city, and . . . the hotels, apartment houses and boarding places will be taxed to their capacities." The members of the Committee on the Comfort of Soldiers and Visitors and the Real Estate Exchange identified several problems that needed to be addressed as soon as possible. Various houses and other rental units in the city had fallen "into a state of dilapidation," and the owners were to be urged to "place them in the best condition" if they expected to rent them. Leopold Strauss, an insurance company executive and chairman of the Committee on the Comfort of Soldiers and Visitors, stressed that "we must work to counteract any movement to charge exorbitant rents. Montgomery has an opportunity to make a great name for itself and every man who doesn't do his duty is a traitor to the city." The Real Estate Exchange members reported real estate agents in the city were "ready and willing to cooperate in the work."[7]

The physical creation of the large camp itself was soon under way. Besides clearing trees and undergrowth from the primarily rural property, the city, as one of its first tasks, extended the city water mains some two and one-half miles to the center of the camp at Vandiver Park. The city had agreed to furnish the camp two million gallons of water daily for its needs.

The unpaved Lower and Upper Wetumpka roads would allow private conveyances—horse-drawn vehicles, automobiles, and trucks—to drive between Camp Sheridan and the city. But groups and individuals, especially the soldiers, relied on the streetcar. To accommodate them, the city commission granted Montgomery Traction and Light a franchise to add a second pair of tracks to Camp Sheridan so that outbound and inbound cars could pass each other. Before it could expand the track, the company had to move its existing switch several blocks east to the corner of Madison Avenue and North Ripley Street. Then it could lay new tracks parallel to those along North Ripley (which changed its name to Lower Wetumpka Road at the city limits) to Pickett Springs.[8]

The *Advertiser* described what had begun at Camp Sheridan under the direction of Major A. W. Reynolds, the constructing quartermaster: "Many miles of company streets will be laid out, additional roads will be built, hundreds of structures will be erected, telephone and telegraph lines, electric light and power lines, long spur tracks, a railroad station." It would be a "city of tents" except for larger structures such as large warehouses, mess halls, the gymnasium, the post exchange, divisional headquarters buildings at Pickett Springs, the hospital complex, the library, the post office, and civilian support buildings such as the Young Men's Christian Association (YMCA) hut. City leaders hoped that wooden barracks would eventually replace the tents. Then the camp could be classified as a "cantonment" that might become a permanent military installation. In the meantime, the camp had to be livable. The tents, large enough to contain cots and footlockers, had wooden flooring and a stove to create warmth and heat water. They were also close to a latrine and a shower constructed of wood. A civilian, Alabama Audit Company president Charles G. Trost, became auditor for construction work at Camp Sheridan. Local firms as well as distant companies bid on the construction contracts. Montgomery's Algernon Blair Company secured most of these bids.[9]

The Algernon Blair Company completed the last of the hospital's two-story ward barracks in the spring of 1918. The health record of troops at the camp was highly satisfactory, with the important exceptions of venereal disease and influenza. As was mandatory for all such camps, the U.S. Public Health Service established a five-mile sanitary zone around the camp in which workers eliminated health hazards and drained both a swamp and its surrounding lowlands to remove the danger of malaria. Within the camp, drainage ditches ensured that the drill fields and parade grounds would not become unusable for days at a time and that they would not be breeding grounds for mosquitoes.[10]

On July 27, 1917, the *Advertiser* characterized the recreational and spiritual aspects of camp life: "It will have its musicals, its movie attractions, its dances, all to enliven the hours of the officers and soldiers when off duty, as well as theatricals and other forms of amusement. To add to the solemnity of the life there will be prayer meetings and preaching. . . . In the line of sports there will be countless baseball and football games, boxing and wrestling matches, horse races." As at other military camps, Camp Sheridan was to have five YMCA huts, each headed by a secretary and a staff of local volunteers. In contrast, the city itself had only one YMCA. A July 3 editorial in the *Advertiser* provided the rationale for this discrepancy, noting that "nothing Montgomery can do—no work for the comfort of the soldiers, no undertaking in the interest of their welfare can be so . . . productive of results as strengthening and sustaining of the

Y.M.C.A." The cost of the buildings was $23,000, one-quarter of which Montgomerians quickly contributed. YMCA national headquarters bore most of the expenses for the buildings, secretaries, and activities.

Jeffers Brothers, a local firm, built the first hut between July 6 and July 18. It was 40 by 129 feet; contained a large auditorium for motion pictures, musicals, plays, and other forms of entertainment; and was a place where soldiers could write letters, receive family and friends, and participate in prayer meetings.[11]

The camp YMCA committee also constructed a brown bungalow they called the Hostess House, which was under the care of Mrs. H. B. Carre, wife of a Vanderbilt University professor on leave with the YMCA in France. The Hostess House provided an area for visits by not only mothers of soldier sons but also other relatives and friends of the soldiers. Among other comforts, the house had a fireplace, shower bath, and kitchen. Two small bedrooms were for Mrs. Carre and her assistant.[12]

The American Red Cross served Camp Sheridan as well. Laura Jones, Amelia Hill, and Katherine Baldwin, young women from prominent Montgomery families, had organized Montgomery's Red Cross chapter in 1916 and enlisted local white women as volunteers. Its primary activity, at first associated with the Allied war effort in Europe and then directed toward U.S. military involvement in the war, was to prepare surgical bandages. It also opened a canteen in downtown Montgomery just east of its railway station, Union Station. Under the leadership of Mrs. Leon Weil, the canteen offered food and a chance to relax to arriving white soldiers, many of whom were assigned to Camp Sheridan. The National Red Cross established a presence in Montgomery, too. It supplied most of the registered nurses to the newly opened camp hospital, supplementing the limited number of noncommissioned military nurses on staff. It also constructed a separate building at the camp that served as an office and dormitory for the nurses.[13]

The local chapter of the national War Camp Community Service (WCCS) also served the bases in or near Montgomery. The WCCS provided travelers' aid to the visiting friends and relatives of men at the military bases, the aid including information concerning boarding and housing, the Hostess House, and other patriotic services. It coordinated the activities of the Red Cross chapter, the Women's League for Service and Motor Corps (which, among other activities, provided transportation for camp patients and others to sightsee and visit downtown entertainment venues), the Patriotic League, the Young Women's Christian Association, and the Girls' Patriotic League. It also linked the community with the camp in the areas of transportation, commanding officers, YMCA, and Knights of Columbus. The WCCS in Alabama extended its services almost exclusively to whites, though a small number of blacks became involved with it.[14]

Most of the WCCS's services affected the troops of Ohio's Thirty-seventh Division. It hardly had time to serve the Alabama National Guard, which occupied the old mobilization camp at Vandiver Park. In August 1917 the Alabama National Guard was federalized. Its 4th Infantry Regiment became the 167th Infantry Regiment of the newly created 42nd Infantry Division, United States Army. After being reequipped and brought to strength, the 167th departed by train to Camp Mills, Long Island, arriving there on August 31. Soon, it left with the Forty-second for Europe. The remainder of the Alabama National Guard units left Camp Sheridan late in August for Camp Wheeler, Georgia, where they were assigned to the recently created Thirty-first Infantry Division. After training, the division arrived in France in the summer of 1918.[15]

Smaller units of Ohio's Thirty-seventh "Buckeye" Division had trickled into Camp Sheridan as the Alabamians left. In September 1917, battalion and regimental staffs and headquarters units arrived, followed in October by the division's four infantry regiments. Only the commanding officer was absent. Major General Charles G. Treat was in France studying trench warfare firsthand. Camp kitchens housed in tents soon served garrison rations while regimental canteens in temporary quarters sold ice cream and soft drinks. Alcoholic beverages were forbidden because Alabama was one of the nation's nineteen states that enforced Prohibition.[16]

On the front page of the *Advertiser* of October 3 was a poem of welcome composed by Montgomerian R. L. Cary, Jr. Its last stanza read:

> Hello Buckeyes! Howdy do!
> Derned if we ain't proud of you,
> Going out to France to fight.
> Armored only with the right.
> Goin' where the shrapnel falls—
> Goin' where the old Flag calls—
> Sons of men who wore the blue,
> Alabama welcomes you.

This poem and an editorial in the same issue may have chagrined Confederate veterans and other devotees of the "Lost Cause." The editor said that the author of the poem "endeavors to give expression . . . to the warmth of welcome of the entire city of Montgomery to the soldiers of Ohio, who have come to fit themselves for the arduous service they are to render on the battlefields of Europe for their country's honor and for the perpetuity of their country's liberty and institutions." He praised Ohioan Newton D. Baker, secretary of war, who chose Montgomery from thirty-two prospective sites "as the training ground of the troops from his own state," and he noted that Ohio "has supplied four Presidents to our nation" and that during the Civil War contributed "Gallant Phil Sheridan, whose name is now honored at Montgomery."[17]

While the Thirty-seventh Division units and troops were assembling at Sheridan, training facilities and a remount depot were still under construction. The latter was necessary because U.S. Army infantry divisions moved almost as much by horse and mule as by foot, truck, train, and ship. Construction of the remount depot commenced early in August 1917 on three hundred acres five miles southwest of Sheridan and two and one-half miles from Montgomery. A Central of Georgia railroad spur linked depot and camp, and a road that ran through the newly developing suburb of Oak Park linked the depot to the city. Designated "Auxiliary Remount Depot No. 312" and commanded by Major Carl J. Schumann, it furnished serviceable horses, mules, wagons, and harnesses to the Thirty-seventh Division and other smaller organizations at Camp Sheridan.

To carry out its duties, the remount depot became a large post in its own right. Its workforce, under the command of several army engineer officers, consisted of forty-one local white men, who soon enlisted in the army, and a varying number of blacks, who remained civilians and worked mainly as laborers and carpenters. The depot's buildings were all wooden and included an administrative office, ten barracks (eight for enlisted men), and three mess halls. Workers placed four latrines and four showers a sanitary distance from the mess halls. The station was ready for occupancy in December 1917.

Other buildings served the depot's basic functions. These structures included a large warehouse with receiving pens, three large-capacity hay sheds, a carpenter shop, and a blacksmith shop, where shoers, teamsters, stable sergeants, and other specialists trained. The depot's veterinary hospital was a veterinarian's paradise. Its stables included a complex of corrals to house different kinds of animals and treat different kinds of diseases.

Its full staff complement included seventy-five enlisted men and a dozen commissioned doctors.

The YMCA opened a hut at the depot in February 1918. YMCA secretary S. T. Banks helped troops form football, basketball, and baseball teams that competed against military teams from Camp Sheridan and civilian teams from Montgomery. Banks also organized schools for the illiterate. A Miss Green and a Mrs. Davis held classes for the white troops at the station, and Professor Beverly of Montgomery's State Normal School, assisted by several black teachers from Montgomery, held classes for black soldiers. Black troops, segregated in their own barracks as they were at Sheridan, performed the most menial depot duties.

Over the two years that the remount depot remained an army facility, it handled a total of 17,285 animals. Of these, 10,256 were issued, most to units at Sheridan, 3,275 were sold to civilians, and 600 died. Ninety-three others, fatally injured or ill, were humanely destroyed by post veterinarians.[18]

Training the soldiers was vastly more important than caring for the horses and mules. Proficiency in weapons—including bolt-action rifles, pistols, the new and deadly machine gun, and artillery—was crucial for survival and military success. The War Department leased four thousand acres in Elmore County for two practice ranges. To reach them, troops lugged their equipment and weapons along the Lower Wetumpka Road and a service road before ferrying them across the Tallapoosa River. Getting to the ranges was time-consuming; a training session often lasted more than one day. This forced troops to bivouac in their pup tents at the range.

Trench warfare demanded specific training, too. When General Treat returned from France in November 1917, he directed that an elaborate battleground be constructed not far from the main camp. This area consisted of two opposing trenches, each with barbed wire and dugouts, that were separated by a no-man's-land complete with imitation shell craters. Troops in the opposing trenches alternated charges across no-man's-land with nearby knee mortars firing over their heads into an unoccupied field. American instructors demonstrated the throwing of hand grenades, and Treat arranged to have a veteran French army noncommissioned officer give instruction in the most effective way to use a bayonet. He also brought in several veteran French and British officers to lecture about the overall nature of trench warfare.[19]

While the encampment and training scenario unfolded at Montgomery's Camp Sheridan, a similar development took place in Alabama's Calhoun County. Influenced by Colonel Charles P. Summerall, an artilleryman, the army had purchased sixteen thousand acres of land there for an artillery range in early 1917, but when the United States entered the Great War, the War Department ordered a machine-gun camp built on the southeast quadrant of the property one mile from Anniston. Like Vandiver Park in Montgomery, the Anniston installation was used originally by companies of the Alabama National Guard. Soon, however, that land became another large divisional training camp named for another Civil War Union general, George B. McClellan.

Other similarities also existed between the divisional camps at Montgomery and Anniston. As in the case with Camp Sheridan, the economic windfall to the community of Anniston outweighed the unpopular name for the camp. Locals wanted to see it named Camp Fred L. Blackmon in honor of the Alabama congressman who secured the Anniston camp in 1917. Blackmon played the same role for Anniston as Congressman Dent had played for Montgomery. These representatives convinced the War Department to choose Alabama for two of the thirty-two division-sized camps built in 1917. Likely, too, these congressmen kept Birmingham and Mobile from being chosen as sites for such camps.

Another similarity between the camps was that Camp McClellan also became a training base for an infantry division newly formed from federalized National Guard units. Just as Sheridan was home to the Ohio Thirty-seventh "Buckeye" Division, McClellan hosted the Twenty-ninth "Blue-Gray" Division, so named because its units came from New Jersey, Delaware, the District of Columbia, Maryland, and Virginia, and thus another division was assigned to a camp located in a former Confederate state but named for a Union general. Both camps were constructed as "tent cities," meaning that they were not likely to be permanent. The War Department calculated that National Guard divisions were already partially trained and did not require a more comfortable wooden camp before being ready for overseas duty. There was one basic difference between the camps, however. The War Department had purchased the Calhoun County acreage for McClellan, whereas it merely leased the land in Montgomery for Sheridan. Some of Anniston's leaders assumed this meant their camp would become permanent.

Aside from the mainly flat land the camps occupied, each had an adjacent terrain feature that played a part in its training. For Sheridan, it was the Tallapoosa-Alabama River system. For McClellan, it was mountains that surrounded Anniston and the camp. "The air at Camp McClellan has a real mountain tang to it," extolled the *Baltimore American* on behalf of the Maryland troops assigned there. More important, mountain streams provided the initial source of water for the camp—Anniston later extended its mains to provide most of McClellan's water—and mountainsides became part of its firing range.[20]

In 1917 Charles L. Dulin, an army major and constructing quartermaster for Camp McClellan, built the machine-gun camp. But a few weeks after the machine-gun companies of the Alabama National Guard arrived there in July, they received orders to return to Montgomery. The machine-gun camp became part of the Camp McClellan complex. Under Dulin's direction McClellan took shape in July and August. The major selected the northwest quadrant of the government-owned land for the camp proper because the terrain was well drained and fairly level, it was traversed by existing roads to Anniston and Jacksonville—a nearby town with a state normal (teachers) college—and it was close to the tracks of the Southern Railway. Dulin persuaded Southern Railway to build a spur to the camp to unload supplies and transport incoming military personnel. This spur bisected the camp; the main portion of the complex was five miles from Anniston.

The time frame for constructing Camp McClellan was similar to that for Sheridan. But a New Orleans–based contractor, John O. Chisholm and Company, received most of the McClellan contracts. Because of Anniston's smaller population, however, Chisholm had more difficulty hiring a sufficient workforce. Carpenters in Anniston were especially scarce. Advertising in surrounding towns and out of state brought in more and more workers, but that situation, in turn, created a problem with housing for the labor force. Mess halls were the first buildings workmen erected. As fast as they completed one, it was temporarily employed to house the workers who were not from Anniston, for whom there were virtually no local quarters available. Ninety-five percent of all mechanics and carpenters were thus affected. In his final report about the construction of the camp, Dulin stated that for the first month "80% of the common negro labor were quartered at the camp, being the highest order of laborers and those used as carpenters helpers, etc." Perhaps unwittingly Dulin revealed that urgent wartime military construction gave African Americans employment opportunities they ordinarily would not have had in a former Confederate state. At the end of August, when construction was widespread, all laborers were told to find quarters off base but were assured of transportation to and from work.[21]

As the mess halls went up, workers built the hospital complex, which became the site of early labor trouble. Two men representing the Industrial Workers of the World (IWW), a radical organization that opposed U.S. entry into the war, gained admittance to the post. They spread a rumor among the workers that there were outbreaks of typhoid fever, yellow fever, and smallpox and that the hospital had inadequate personnel to cope with these problems. Military police seized the two men and turned them over to the Calhoun County sheriff, who put them on a train bound for Atlanta. But the rumors led to a strike by seven hundred out of the several thousand workers. Dulin promptly met with the workers in the mess halls, assuring them that there was not a single case of contagious disease in the hospital. Furthermore, the hospital had two registered nurses and a resident physician on duty as well as a visiting physician on call at all times. The men returned to work within the day.[22]

Camp McClellan, like Camp Sheridan, had a remount depot to supply the horses and mules required by the infantry division. The construction, layout, nature of personnel, and duties and responsibilities were the same at both camps. Located near the former machine-gun camp, the McClellan remount depot had a Southern Railway siding.[23]

From the beginning, transportation between Camp McClellan and Anniston was a problem. The road connecting the town and camp, known as the Jacksonville Pike, was unpaved. Major Dulin and the Anniston Chamber of Commerce proposed that the operator of the local streetcar system, Alabama Power Company, extend its tracks to McClellan. The company balked, claiming it did not have sufficient funds for such a long extension. It was obvious that there had to be an effective way for the troops to get back and forth if the city's economy was to benefit from their presence. While Alabama Power conducted a study of its finances, Dulin arranged to pave with brick the road between town and camp.

Town and camp had other mutual problems. More so than at Montgomery, housing in Anniston for family members who wished to live close to their soldiers before they went overseas was extremely scarce, as were temporary rental quarters for visiting relatives and friends. The chamber of commerce surveyed available housing in the city, and some landowners began constructing houses. Some wives and mothers found rental property in the nearby towns of Jacksonville and Oxford, and other relatives had to quarter in Birmingham, sixty miles away. The problem lingered.

When the troops began to arrive—a few in July, more in August, and a flood when the infantry regiments of the Twenty-ninth Division came in September—entertainment, morale, and morals became important issues to officials. The Anniston Chamber of Commerce laid plans for "good, clean" entertainment, and the Anniston Country Club admitted two categories from Camp McClellan: commissioned officers and individual units, the latter to sponsor dances. Local organizations such as the Girls' Patriotic League held picnics and dances for the troops. When the soldiers of the Twenty-ninth Division received passes at noon on Saturdays, they crowded downtown streets and filled the movies, restaurants, and shops. Military and local police cooperated in enforcing law and order. The city fathers passed an ordinance on August 23 making it unlawful for "chauffeurs and taxi drivers" to take soldiers to "immoral houses for a consideration."[24]

Other groups and individuals smoothed relations between town and camp. The city appointed city leader W. F. Acker as its liaison with military authorities, and he was noticeably successful in holding down rents that affected soldiers' families. The Anniston chapter of the American Red Cross, founded by Mrs. William A. J. Kopp and Miss Anne Kilby in July 1917, not only rolled bandages and knitted warm garments but also aided soldiers with problems such as communicating with family members. As at Camp Sheridan, the Red Cross constructed a building on the post and aided the U.S. Public Health Service in establishing a five-mile sanitary corridor around the camp. Red Cross registered nurses from across the country formed the core of the nursing staff in both camps. But McClellan differed in one way from Camp Sheridan and from most other camps, too. On its hospital staff served one of the army's first commissioned female medical doctors, First Lieutenant Ollie Josephine Baird.

For its part, the YMCA erected five huts at McClellan and conducted similar activities to those at Sheridan and other camps. The WCCS furnished sports equipment and organized teams of the various units that competed with each other as well as with teams from Sheridan and other camps.

Troops of the Twenty-ninth Division trained for the most dangerous game of all, trench warfare. Division commander Major General Charles G. Morton went to France in September 1917 for field training.

While he was gone, infantry officers consulted a War Department pamphlet titled "Notes for Infantry Officers on Trench Warfare." The *Anniston Star* reported that "several hundred American negroes will soon be in the trenches, not in France but at Camp McClellan," digging "several hundred yards of target and firing trenches on the range grounds in the northern part of the reservation." At three separate rifle ranges of different distances, soldiers in the trenches fired at disappearing targets on a mountainside. At both McClellan and Sheridan, poison gas training—beginning with the proper use of the newly issued gas masks—began. When Morton returned to McClellan in October, he ordered the construction of a network of trenches, dugouts, and no-man's-lands for live-action exercises.[25]

The training of the Twenty-ninth's citizen-soldiers paid off. This federalized National Guard unit established in the short span of World War I a tradition of valiant service. Twenty-six years later, on June 6, 1944, the Twenty-ninth formed half the main assault force at Omaha Beach. On D-day its 116th Regiment suffered the highest number of fatalities of all Allied units landing on Normandy's beaches, including twenty-two of the "Bedford Boys," thirty-five soldiers in the same company who hailed from the eponymous hamlet in Virginia. The renumbering and reorganization of the Twenty-ninth Division units that produced such courageous soldiers began at Camp McClellan in 1917.[26]

At both McClellan and Sheridan, draftees fleshed out the newly reorganized divisions. The Selective Service Act of May 1917 required all men between the ages of twenty-one and thirty—later expanded to ages eighteen to forty-five—to register for call-up, mainly for army service. In the Great War, draftees were called "draft men" or "selectmen" and, with wartime volunteers, made up the "National Army." In contrast, the "Regular Army" consisted of West Point graduates, officers and enlisted men of the army reserve, prewar volunteers, and federalized National Guard units. Eventually, all units received draftees and wartime volunteers.[27]

At both McClellan and Sheridan, African American enlistees and selectmen trained and served in segregated units. At McClellan, the federalized Maryland National Guard's First Separate Negro Company trained in trench warfare techniques and in December 1917 joined the 372nd Infantry Regiment at Camp Stuart, Virginia. Sheridan sent the federalized Ohio National Guard's Ninth Battalion of Infantry Colored, also trained in trench warfare techniques, to a similar unit at Camp Stuart that same month. Both regiments joined the black Ninety-third Infantry Division, which was led by white officers and which General John Pershing of the American Expeditionary Force sent to fight under French command. Despite this slight, the Ninety-third fought with distinction. During the Great War, the state of Alabama had no black National Guard troops.

Similarly, neither Sheridan nor McClellan had black Red Cross personnel. Nonetheless, the national headquarters authorized blacks in Anniston to create their own chapter, and though Montgomery and Camp Sheridan had no black Red Cross chapters, African Americans there supported the Red Cross and the general war effort. In June 1918, black civilian laborers at Camp Sheridan pledged $479.33 during a Red Cross nationwide fund-raising drive. A resolution accompanying the pledge sent to the Montgomery chapter's headquarters stated: "We, the colored laborers at Camp Sheridan, Montgomery, Ala. . . . feel it our patriotic and bounden duty and obligation to render what assistance is within our power to assist in aiding the Red Cross. . . . Therefore, each of us do, of our own free will and accord, hereby pledge to give and donate one (1) day's wages to the Red Cross . . . for the great work being done by the Red Cross for our boys overseas." These laborers in the Fuel and Forage, Warehouse, Transportation, and Sanitary departments and cooks and waiters at the quartermaster reclamation mess followed through. The workers' finance committee, chaired by a Mr. Reese Jones, handled the transaction.[28]

Like African Americans' efforts, women's contributions were channeled toward serving the needs of white soldiers slated for line duty. But in October 1917, Ruth Law stepped beyond her gendered role. An aviation pioneer, she became the first aviatrix to take off and fly over Anniston and Montgomery when she gave an exhibition at Camps McClellan and Sheridan. The *Montgomery Advertiser* described her performance there: "Miss Law made a practice flight. . . . While above the camp she put over several feats that caused watchers' hearts to miss a beat."[29]

Camps McClellan and Sheridan trained infantry, but Alabama also hosted training sites for "knights of the air." On November 28, 1917, Congressman Dent telegraphed W. T. Sheehan, editor of the *Advertiser,* that "Montgomery selected this afternoon for aviation camp. Location near Pike Road." Dent's lobbying efforts had resulted in a new Army Air Service flight training field to be built in the Montgomery area. The War Department dubbed it Taylor Field in honor of Captain Ralph L. Taylor of Connecticut, an Army Aviation Service pilot who died in a New York State accident in August.[30]

It took only a few weeks for Montgomery to reap the benefits of Taylor Field. The War Department had leased eight hundred acres of flat prairie cotton land near Pike Road in east Montgomery County, eighteen miles from the capital city. The James Alexander Construction Company built Taylor Field along the same lines as Camps Sheridan and McClellan. Taylor, however, was not a tent city. Along one side of its takeoff and landing area was a line of sixteen large hangars. To the east of the hangars were shops—repair, woodworking, wing construction, and motor—as well as warehouses, ground school buildings and quarters for the air cadets, quarters for officers and enlisted men, mess halls, recreation halls, a YMCA hut, an athletic field, and a concrete swimming pool. Most of the buildings were wooden, but the last four hangers constructed were steel, indicating that Taylor Field was to be permanent. The field was ready for occupancy by March 1918.

The War Department was under pressure to turn out airmen who could defeat the veteran German air force. The army modeled its air crew training on European experience but added such innovations as the cadet system, borrowed from the U.S. service academies. Air cadets spent several weeks in a classroom at such colleges as Georgia Tech learning the mechanics of flight and the basics of aviation. Then they were tested, and those who passed received flying training at a field such as Taylor. The need for flyers was so great, however, that many cadets were assigned to Europe for all their flight training.

Training at Taylor, as at all primary flight training fields in the United States and abroad, was about more than just flying airplanes. Cadets learned to disassemble and reassemble aircraft engines. They learned military protocol as well, practicing close-order drill and the manual of arms. They also marched in formation from place to place during duty hours.

Nevertheless, flight training was the most important part of their preparation for combat. During the first eight hours of flight time, a cadet, whose status was a cross between a student and an officer candidate, flew in a dual-control biplane trainer with an instructor. This commissioned officer-pilot taught cadets the rudimentary maneuvers of banking for a turn, climbing, and ascending. Finally, a cadet learned how to take off and land. A cadet who failed to grasp these maneuvers at the end of eight hours of flight training failed the program.

Next on the training agenda were twenty more hours of flight time during which a cadet flew solo and cross-country. Cadets' first solo takeoffs and landings were the most tense moments of training. During cross-country flights, cadets practiced elementary formation flying. Again, a cadet who failed to learn these maneuvers "washed out." The final phase of primary training involved basic aerobatics: sideslips, tailspins, nosedives, and loop-the-loops.

Cadets who successfully completed primary training were assigned one of three duties. Because the need for combat pilots was so great, a small number—mostly those with the best records—received commissions as second lieutenants immediately after primary training and went overseas. Other newly minted second lieutenants served as instructor pilots in the United States after advanced training. But the majority of those who completed primary training at Taylor and other stateside fields went overseas for advanced combat training, including gunnery training, at fields not far from the front lines at French, British, and Italian airfields. Successful completion of training led to the silver wings of an Army Air Service pilot and the gold bars of a second lieutenant. In France the new pilot became a member of a pursuit (fighter), bomber, or observation squadron and flew his initial combat sortie.[31]

Signifying the importance of aviation in the war, Montgomery received a second Army Air Service station in April 1918. Influenced by Representative Dent, the War Department authorized a repair and maintenance base beside the Alabama River two miles west of downtown Montgomery. Locals called the area Wright Field, for it was the site of the Wright Brothers' civilian flight training school in 1910, the first of its kind in the United States and the place where Orville Wright made the first airplane flight in Alabama. It was one of three such fields in the United States, and the Army Air Service named the base Aviation Repair Depot No. 3 and charged it with serving the seven army airfields in the Southeast. Its fifty-two buildings were all painted green and made of wood, including hangars—metal hangars hinted that a field might become permanent—repair shops, barracks, an infirmary, a post exchange and commissary, and a headquarters building connected by three miles of tarvia-surfaced roads. The fourteen hundred soldiers and civilians who began arriving at the depot in June served its mission as engine mechanics; carpenters; wing, tail, and fuselage canvas cover specialists; military police; commissioned test pilots; and commissioned and enlisted administrative personnel.[32]

The depot's first commanding officer was Major Stiles M. Decker, a Texan. In August 1918, when the depot officially opened for business, the *Advertiser* used a biblical analogy to describe its principal activity: "When an airplane is received by the depot for repair, it is systematically dissembled, and likened unto the Day of Judgment, the sheep are separated from the goats, meaning the good parts are collected and sent to the store room, and the bad parts are condemned to the scrap heap." A third class of parts was the group "capable of being repaired." These parts "in the religious language might be likened unto back-sliders, and most of the efforts of the depot, like the efforts of the church, are devoted to the reconstruction of these particular parts." When enough parts were available to assemble a whole airplane, mechanics put it together, and then a test pilot risked his life by taking it up and trying it out.[33]

Taylor Field and Repair Depot No. 3 were the only military air bases in Alabama during the Great War, although Mobile Bay's Fort Gaines trained antiaircraft gunners. Taylor Field saw operational changes in June 1918: spring rains turned Taylor's landing area into a quagmire; the wheels of planes taking off and landing often stuck in the mud, causing the planes to nose over. Workers remedied the problem by spreading sand on the takeoff and landing area. The field had also become congested with more than a hundred planes and an increasing number of cadet classes. To manage the traffic, commanding officer Major E. L. Hoffman had an observation tower erected. He also assigned each plane a number, which was posted on the tower when it was a plane's turn to take off. To reduce the possibility of collisions in landing, Hoffman divided the field in half: one side was to be used by cadets and their instructors, the other by cadets who had flown solo.

Taylor Field suffered no fatal aircraft accidents during its first two months of operations. But on May 31, Cadet George H. Lacoaker from Michigan, who had soloed, was preparing to land a Hall-Scott biplane trainer when, at two hundred feet above the field, the engine burst into flames, and the plane dove straight into the ground. Lacoaker was the first person killed in an air crash in the Montgomery area since 1912, when an aerial barnstormer died during a stunting routine at the Vandiver Park fairgrounds. On June 4 Cadet George O. Mills, who also had soloed, was flying in a Hall-Scott trainer several miles from the field when his engine, too, burst into flames. Two sharecroppers witnessed what followed. Mills attempted to escape the flames by executing a sideslip and then cutting off the motor. He eased out of the cockpit and held onto his seatbelt while he dangled. The flames died away, and Mills tried several times to climb back in, but the trainer plunged to earth before he succeeded.

With this second tragedy, Major Hoffman ordered all training flights suspended. A panel of investigators determined that the Hall-Scott engines were defective, so Hoffman had Taylor Field's entire fleet of Hall-Scotts crated and returned to the factory. He replaced them with Curtiss JN-4s—the famous "Jenny"—a biplane trainer that had a low rate of mechanical failure. Flight training resumed in late June.[34]

Camps Sheridan and McClellan also went through significant changes in June 1918. Their infantry divisions packed up and headed for a port of embarkation (the Thirty-seventh replacing General Treat with Major General Charles S. Farnsworth before leaving), spent several weeks crossing the Atlantic under U-boat threat, and assembled in the deadly trenches of the western front. Many residents in Montgomery and Anniston, for economic, social, and personal reasons, were sad to see them go, but they were thrilled by the troops singing the rousing George M. Cohen patriotic tune that proclaimed, "Over there, over there, send the word . . . the Yanks are coming," despite the word "Yanks."

Years later, the soldiers remembered their time in Alabama. A veteran of the Thirty-seventh Division, J. F. Weadock, twenty-six years after the departure, recalled, "They opened their hearts to a lot of lonely kids, and the majority were pretty much kids. . . . We were entertained at dances and they visited the camp to join in our parties there, arriving by the truck load and dancing until dawn. . . . A hospital grew up out in those cotton patches and it was far from the homes of the men who were in it. But it never lacked for visitors. . . . In the downtown stores, in theaters and parks the Yanks of 1917 received friendly and courteous treatment from young and old alike." Images of the doughboys from Ohio in their garrison hats, khaki uniforms, and wraparound leggings lingered for decades.[35]

Unfortunately, the Thirty-seventh's leave taking was marred by a health crisis of major proportions that alarmed both civil and military authorities. Brigadier General W. R. Smith of the Thirty-seventh imposed a quarantine on the camp on June 6 as the division began to depart unit by unit. At a meeting that same day with the advisory board of the WCCS at the downtown Gay-Teague Hotel, Smith laid out the facts. Camp Sheridan's troops, like those at most military camps, suffered from an epidemic of venereal disease. Citing a recent report, he noted that over a seven-month period, there were 1,853 cases of venereal disease isolated at Sheridan's detention camp. He blamed "social functions in Montgomery [that] have been used by prostitutes to meet the soldiers in the practice of their trade" as well as taxi drivers who, he claimed, were the "most active agents" in aiding and abetting prostitution. The "amount of intercourse with negro women" was relatively small, Hoffman continued. White prostitutes were the major culprits, "100 of whom" were known to be infected. As in most urban areas with newly built military bases, the number of prostitutes, both local and from outside, grew.

Advertiser editor W. T. Sheehan addressed the crisis on June 9, writing that "Montgomery has nothing to be ashamed of in its record as a camp city, compared with other cities which have large training camps," ranking "in health at or near the top . . . [but] in the statistics relating to disease resulting from vice, Montgomery is seventh in a list of fourteen camp cities." The venereal disease crisis posed a threat to "the immediate future of Montgomery as a military post."[36]

On June 10 officials of the WCCS sponsored a meeting of one hundred prominent Montgomery business and professional men at the Gay-Teague Hotel to discuss ways of combating this scourge. The assembly passed a number of resolutions. One, offered by Jack Thorington, a prominent local attorney and businessman, asked the War Department to send secret service agents to various camps to determine whether "camp followers" (i.e., prostitutes) were German agents. Other resolutions were based on War Department recommendations for "the absolute abolishment of all houses of ill-fame," a shelter home for "young and irresponsible girls," a detention camp for prostitutes where they "can be isolated and medically treated until cured," and a clinic "under Federal control for the free treatment of all persons infected with venereal disease."[37]

Federal district judge Henry D. Clayton in Montgomery contributed to the effort on June 12, when he held what the *Advertiser* termed "vice" day in his courtroom. He tried two types of cases before the all-white, all-male juries: one for the illegal sale of alcoholic beverages, especially to soldiers, and the other for the illegal sale of sex, especially to soldiers. A number of cases resulted in convictions for illegal sales of alcohol, but the only convictions for the illegal sale of sex were of four black madams, despite the Camp Sheridan report that blamed white prostitutes for transmitting the most cases of venereal disease there. Judge Clayton congratulated the jurors for "the devotion which you have given to the discharge of your duties" and told them that "the fallen women and those who help the fallen women in their business, their unholy occupation of tempting these young men, and participating with them in the violation of God's law and man's law, as well—those fallen women, the taxi drivers, the hack drivers, those people who have houses for these women to resort to—they are all pro-German." But particularly, he emphasized, "these lewd women . . . are to be treated as pro-German."[38] The camp commander lifted the quarantine a week later, but remaining troops who sought sex for sale in Montgomery found the sources temporarily cowed.

Neither Camp McClellan nor the city of Anniston experienced a similar crisis. As noted earlier, Anniston was a much smaller community, and thus houses of prostitution were more visible and easier to police. City and military officials there had recognized early on that taxi drivers were the "most active agents" in fostering prostitution and set out to foil them.[39]

Back at Camp Sheridan, the newly activated regular army Ninth Infantry Division arrived in increments to replace the Thirty-seventh. On Sunday, July 23, at the weekly community sing in the city auditorium, merchant and chamber of commerce president Emmanuel Meertief officially welcomed the Ninth's regimental and divisional staffs. Citizens there sang old Southern melodies, and a regimental band gave a concert of marches and popular patriotic songs. Most of the division's units soon settled into a rigorous training routine.[40]

The men of the Ninth not only trained for overseas duty but also quickly picked up the social reins recently dropped by the men of the Thirty-seventh. One particular relationship, between a Sheridan-based soldier and a local young woman, would become world famous. On the night of July 15, 1918, Second Lieutenant F. Scott Fitzgerald, a young infantry platoon leader, finagled an invitation to a dance at the Montgomery Country Club. As Fort Leavenworth Officer Training School captain Dwight D. Eisenhower noted, Fitzgerald was an indifferent officer. He was much more interested in writing a novel than soldiering.

He was also interested in pretty and vivacious young women and focused on Zelda Sayre, the darling of the Taylor Field flyers. A biographer called her "a child of nature, her spirit had something in common with the Greek poetic idea of the demigod or super-human, who is free from that terror of environment which makes for conformity." Fitzgerald was entranced, she less so. But in the months that the Ninth Division trained at Sheridan, they came together. Fitzgerald also found time to pursue his other love. In the post library he worked on his first novel. Zelda later described him as a "blonde lieutenant" who seemed to have "some heavenly support beneath his shoulder blades that lifted his feet from the ground in ecstatic suspension, as if he enjoyed the ability to fly but was walking as a compromise with convention."[41]

Things were different in Anniston. The army did not immediately replace the Twenty-ninth with another division, so much of Camp McClellan lay vacant for a long period. Troops who did arrive were mainly draftees from New Jersey, New York, and the New England area, many of whom were African Americans slated for stevedore duty. They occupied tents vacated by the Twenty-ninth and received basic training in the camp's development battalion. White commissioned officers and noncommissioned officers trained black noncommissioned officers. Because of the increasing number of black troops, a black YMCA secretary, Professor M. R. Powell, and staff took over one of the camp's YMCA huts.[42]

Like the soldiers in Montgomery, these draftees and the men of the Twenty-ninth before them established some lasting social ties in Anniston and Jacksonville. The Battle family of Jacksonville, like other civilians, "were encouraged to open their homes to military men." Mrs. Maude Battle "walked around the square in Jacksonville and selected four men whose faces she liked and invited them home for Sunday dinner. These four, 'Ray, Eddy, Spag, and Van,' became regulars, attracted by the family warmth, the good food, and the young ladies." One of the four soldiers, Howard P. Van Tassell from New Jersey, returned after the war and married one of the Battle daughters, Willie Maude.[43]

Regardless of sociability, war yields death, and the Great War was particularly bloody. In July came news from the western front of the deaths of men once stationed at the mobilization camp at Vandiver Park. September brought casualty lists from the divisional troops formerly stationed at Sheridan and McClellan. The 167th Infantry Regiment of the 42nd "Rainbow" Division, the old 4th Alabama National Guard Regiment, helped stop the final German offensive and took part in the Allied counterattack that marked the beginning of the end of the war. Several Montgomerians died in the battle of the Croix Rouge Farm of July 26, 1918. The 167th lost Captain Julien M. Strassburger, commander of a machine-gun company, Corporal Pearson Wynn, and Private Ferrall Smith to a hail of enemy artillery and machine-gun fire. Friends in Montgomery and in Anniston learned in September of the deaths of Thirty-seventh and Twenty-ninth Division soldiers in the final Allied push, the Meuse-Argonne offensive, in which American casualties were very heavy.[44]

Another international casualty-producer affected Alabama beginning in September 1918. This was the Spanish flu pandemic, a version of swine flu, which actually began in the United States and was carried overseas by the American Expeditionary Force. Historian Wayne Flynt described its effect on Alabama: "With soldiers lacking immunities and packed together in places like Camp Sheridan, the virus spread like wildfire . . . killing thousands in Alabama before it subsided." Base commanders drastically reduced training schedules as base hospitals filled with hundreds of patients. Inevitably, deaths occurred in the cities and at the bases. On a single day in October, for example, twelve Camp Sheridan soldiers died of the flu. The other Alabama camps had similar numbers of flu deaths.[45]

As the war dragged toward its end, and the flu burned itself out, Camp Sheridan, Camp McClellan, and Taylor Field managed a moderate level of training activities. In October the Ninth Division left Sheridan for Camp Mills, Long Island, in preparation for shipping overseas. At McClellan, the Sixth Infantry Division arrived. That same month, Montgomery became the headquarters for all Army Air Service bases in the states of Alabama, Tennessee, Georgia, Mississippi, and Florida. Commanding officer Lieutenant Colonel Frank M. Andrews established his headquarters in the Bell Building downtown, but the Army Air Service closed his office in an overall reduction in force several months after the war ended.[46]

Hostilities ceased with the armistice of November 11, 1918. The celebration in downtown Montgomery was wild. Planes from Taylor Field flew over the city and dropped roses on the crowd. Anniston had a less-boisterous celebration. The Ninth Division returned from Camp Mills in December. Scott Fitzgerald was disappointed that he had not seen action on the western front but was happy to return to his courtship of Zelda Sayre. The Sixth Division at McClellan had undergone little training and did not deploy overseas.[47]

Months before the end of the war, congressional backers of Camp Sheridan and Camp McClellan, respectively, jockeyed to have their favored base made permanent after the war. Montgomery and Anniston newspapers periodically emphasized that improvements at their camps likely signalized the longed-for permanence. But Montgomerians paid less attention to the postwar prospects of Taylor Field and Repair Depot No. 3. The former was many miles away in the county, and the city had not benefited as much as it had from Camp Sheridan. As for the repair depot, Montgomery had barely become accustomed to it before the war ended.

In May 1918, Montgomery city leaders thought they saw evidence that Camp Sheridan was to become a permanent cantonment. Representative Dent's office announced that the Algernon Blair Company received $772,700 to build a sewer system for the entire camp. The contract called for a fifteen-mile-long main line that would be connected with the base hospital and then run across the camp and discharge into the Alabama River. Construction was unfinished when the war ended.

Even with hope high that Sheridan was to become a cantonment, the mayor and the city commission hedged their bets with a plan to annex the county land on which Camp Sheridan stood if the federal government demobilized the camp. Early in 1918, city lawyers brought condemnation proceedings in federal court to obtain part of the Camp Sheridan property, including Vandiver Park. In June 1918, the court awarded Vandiver Park to the city, which then paid $33,000 to its owners, the First National Bank of Montgomery, the Fourth National Bank of Montgomery, and the Western Railroad of Alabama. The War Department authorized Mayor Robertson to renew the leases, due to expire on July 1, for the remaining campsite.[48]

Montgomery had hedged its bet well, for Camp Sheridan was not destined to be a cantonment. Soon after the armistice, the War Department designated the camp a demobilization and war surplus center. In May 1919, the city bought the leases of the Camp Sheridan property from the federal government for $10,000. After the leases expired in July, the city brought condemnation proceedings in federal court against the property owners. But that process took a year and a half to complete. In 1920, after appeals by the property owners were unsuccessful, Montgomery absorbed the former campgrounds.[49]

Flight training at Taylor Field ceased shortly after the armistice. The buildings were sold and the land returned to the property owners. In World War II, army aviation cadets from nearby training fields used Taylor Field's still-undeveloped landing area to practice touch-and-go landings. Montgomery's third military base, Repair Depot No. 3, survived the postwar downsizing and, despite War Department efforts later in the 1920s to close it, became permanent through the efforts of Representative Lister Hill, a worthy successor to Stanley Dent. Through a long evolutionary process it has become Maxwell Air Force Base and home of Air University, the doctrinal, intellectual, and educational center of the United States Air Force.[50]

Camp McClellan did become permanent. In June 1918, the *Anniston Star* reported that construction of a sewer and plumbing system had begun there at a cost of one million dollars. Plans called for the contractors, local firm Lebarre and Edwin, to install a large septic tank to receive the sewerage. They completed the system before the end of the war. In June the Alabama Power Company finally agreed to extend its tramline to provide service from Anniston to the camp, but withdrew its offer in July. Representative Blackmon and the local Rotary club pressured city leaders to find an alternative, and by September local funding enabled an extension of the streetcar line to begin. Also in September, Blackmon's office announced that all tents at McClellan would be replaced by wooden barracks. The camp had become a cantonment.[51]

But its future was uncertain until 1920, when the War Department designated it a permanent regular military camp. It was upgraded in 1929 to become Fort McClellan, serving as a regular U.S. Army post in World War II and the Korean and Vietnamese conflicts. The fort was decommissioned as a regular army installation in the 1990s, but part of the McClellan complex now serves as a National Guard training center, returning full circle to the function of Alabama's few small military encampments at the beginning of World War I.[52]

The War Department decommissioned both Fort Gaines and Fort Morgan after the Great War, turning them over to the State of Alabama. In the twenty-first century, they have become important tourist attractions under the auspices of the Alabama Historical Commission.

Once the United States entered World War I, three of the four new military bases constructed in Alabama trained thousands of ground troops and hundreds of Army Air Service pilots. Many of these infantrymen saw action on the western front in the final campaigns against Germany. Although much smaller in number, pilots trained at Taylor Field flew in combat above the trenches in France. Perhaps equally as important to the residents of the cities near the bases, these soldiers and airmen interacted socially with them, shared their own backgrounds and perspectives, married some, and contributed greatly to the local economies. Civilian and military personnel alike shared the horrors of the flu pandemic in 1918, heightening local awareness of the humanity of these strangers. Especially important was the presence of large numbers of soldiers and airmen from the East and Midwest, a presence that helped mitigate the locals' prejudice against "Yankees" that had lingered since the Civil War. Not all such interactions were positive, of course; the relationship between military personnel and prostitutes in nearby cities is one example.

Of the military bases during World War I in Alabama (Fort Gaines, Fort Morgan, Camp Sheridan, Camp McClellan, Taylor Field, and Army Air Service Repair Depot No. 3), only Repair Depot No. 3 remains active as a military base in the twenty-first century. Though the least significant of the newly created federal military bases in Alabama during World War I, as Maxwell Air Force Base it has become one of the country's most important U.S. Air Force installations.

4
Alabama's Black Baptist Leaders, the Progressive Era, and World War I

Wilson Fallin, Jr.

The period from the beginning of the twentieth century to 1917, the year the United States entered the Great War, was a time of subjugation and oppression of blacks in Alabama. Although called by some historians the Progressive Era because of agitation for social and political reform, it was a progressivism that did not seek basic changes in race relations. In Alabama, Progressives sought to improve education, standardize business and medical practices, institute child labor laws, and promote Prohibition. But these reforms were for whites only. In 1901, in the name of purifying the state of voting fraud, Alabama ratified a new constitution that disfranchised blacks and poor whites. Prior to the constitutional convention, more than 100,000 blacks were registered to vote. Following ratification and the institution of the poll tax, all but 3,572 blacks were removed from the voting rolls.[1] Shortly afterward, laws emerged that mandated legal segregation. Alabama cities and streetcar companies passed regulations that placed blacks in separate cars and separate geographical locations in towns. As a result of these new restrictive measures, blacks were increasingly forced to build their own communities. It was within these communities—led by ministers—that black Alabamians experienced the full impact of World War I on the home front.

To understand the importance of black Baptist leaders in the black community of Alabama, it is necessary first to look at the place and role of the church, particularly Baptist churches. Churches were at the heart of the segregated communities that blacks developed. Leaving white churches and forming their own after slavery, black churches formed conferences and conventions during the period of Reconstruction. The largest and most influential of the black religious groups were Baptists.

A desire for independence and self-determination motivated blacks to establish their own churches and to exercise their right to free worship. Having developed their own worship style, blacks wanted a setting in which they could listen to and react to their own preaching, singing, dancing, and shouting. In their own churches, they could do so without being criticized or looked down on by whites. Their churches also promoted equality. Previously, black members had been relegated to balconies and separate seating areas and prohibited from voting on church matters. By organizing their own churches, freedmen gained some measure of freedom over their own lives and an opportunity to develop pride and self-respect. In addition, with the dissolution of the old communal bonds, churches provided former slaves with a caring community of their own creation. By 1868 there were approximately fifty such churches. In that year, twenty-seven delegates from Alabama churches came together and formed the Alabama Colored Baptist State Convention.[2] After the convention, delegates went back to their communities and formed local associations. Ten years later, the convention created the Alabama Baptist Normal and Theological School to train teachers and pastors for the black community. In 1908 the school became Selma University.

There were many reasons for the rapid growth of black Baptist churches over other denominations. One of the most important was the leadership that pastors from within the state provided. In fact, when the state convention formed, a few men from the all-black American Baptist Missionary Convention offered some advice, but they gave no guidance beyond the initial meeting. In contrast, other denominations in Alabama, including the black Methodists who constituted the second largest group, selected leaders primarily from outside the state. Another advantage for the Baptists was that their ministers came from the bosom of the people and sought to minister to the needs of their congregations. Many of the early black Baptist leaders had been slave preachers, and others had gained their personal freedom but continued to minister to slaves. This experience gave black Baptists a tremendous advantage over other denominations and helped give their leaders credibility as spokesmen for their people.

Representing the largest religious group in the state among people of color, black Baptist leaders generally spoke out against what they saw as the excessive oppression of blacks. Leading up to World War I, black Baptists issued protests against both segregation and disfranchisement and worked to defeat both. In Mobile and Montgomery black pastors led and supported bus boycotts against the segregation of streetcars. Although both movements received only temporary and limited success because of internecine conflict and the upsurge of racism across the South and the nation, blacks took solace in the fact that they had shown their disapproval of such measures.[3]

When Europe descended into war in August 1914, Alabama blacks had been marginalized socially and politically, and because they were preoccupied with other pressing issues, they made few comments about the war in the official proceedings of the Alabama Baptist Convention or in associational records between 1914 and 1917. Most black Baptist leaders believed that the war was primarily a European conflict and had little to do with blacks in the United States. Woodrow Wilson pledged in his 1916 campaign to keep America out of the war. Many blacks had abandoned the Republican Party and had supported him but were disappointed that he had resegregated facilities in federal buildings and had not championed their cause. Nevertheless, most blacks had no reason to believe that the United States would enter the war. In addition and most important, black Baptists were concerned with issues they perceived to be of greater significance or to be directly pertinent to their survival—lynching, disfranchisement, segregation, and the lack of education—to worry about Wilson's foreign policy vis-à-vis Europe.

In spite of black Baptist apathy toward the war before the United States entered it, mention of the war did begin to creep into their associational and convention minutes. The price of cotton was of special concern to blacks because most continued to live in the Black Belt as small farmers and sharecroppers. In his 1914 annual report to the Alabama Colored Baptist State Convention, President William Gilbert of Selma University blamed the war for an economic depression that had brought on hard times at Selma University. He urged the convention to undertake a special rally in January to enable Selma University to operate during the winter months.[4]

Black Baptists also discussed the war as a theological problem—they saw the war as the work of Satan. In 1914 the New Hope Association blamed the war directly on the devil; its moderator said that "sin and the work of the devil were at the heart of the conflict, and there was now war within and outside the church."[5] One year later the Mt. Pilgrim Association of Birmingham agreed that sin was at the heart of the war, but also added that Germany was the aggressor and the "deification of Satan's work."[6] One speaker at the association agreed with some national Baptist leaders that the war was God's revenge on Europe for the colonization of African nations. These leaders insisted, for example, that Germany's devastation of Belgium was just retribution for King Leopold's brutal reign in the Congo. The government of Belgium, having reaped rewards through greed, brutality, and the suffering of others, had to pay for its callousness and oppression.[7] In making sin and Germany the cause of the war, black Baptists were in agreement with many white Baptists in the state. As war clouds gathered over Europe, white Baptists spread the blame among all European nations, but as German submarines attacked American ships, sentiment turned against the Kaiser.[8]

The emphasis among black Baptist leaders on sin and Satan as the cause of the war is not surprising in the light of major theological ideas in the Baptist community. Beginning with slavery, blacks developed a liberation theology in which they identified their plight with that of the Israelite slaves in the Old Testament. They were convinced that if they remained faithful and patient, God would deliver them as he had the Israelites from Egyptian bondage. Sermons of black pastors and the singing of the spirituals reflected this liberation theme. Slavery and segregation were identified as the work of Satan as was all evil in the world. War was also the devil's work brought to earth as a result of man's selfishness and greed. In the end, however, good would triumph over evil. Being a God of justice and power, His will would finally reign supreme, and sin would be destroyed. It was this faith that gave blacks hope amid slavery, segregation, and war.

President James H. Eason of the Baptist convention noted the sinking of the *Lusitania* and regretted the awful loss of life in his annual address in 1915. He contended that because of the war both the high and the low were tasting the grim reaper, death. To him this incident was not enough to bring the United States into the war, and his highest concern remained the survival of blacks in Alabama. Even though he lamented the many deaths caused by the war, Eason was more perturbed by that year's death of Booker T. Washington and what the loss of such a leader meant for the future of blacks in Alabama and the nation. The convention that year paid special attention to Washington, calling him "the greatest man of his time."[9]

When the United States finally entered the war in 1917, Alabama Baptist leaders began to give it priority among their concerns. The main theme of leaders during the conflict was loyalty. In his address at the 1917 jubilee session of the convention, David V. Jemison, who had succeeded James

Eason as convention president in 1915, urged Baptists in the state to remain loyal to the war effort. He reminded the delegates that blacks had served faithfully in every war. Using the example of the Revolutionary War, he reminded his audience that Crispus Attucks, a black, was the first person to die for the revolutionary cause. He also recounted black contributions in the War of 1812, the Civil War, and the Spanish-American War. Jemison insisted that blacks could do no less in World War I. He was convinced that support of the war effort would bring greater rights to blacks in the state, for whites would see black loyalty and out of a deep sense of appreciation grant better treatment. He maintained that God was working through the war to bring about the greatness of the black race. Through black loyalty, Jemison asserted, "Ethiopia was stretching forth her hands unto God."[10]

Jemison's statement reflected a theological stance in the black religious community known as Ethiopianism, which emerged in the nineteenth century and was prominent in the sermons of African American clergy. Ethiopianism served as a deterrent to racism and a counter to those who posited black inferiority. Based on Psalms 68:31, "Princes shall come out of Egypt, and Ethiopia shall stretch forth her hands to God," the movement idealized both Egypt and Ethiopia. Black clergymen and scholars insisted that the African race, represented by both Egypt and Ethiopia, had a glorious civilization in the past. Ethiopianism thereby sought to destroy many pseudoscientific beliefs that had emerged during the Progressive Era, most prominent of which was the notion that blacks were genetically inferior to whites and could not elevate themselves. Instead of the curse on Ham, black leaders insisted that Psalms 68:31 pointed to a magnificent past and a rising future. That future included the redemption of Africa from colonialism and a worldwide mission for black people to humanize the world through the imitation of Christ's humility.[11]

Some Alabama Baptist clergymen pointed to the rise of great leaders such as Booker T. Washington and Richard Boyd of the National Baptist Publishing Board as evidence of increasing achievement and elevation of black Americans. The growth of black educational institutions also showed the emergence of the race. As a result, Ethiopianism advanced the call for black pride and for blacks' control of their own institutions. For Jemison and others, the Great War was a part of God's design to elevate blacks and give them greater rights.

Others joined Jemison at the 1917 jubilee session of the convention in urging loyalty. The Reverend C. First Johnson gave a report titled "The

Future of the Convention." He said that "blacks should leave nothing undone that would have our loyalty questioned." Charles L. Fisher gave the jubilee sermon and again called for black support of the war effort. He added that the "cause of the war was not the failure of Christianity, but the result of men not heeding the gospel especially the fatherhood of God and the brotherhood of man." Yet he insisted that black loyalty would cause the nation to elevate the race.[12]

Also giving a speech at that jubilee session was Robert R. Moton. Moton had succeeded Booker T. Washington as principal of Tuskegee Institute in 1915. Although not the premier race leader as was Washington, Moton was aware that the job carried with it an implicit leadership position among blacks. Because Washington had built and maintained strong support from the Baptists of the state, it is not surprising that his successor would be asked to address the convention during its anniversary meeting. Both parties were anxious to maintain the good relationship between Tuskegee and the convention, especially as Moton's visibility increased during the war. The Federal Council of Churches appointed him to its Committee on the Welfare of Negro Troops, and President Wilson sent him to France to investigate actions of black troops. Moton's address to the jubilee session fortified his audience. Knowing not only the financial struggles of Selma University but also its value as an institution for training ministers and teachers for Alabama pulpits and schools, Moton urged the convention to keep the institution alive. His remarks regarding Selma drew great applause. The delegates were happy to know that this eminent black leader, who was highly influential among white educational philanthropic foundations, thought well of their institution. Moton also told the delegates that the war provided opportunities that blacks must take advantage of, especially in industry. Blacks, he insisted, "must become so indispensable that foreign labor could not replace them."[13]

Statements of loyalty expressed by Jemison, Moton, and other Baptists in the state were well in line with opinion in the general black community. Although A. Phillip Randolph, a black socialist and president of the large and influential Brotherhood of Sleeping Car Porters, opposed the war and blacks' participation in it, most blacks supported the notion of loyalty. Among these were W. E. B. DuBois, editor of the NAACP's magazine, the *Crisis*, and one of the most militant blacks of his day. He urged blacks to close ranks with whites and present a unified front during the national emergency. "Let us," he editorialized, "while this war lasts, forget our special grievances and close our ranks shoulder to shoulder with our own white fellow citizens and the allied nations that are fighting for democracy. We make no ordinary sacrifice, but we make it gladly and willingly with our eyes lifted to the hills."[14]

Their loyalty in other U.S. wars appeared to blacks to have brought some positive benefits, justifying their hopes that loyalty in the Great War would do the same. The service of five thousand black soldiers in the Revolutionary War advanced the cause of abolition in the North, and the Civil War, in which 180,000 black soldiers fought for the Union, had garnered emancipation in the South. With all the rhetoric about making the world safe for democracy, most blacks in Alabama and the nation supported the war with the hope that doing so would improve race relations.

Heeding the call of their leaders, blacks volunteered in large numbers. Of the 750,000 men in the regular army and the National Guard at the beginning of the war, approximately 20,000 were black. Ten thousand were in black units of the regular army, and ten thousand were in various units of the National Guard. African Americans were among those who thronged the recruiting stations in April 1917, but for the most part they were rejected. Approximately 2.3 million blacks registered for the draft, and 367,000 were called to duty, some 13 percent of the nation's 2.8 million draftees. In all, more than 400,000 blacks served in the United States armed forces during World War I.

Loyalty among black Baptists on the Alabama home front expressed itself in several ways. In communities where black soldiers trained, churches provided assistance and encouragement. The black churches in Montgomery organized the Central Committee of Colored Montgomery Citizens to devise ways to "entertain the colored soldiers stationed in the area." Black Baptists were active on the committee, especially members from the Dexter Avenue Baptist Church, such as committee chair and Montgomery businessman Victor Hugo Tulane, along with prominent community leaders W. F. Watkins, J. W. Phillips, and H. C. Scott. The Dexter Avenue Baptist Church choir, with participants from other black churches, created a 250-voice chorus to entertain the troops with practices and programs held in the Dexter Avenue sanctuary. Dexter Avenue superintendent of the Sunday school, J. W. Beverly, was in charge of directing the food conservation program among Montgomery's African American community, and in November 1917 the congregation expanded its participation in the war effort to include national as well as state involvement. Kelley Miller, dean of Howard University, organized the Colored Comfort Committee in order to "aid the dependents of our soldiers and sailors" who were killed or disabled fighting for the nation. Churches in Montgomery, including Dexter Avenue, scheduled programs to raise money for this cause.[15]

Black Baptist churches also actively promoted the four Liberty Bond drives during the war to raise revenues to prosecute the military effort. Among the many churches that promoted bond drives, two were very active: the Dexter Avenue Baptist Church of Montgomery and the Sixth Avenue Baptist Church of Birmingham. John Goodgame, pastor of the Sixth Avenue Baptist Church and treasurer of the Alabama Colored Baptist State Convention, agreed with convention president Jemison and others that loyalty would create better opportunities for blacks. One important way to show loyalty was to purchase bonds.

Providing money was not the only way Alabama's black Baptists showed their loyalty while helping the war effort. They were active in the speakers bureaus that worked closely with the federal Committee of Public Information and its Alabama equivalent. Because ministers were leaders of the black community, many served as "Four Minute Men" (so named because they dispensed information about the war in four-minute speeches). Oscar W. Adams, editor of the *Birmingham Reporter,* was chief of the "colored division" of the Four Minute Men in Birmingham. He sent speakers to churches and civic meetings to discuss why blacks should support the war by buying Liberty Bonds and War Stamps. For Adams and these speakers, support for the war was more than just a patriotic duty. Like Jemison, they had faith—and promulgated that faith—that if blacks were loyal to U.S. interests, white society would reciprocate by granting greater rights following the war. Several prominent Birmingham pastors—W. L. Boyd, pastor of Trinity Baptist Church, G. L. Glanton, pastor of Twenty-third Street Baptist Church, and A. C. Williams, pastor of the Sixteenth Street Baptist Church—served in this vital capacity and made these important presentations.

Blacks made a very public showing of their loyalty when they, led by their churches' congregations, gave rousing send-offs to black soldiers who had been drafted into the military. One such rally for black "selectmen" from the Black Belt in April 1918 provides an example. A total of 160 Dallas County draftees joined 148 from Marengo County, 110 from Clarke County, 72 from Hale County, and 70 from Perry County in Selma on April 9 to be trained at Camp Dodge, Iowa. The night before they were set to leave, Tabernacle Baptist Church, headed by Pastor David V. Jemison, hosted a mass rally in their honor. The next day some five thousand persons, including whites, came to cheer the selectmen as they boarded trains to Camp Dodge.[16]

Churches were also the meeting places for patriotic rallies held by the state organization formed in 1918 by Robert Moton to support the war. Serving on the state committee was A. F. Owens, dean of theology at Selma University. Owens had served in the Spanish-American War and had formed a military unit when he served as pastor of St. Anthony Church. He was the main speaker at patriotic rallies that Moton sponsored in local Baptist churches in Birmingham, Bessemer, Opelika, Selma, and Mobile. Speaking at a March 1918 rally in Opelika, Owens listed four ways that the war provided the greatest opportunity for blacks to show loyalty and patriotism: (1) by serving his county the person is advancing Christianity and civilization; (2) military service gives blacks an opportunity to gain recognition in the eyes of the world; (3) the war is a way of destroying autocracy and advancing democracy and freedom; and (4) service in the military and war industries provides an opportunity for blacks to receive sufficient monetary compensation to secure a better place in society. In June 1918, Owens sponsored a rally at the First African Baptist Church of Tuscaloosa that raised $1,500 to support the troops and war work.[17]

Black Baptists from Alabama served not only on the home front but also in the Allied trenches. Of course, some prominent black ministers saw action with them. The most well-known case was Uriah J. Robinson, pastor of the Mt. Olive Baptist Church in Anniston. The church granted him a leave of absence so he could become a chaplain in the American Expeditionary Force's 365th Infantry Regiment from the time of its organization until its demobilization. He saw more than ten months of service in France and Belgium and was with the 92nd Division during its battles in the Argonne Forest and Metz. Wounded at Metz, Robinson refused to leave the field. On his discharge from active duty, he returned to Mt. Olive Church as pastor and also continued as a chaplain in the reserve officers' corps. Robinson later became president of the Alabama Colored Baptist State Convention.[18]

Black Baptist women responded patriotically to the war in their own ways. They supported the Liberty Bond efforts and served with the speakers bureaus. Possibly the most significant work came from women who were part of the Women's Committee of the Council of National Defense (WCCND). Mrs. Alice Dunbar Nelson, widow of the famous Negro poet Paul Lawrence Dunbar, came south to help black Baptist women organize their efforts. In several sections of Alabama she found women's organizations hard at work on their own and in close association with women in churches. In Selma, local women sold Liberty Bonds and War Stamps, but their work was unorganized. Mobile was a bit better; women had established a "war service club," but it was not a part of any existing state or national group. Overall, few nonchurch state or national associations operating in the South tried to organize the black community. For example, the Alabama Red Cross refused to allow black women to do canteen work at railroad stations because doing so would have required them to wear special uniforms, which would give them status similar to white women.

The most productive work among women that Mrs. Nelson found was in Bessemer, Birmingham, and other areas of Jefferson County. In both Bessemer and Birmingham, women had active chapters of the WCCND that "made comfort kits for soldiers with a Bible in each kit." These chapters helped women whose husbands had gone to camp, paying particular attention to expectant mothers. The WCCND pressed its chapters to do all in their power to conserve and enlarge the existing food supply. The Bessemer unit responded by canning one thousand quarts of perishable foodstuffs.[19]

One reason black women supported the WCCND was to promote social reform, some of which began before the war. Health care was one of these areas that needed attention. Infant mortality and the health of babies was a real concern among black women in Alabama. The members of the WCCND weighed and measured babies to promote good health. Clinics were often set up at churches. In Birmingham, three separate black units were involved in this work. Another area of interest for reformers was the creation of better recreational facilities. At the Shiloh Baptist Church, Birmingham's largest black congregation, the WCCND, with Mrs. Nelson as the primary speaker, talked about not only better recreation but also measures to be taken to safeguard black women working in industry.[20] These activities were similar to those of the white Alabama Federation of Women's Clubs. Inspired by Margaret Murray Washington, wife of Booker T. Washington, Alabama's black women's clubs focused on social services to lift up the race, paying particular attention to the social, economic, and moral uplift of black women.[21]

As the war continued, black Baptist leaders became more assertive in discussing what they hoped would come from the war and in calling for fair play for blacks in the military. James Eason gave the annual Emancipation Day speech in Bessemer on January 1, 1918. Emancipation Day was a noteworthy event in the black community, for it celebrated the Emancipation Proclamation that took effect on January 1, 1863, during the Civil War. In addition to being a celebration, Emancipation Day was a time to project what African Americans must do to enhance and attain full freedom. Eason titled his discussion "What the Negro Expects from the War." He listed four anticipated results: the chance to work; better educational facilities; the "chance to live," by which he meant better health facilities for blacks; and the ballot. Eason made it clear that blacks would not be satisfied with anything less than these four things.[22] For him the loyalty of blacks in the war meant that these rights were deserved and just.

David Jemison, in his 1918 address before the Alabama Colored Baptist State Convention, again stressed the need for blacks to show loyalty, but he also called on the nation to be sure that blacks were treated with greater respect and courtesy. He deplored the continuing violence against blacks, especially lynchings. He ended his comments by maintaining that "while blacks had been loyal, the government had a responsibility to protect them."[23]

Black ministers and their organizations pressed for greater rights for blacks as they served in the army. In March 1918, the Interdenominational Alliance made an appeal to the Birmingham Railway, Light, and Power Company to improve the transportation of blacks on streetcars in the city. Among those making the appeal were James Eason, R. N. Hall, A. C. Williams, and John Goodgame. Hall, along with the others, as noted earlier, was a pastor of a large Baptist church in Birmingham and an active member of the state Baptist convention. Each insisted that "the kind of abuse and negative treatment that blacks were receiving on Birmingham's streetcars was doing more to hurt the cause of the war than German propaganda."[24]

But such calls and appeals fell mostly on deaf ears. Many whites were determined to see that there would be no wholesale distribution of the blessings of liberty. Most symbolic of white resistance to such change was the revival of the Ku Klux Klan after 1915. Its growth was slow until the end of the war, at which time it came forth with a broad program of uniting native-born white Christians for concerted action in the preservation of American institutions and the supremacy of the white race. Although the revived Klan was not as strictly antiblack as had been the first Klan—it added a leavening of anti-Catholicism and anti-Semitism—it used beatings and lynchings to punish those blacks perceived as being "out of line." Moreover, Alabama blacks felt especially threatened by the Klan because of the activities of the post-Reconstruction group. The Alabama Klan grew rapidly after the war. By 1925 it had 95,000 members and had become a powerful political force in the state.[25]

In addition to the extralegal threats from the Klan and other violent groups, Alabama's segregation laws and disfranchisement grew. Much of this broadening of racist attitudes occurred from changes brought about by the end of the war. For example, after the war ended, organized labor decided the time was right to secure higher wages for its workers. Employers, on the other hand, sought to rescind some of the benefits they were forced to grant during the war. This conflict led to a rash of labor strikes, many of which occurred in the steel industry. The strikes also helped spark the Red Scare, the belief that Communism had infiltrated labor and other organizations. At the same time, the United States was experiencing racial unrest that grew from blacks returning from the war and seeing that their sacrifices were not leading to the equal rights they had hoped for and expected. As blacks moved north, too, resentment grew, and race riots broke out. All these events created a heightened atmosphere of hostility toward blacks in Alabama. In the early 1920s, Birmingham easily enacted several ordinances mandating rigid segregation in housing and on streetcars, further marginalizing blacks both socially and spatially. Furthermore, the Alabama constitution of 1901 had done its job—to remove the political voice of African Americans from the state. In the Birmingham of the 1920s, only 352 blacks out of a population of 85,280 were eligible to vote.[26] In some Black Belt counties in Alabama, no black was eligible to vote in the 1920s and 1930s.

Despite white oppression, African Americans' loyalty to the war effort strengthened in black Baptists, and in the black Alabama community in general, a determination to advance themselves. For example, Robert Moton was successful in acquiring a new hospital for black veterans at Tuskegee Institute. No sooner had the hospital opened than there emerged a power struggle over the staff. Tuskegee whites demanded an all-white staff, while Moton firmly insisted that it should be black. Moton and the blacks of Tuskegee won the debate. The presence of so many highly trained blacks and other professionals frightened local whites, but Moton and the other blacks stood their ground and won in spite of protests from the Ku Klux Klan and various Alabama political officials.[27]

Alabama's black Baptists were a part of the growing activism of the race. In the convention one year after the end of the war, Dr. R. T. Pollard, president of Selma University, reported that the enrollment at Selma

University had increased that year. He saw this increase as black determination to persevere in spite of opposition. Pollard, who had vigorously supported the war, stated that "all kinds of inducement were held out and promises made to our people as to what might be expected when the war was won, yet it seemed that never before in the history of the race had there been such a united effort on the part of some to hinder our progress and subject the race to humiliation and disgrace." He further added that "instead of defeating the spirit of blacks it has brought greater activism among them. Never will blacks resort to things as they were."[28]

David Jemison issued several strong calls for justice and fairness. In his 1921 address Jemison noted that blacks, most of whom had been loyal during the war years, were discontent. One of the major reasons was unfairness, especially in the courts. He made it clear that he opposed crime, but he insisted that black crime was exaggerated because of injustices in the courts. Blacks did not receive fair trials, and that fact accounted for their disproportionate numbers in penal institutions. In addition, Jemison maintained that white policemen had been so unfair to blacks that they had lost the respect of the black community. He demanded that the legal system and the courts administer equal justice to both blacks and whites.[29]

The stronger call for fairness did not lead black Baptist leaders to embrace radical social and economic movements, such as Communism, that sought inroads into the African American community after the Great War. Protest and self-help rather than radicalism or revolution continued as an important part of black Baptist ideology. Consequently, ministers and other leaders reflected this theme in their writings and sermons. Charles L. Fisher, who served as pastor of the Sixteenth Street Baptist Church, dean of theology at Selma University (succeeding A. F. Owens), and chair of the trustee board, preached that black Baptists should thank God for such leaders as William McAlpine, Charles O. Boothe, and William R. Pettiford, all of whom laid the foundation for great institutions. Pettiford, for example, helped found both a children's hospital and a senior citizens' home in Birmingham in the 1890s even though neither the city nor the state provided funds. But Fisher especially singled out the contributions to the race made by Booker T. Washington and his articulation of racial self-help that made him, in Fisher's mind, the greatest man of his time, either black or white. Because they implemented the philosophy of self-help, blacks often provided for themselves when they could not get an equal share of taxes for education or social services. Fisher's gratitude for self-help, however, did not stop him from demanding fairness from the government. He joined Jemison and others in calling on the government of Alabama to return the franchise to all who qualified, blacks as well as whites.[30]

In addition to Fisher, John Goodgame called on blacks to develop self-help traits and habits that would advance the race. He admitted that blacks lived in an age of renewed prejudice and discrimination. He pointed to job discrimination, the lack of funds for schools, lynchings, police brutality, and the growth of the Ku Klux Klan as evidence of this renewed hostility. Therefore, Goodgame said, blacks needed to develop strong values: frugality, religion, education, and racial solidarity. With these virtues blacks would excel in spite of the times.[31]

Some black Baptist leaders went beyond resolutions and speeches and took a more activist approach. Protest became stronger among them. For example, in 1919 R. T. Pollard and several prominent black religious and civic leaders formed the Negro Betterment Association. They petitioned, however unsuccessfully, the Alabama legislature to create greater justice for blacks.[32]

Nothing represented the postwar activism in the black community and black church more than the emergence of the NAACP. Founded in 1909 in Springfield, Illinois, in response to a race riot in that city, the interracial group challenged discrimination in the courts. It rejected the accommodationism of Booker T. Washington and called for full rights for blacks. It established branches in Birmingham in 1916 and in both Montgomery and Mobile in 1919. Among its earliest activities in Alabama, the group petitioned the state legislature to provide better public education, improve conditions for Negroes on trains, take action to deter lynchings, and give blacks the right to vote.[33] The NAACP became the most successful civil rights organization in the state, and its fostering of the *Brown v. Board of Education* case in 1954 essentially destroyed legal segregation in the nation.

When the Great War began in 1914, Baptists were the largest denomination among people of color in Alabama. Baptist churches, associations, and the state convention had provided blacks with educational and benevolent institutions, together with a theology of hope and liberation as well as protest against racial injustice. At first, black leaders were not especially concerned with the problems of Europe, so preoccupied were they with issues they viewed as essential to their very survival—lack of education, disfranchisement, and threats from militant white racists who referred to them as less than human beings and sought to deny their basic civil and human rights. When the United States entered the war in 1917, black Baptist leaders called on their communicants to be loyal in every way. Leaders saw the war as a chance for a quid pro quo. Blacks would show their loyalty to the country and thereby garner greater rights. Black Baptists leaders led the way by urging their congregations to buy Liberty Bonds and by serving as speakers at rallies and patriotic programs. Baptist women contributed to the war effort in important ways through the Women's Committee of the Council of National Defense and localized efforts in support of the war and soldiers' families. Many of their meetings were held in black churches and were concerned with social reforms such as health and recreation.

Blacks were highly disappointed when, after the war ended, it became clear that their expectations of greater rights would be unrealized. Nevertheless, this reality did not destroy their morale. Armed with their liberation theology and convinced that God was on their side and that He would bring ultimate justice, black Baptist leaders protested through petitions to government officials while still championing self-help. In 1916, the NAACP began to form chapters in the state with aggressive black laymen and pastors working together. The black Baptist church's theology and leadership that helped sustain blacks during the turbulent progressive years in Alabama and during World War I would also motivate them to seek greater changes in the mid-twentieth century.

5
A Call to Arms for African Americans during the Age of Jim Crow
Black Alabamians' Response to the U.S. Declaration of War in 1917

David Alsobrook

On April 2, 1917, when President Woodrow Wilson asked Congress for a declaration of war against Germany "to make the world safe for democracy," his noble words rang hollow for African Americans across the nation. Wilson's patriotic call to arms "for the ultimate peace of the world and the liberation of its people" was especially galling for blacks in Alabama. Virtually erased from political participation by the constitution of 1901 and brutally subjugated by more than two decades of Jim Crow rule and mob violence, black Alabamians were ambivalent at best about fighting overseas for freedoms they had not known at home.[1] Moreover, by the spring of 1917, they had no faith in Wilson's commitment to "Negro Issues," such as equality in the courts, public transportation and accommodations, black compulsory education, and federal protection against lynchings. Wilson's glowing endorsement in 1915 of D. W. Griffith's controversial film *The Birth of a Nation* and his administration's segregation of federal employees' restrooms, cafeterias, and other facilities in Washington, D.C., spoke volumes about the president's racial views.[2]

Yet, many African American leaders sought to demonstrate to whites that the black masses were loyal, patriotic, and eager to contribute to the war effort. They believed that such public acts would dilute Jim Crow's horrific effects and provide blacks with some measure of equality after the war.[3] These leaders feared that unless blacks appeared to be "true Americans," they might suffer even worse injustices than they had during the previous twenty years. They followed in the tradition of Booker T. Washington, the post-Reconstruction accommodationist who frequently appealed to blacks to show white society that they were moral, industrious, and productive and thus worthy of the fruits of citizenship.[4] In employing their own conciliatory approach to race relations in 1917, however, Washington's successors underestimated whites' fears of black revolts inspired by German spies.

With war fever rising in the early spring of 1917, the *New York Times* and other reputable white newspapers published accounts of German schemes to attract southern blacks to Mexico, where German military officers would arm and train them for an insurrection against their white oppressors in the United States. Such stories fell on fertile ground among white southerners who had harbored obsessions about vengeful, armed blacks since slavery days. Sensationalized press coverage of the famous Zimmermann telegram, allegedly a secret German cable promising Mexico the return of its lost territory in the United States in exchange for supporting Germany, and the San Diego Plan, a German-Mexican conspiracy to launch a race war in the Southwest, exacerbated these white phobias. Though unsubstantiated, such accounts captured the attention of at least two federal offices in Washington, D.C.—the Justice Department's Bureau of Investigation (BI), the forerunner of the FBI, and the War Department's Military Intelligence Division. In early April 1917, the BI and the Military Intelligence Division dispatched special agents southward to investigate. In York, Alabama, two white men identified as representatives of a Wisconsin orphanage were reportedly organizing blacks to join a German plot in Mexico. Federal agents tracked the men to Blocton, then detained them, questioned them, and placed them under surveillance. In another case, BI agents in Birmingham interrogated a white man and a black man "posing as bible salesmen and ministers of the gospel" who were allegedly recruiting blacks across the South for migration to Mexico by train.[5]

White Alabamians' reactions to press articles and rumors of a German conspiracy in Mexico involving blacks ranged from skepticism to great alarm. These reactions also revealed many whites' paternalistic views about blacks. One *Montgomery Advertiser* reporter confidently assured his readers that German agents' clandestine efforts among blacks were wasted because "the average negro would patiently hear the appeal of a 'German spy' and immediately report the full conversation, with embellishments, to his white friends."[6] The *Birmingham Ledger* asserted: "The idea of Negroes rebelling against the United States is one of the wild rumors that always precede[s] war. . . . The Teuton would be losing his time in trying to create a Negro uprising, and we do the Negro race a great injustice when we credit the reports we hear. . . . They will not go into such plots except a few, and death would come quickly to that few. The Negro does not like such crimes as treason and rebellion. His faults do not lie in that direction."[7]

Adherents to the *Ledger*'s position included journalists, businessmen, ministers, and educators—all leaders among Alabama's nascent African American middle class and spokesmen for the unlettered black masses. Tuskegee principal Robert Russa Moton, who succeeded Booker T. Washington after his death in 1915, declared that a "few malcontents" could be "misled by Teuton intrigue" but that other blacks would deal harshly with them.[8] G. T. Buford, a business owner who also had a long career in Birmingham's black press, tersely affirmed the *Ledger* and Moton but added his own cautionary note. As the *Birmingham Weekly Voice*'s editor, he wrote, "[The] Kaiser with all his hordes might come and sojourn among us for a decade here in the South and he could not raise a decent corporal's guard among us. . . . There will be no need for protection against Negroes in the South, but we Negroes believe there are many white men who would bear watching."[9] Later that month he added, "We are here to remain, no Mexico or any other country for the Negro."[10]

About the same time that Buford penned his remarks, Alexander D. Pitts, the U.S. attorney in Mobile, notified the Justice Department that local blacks were planning a trip to Mexico via New Orleans: "The white people are very restless and disposed to be violent. . . . I can keep down mob law, but I would like to know what I can do with these [Negro] fellows for an example."[11] Blacks in Decatur, led by N. E. Cashin and J. A. Wilson, bitterly petitioned Governor Charles M. Henderson for an immediate investigation into press reports about the Mexican intrigues. The governor ignored their request.[12]

For their own part, white Alabamians aggressively lobbied Henderson on behalf of various schemes to prevent German-inspired black revolts. Prominent merchants in the Black Belt city of Demopolis, fearing a large, unemployed black population, advocated raising a black cavalry regiment commanded by white officers.[13] Cotton wholesaler John C. Webb assured the governor that blacks in Marengo County "are expressing a desire to volunteer for service, and cavalry especially appeals to them as they are born riders."[14] One of Webb's friends told Henderson this regiment's recruitment "will in a way solve the problem of an uprising in this community."[15] In other words, these business leaders believed that removing Demopolis's unemployed black men and subjecting them to military discipline under the guidance of white officers would make them less inclined to rebel. The governor claimed that because he was awaiting guidance from the War Department and Congress, he could not issue a statewide call for additional volunteers.[16]

Whites outside the Black Belt also feared an African American insurrection. On April 8, 1917, Colonel W. F. Garth, a Huntsville horse breeder, confided to the governor that although he had "great faith in the loyalty of our Negro population, there is . . . no question that they are being tampered with by German ag[en]ts." Garth proposed creating an Alabama Home Guard composed of draft-exempt men aged thirty to sixty. The Home Guard, he explained, "would have a very salutary effect upon any young Negroes who are disposed to be poisoned by the wiles of these German agents, or our disaffected population, . . . [and] would cause the Negro to turn a deaf ear to their persuasions, and . . . make our poor Germans very loyal." In Garth's plan each county would recruit two cavalry and two infantry companies to bolster the local sheriffs' departments. Subject to the governor's call to action, the Home Guard, Garth argued, "would anticipate any trouble real or imaginary that might come up."[17] Henderson replied that although state laws did not authorize him to create a Home Guard, several counties had already deputized special sheriffs' auxiliary units to perform the duties described by Garth.[18] The governor failed to mention that the federal government was already making plans to organize the Alabama Council of Defense. As in other states, the Council of Defense later investigated any alleged "disloyal activities" among African Americans, immigrants, socialists, and labor organizers.[19]

By late April 1917, much of the public hysteria over German–African American plots had subsided. Federal and state officials failed to produce any hard evidence of such plans and prosecuted no suspected provocateurs. Yet these events proved how easily during wartime half-truths and rumors can acquire credibility with whites who were prone to fear and distrust blacks.[20] The truth was less sensational, as one white Birmingham resident observed: "When this is boiled down, we will discover the German agents so-called are for the most part ordinary labor agents making an effort to increase the Negro exodus from the South to northern and eastern fields."[21]

This "Negro exodus" from the South to northern cities actually began as early as 1910, and by 1917 journalists and scholars had already labeled it the "Great Migration." Between June 1916 and September 1917, about eighty-five thousand African Americans left Alabama for the North. During the first six months of 1917, Mobile County alone lost about three thousand blacks to the movement. Nevertheless, probably because of plentiful jobs in the mining and steel industries, Jefferson County's black population figures held firm during this era. White Alabama landowners and industrialists who depended almost exclusively on abundant black labor blamed the Great Migration on the war, the boll weevil, and floods—factors that crushed the cotton market—and on greedy northerners who were luring blacks from the state with false promises of jobs, equality, and better lives.[22]

Such promises, whether they were true or exaggerated, fueled the Great Migration. White southerners seldom read African American newspapers or paid much attention to black leaders' opinions. As one contemporary black sociologist noted, decades of Jim Crowism had created "a sharp distinction between whites and Negroes, living and dead; there is growing up in the cities of America a distinct Negro world, . . . little known and understood by the white world."[23] Consequently, whites ignored the Great Migration until the steady drain of black labor began to have a negative effect on the southern economy. Even then, however, whites tried to minimize the migration's significance while claiming that blacks were better off in the South. For example, on April 15, 1917, the *Mobile Daily Register*'s Erwin Craighead mirrored his readers' racially skewed view of blacks and the Great Migration in an editorial titled "Jim Is Coming Home": "A curious people, child-like in some aspects, and helpless in many ways. The South is the place for them. No others understand them as do the Southern white people. Certainly, no where else will the negroes in trouble find that sympathy and help that is always extended to them by the white people of the South."[24]

George M. Cruikshank, the *Birmingham Ledger*'s editor, although arguing that the Great Migration was virtually over by April 1917, grudgingly admitted: "Those negroes who are dissatisfied in the South are going North. The United States is large and they can go where they please."[25] He added that the black southerner cannot find work as a barber or a locomotive fireman in the North, where "individual white men accord him the intimacy which we would grant a monkey, a dog, or a parrot." But in the South, the editor urged, with the black man's economic opportunities running "parallel with . . . [but] never touching the white man, in his private affairs, he conducts himself according to his own tastes and propensities, [and] his enjoyments are twice as great for being concocted . . . by himself with racial color."[26]

This idyllic white view of southern blacks' existence contrasted sharply with how African Americans saw their own plight. A 1917 report by George E. Haynes, an African American sociologist who briefly directed the U.S. Labor Department's Bureau of Negro Economics, listed the primary reasons blacks left the South: low wages, bad treatment by whites, tenant farming's inequities, and "more dissatisfaction than formerly with these conditions, in the light of the world movement for democracy." In Haynes's lexicon, "bad treatment by whites" encompassed a variety of abuses associated with Jim Crow, from racial slurs to mob violence.[27]

Contemporaneous black accounts of the Great Migration also contain poignant testimony about "bad treatment" and the overwhelming desire by African Americans to earn a living wage and a measure of self-respect. The *Chicago Defender,* one of the era's leading black newspapers, published letters from potential migrants scattered throughout the South. A black janitor wrote from Mobile in January 1917 that he was "anxious to leave this part of the country and be where a Negro man can appreshate *[sic]* beaing *[sic]* a man."[28] In late April, a twenty-five-year-old black woman with five children informed the *Defender:* "My husband can hardly make bread for them in Mobile. . . . This is my native home but it is not fit to live in. . . . I want to get out of this dog hold *[sic]* because I don't know what I am raising them up for in this place."[29] A black brick mason in Mobile seeking work in Detroit wrote, "There is nothing here for the colored man but a hard time w[h]ich these southern crackers give us."[30] In Daphne a black man speaking for about twenty other families graphically described their situation: "We see starvation ahead of us here. . . . We are treated like brute[s] by our Whites here. . . . We can't talk to you on the phone here. We are afraid to. They don't want to hear one say that he or she wants to leave here. If we do we are apt to be killed. They say if we don't go to war they are not going to let us stay here with their folks, and it is not anything we have done to them."[31]

African American newspapermen warned whites that the migration would continue until Alabama's political leaders took action to remedy the deplorable racial conditions in the state.[32] G. T. Buford asked what was the "Negro's reward" for his labor in rebuilding the South since 1865. His answer: "Race hatred, poor wages, poor homes, poor schools, lynching, mob violence and no protection. This is why he is leaving. This will be the cause of the ruination of America if somebody don't take a hand and do something."[33] While bowing to the reality of Jim Crow's pervasiveness, Buford also discussed what blacks really wanted: "Any man capable of bearing arms for his government and . . . uphold[ing] his country's flag should have the right to vote. The great cause for the exodus of the Negro north is not money, not social equality, but political equality, and equal school advantages. . . . We simply want a school curriculum and building equal to those of the whites here."[34]

Despite such impassioned pleas as Buford's, neither state nor federal officials in Alabama appeared capable of fathoming the Great Migration's actual causes or of formulating practical responses. Rather than analyze why blacks left Alabama, local BI agents investigated northern labor agents' activities or white-initiated concerns. For example, in June 1917, the Birmingham BI office reported to headquarters that labor agents were promising draft exemptions for blacks who went north. Also in Birmingham, the Tennessee Coal, Iron and Railroad Company complained to the BI that Mount Pilgrim Missionary Baptist Association ministers preached to their flock to "Go North." After investigating, the BI special agent concluded that his office had no jurisdiction in the matter because no federal laws had been violated.[35] Thus, during the most dramatic period in the Great Migration, BI agents primarily functioned as chroniclers and observers of the movement.

By the time this exodus finally ebbed in the early 1920s, more than a half-million African Americans had moved to the North. Between 1916 and 1918, approximately one hundred thousand black Alabamians joined the "Great Migration." But conditions in the South changed little, so during the late 1930s, throughout the 1940s, and again in the early 1950s, similar migrations followed.[36]

For the thousands of African Americans who remained in Alabama after the 1917 declaration of war, their public responses to the crisis were unequivocally positive and patriotic. Black ministers, editors, businessmen, and educators exhorted their followers to lay aside any "past grievances" and "do their bit" alongside whites to win the war. They often cited W. E. B. DuBois's famous *Crisis* editorial, "Close Ranks," as exemplifying how even more outspoken blacks could postpone their own agendas for racial advancement for the war's duration.[37] Primarily through public addresses, letters to newspapers, and participation in patriotic rallies, African American leaders conveyed a message that was palatable for white audiences. Speaking at a public assembly in Mobile in early April, black Baptist minister W. H. Hunt averred: "[The Negro] is willing to trust the government under which he now lives for his future good. His rights and wrongs are not the issue, but the rights of the government which concern all."[38] Robert Moton released to the press his letter to President Wilson that offered assurances of complete black loyalty. On April 21 Moton also delivered an emotional speech to two thousand black farmers at the Autauga County courthouse in Prattville. He challenged his audience to produce "the fullest and most bountiful crops" and to contribute "everything possible to the aid and support of the country." "That's patriotism," Moton asserted. He also urged black farmers to seek "counsel and advice" from whites about livestock raising and other technical areas of food production. He concluded with a tribute to black courage and loyalty: "If necessary [the Negro] would die willingly for the flag, and that under all circumstances and conditions brought on by the war, no matter what test might be applied to him, he could be counted on to do his fullest duty." A white reporter in the crowd characterized Moton's hour-long address as "sane, practical and far-reaching," reminiscent of Booker T. Washington's "doctrine of optimism and hope" for both races.[39] Other black educators offered pledges of loyalty and support to the state and nation. Walter S. Buchanan, president of State A&M College at Normal, asked Governor Henderson for authority to recruit a black volunteer naval unit: "We do not feel that you could muster a more loyal body of [troops] than can be gathered from the Negroes of our native State; and here . . . we stand ready to render whatever service we can at this critical moment."[40] Instead of reminding Buchanan that the U.S. Navy recruited blacks solely as officers' mess stewards, the governor suggested that he contact the secretary of the navy.[41]

Pledges of loyalty from the state's black educators and other leaders constituted an important element in their plan for publicly responding to the war, but blacks also participated in elaborate patriotic rallies throughout the spring of 1917. These public meetings usually followed the same format in each city and town: speeches and loyalty pledges, musical interludes featuring a band or orchestra, and the adoption of patriotic resolutions. On April 25, one such rally organized by dentist W. F. Watkins and attorney Julian P. Rodgers drew four thousand African Americans to Montgomery's Old Ship Church on Holcomb Street. Governor Henderson spoke first, followed by four members of the Colored Citizens Committee: attorney Rodgers, John W. Beverly, president of the State Normal School for Negroes; postal worker E. M. Dale, and the Reverend E. L. Hatcher, A.M.E. Church, Dothan District. After the speeches, the Tuskegee Institute Band performed, under the direction of a "Capt. Dryer," former bandmaster of the Tenth U.S. Cavalry. Watkins and Rodgers concluded the festivities with the presentation of resolutions paying tribute to President Wilson and pledging blacks "to uphold the honor of our country" through military service and the production and conservation of food.[42] Each rally usually included some kind of symbolic gesture to underscore blacks' loyalty and commitment to the war. In Montgomery "Capt. Dryer" the bandmaster served as a reminder that African Americans had served bravely in past wars—the Tenth Cavalry troopers had fought with the Rough Riders in Cuba in 1898. To whites, John W. Beverly's presence was a more powerful symbol of black loyalty. He had been born a slave in 1858 on a plantation in Greensboro.[43] Several other rallies employed these living memorials of the Old South, including ex-slaves marching with groups of uniformed Confederate veterans. On May 8, a crowd of three thousand blacks and whites listened to speeches and "numerous patriotic airs" at the Corona Industrial and Normal School in Walker County, then cheered wildly as a former slave raised a large American flag.[44] Although large racially mixed audiences attended loyalty rallies in the spring of 1917, Jim Crow in Alabama was hardly on the wane. On the contrary, both races simply played their traditional roles in these well-rehearsed patriotic tableaux.

In Mobile, black businessmen C. First Johnson, James T. Peterson, and Charles Peters, dentist Dr. E. T. Belsaw, and school principal Dr. W. A. Caldwell organized a series of loyalty meetings in April. After the customary preliminary speeches at an April 15 assembly of Mobile's "citizens of color," these leaders announced the formation of several war preparedness committees: "Food Production," "Home Guard and Militia Drill," "Patriotic Assemblies," "Auto Practice and Mechanics," "Hospital Service," and "Horsemanship and Practice Camps."[45] One white observer, editor Erwin Craighead, later remarked on the "eloquence and force of the speeches, . . . the genuine sympathy shown by the great assembly present, . . . and an enthusiasm that testified very strongly to the sincerity of the feeling of affection for the union and its flag."[46]

Existing evidence indicates that influential whites such as Craighead functioned as more than merely observers at some black loyalty rallies. On June 27, 1917, more than one hundred African American miners employed by the DeBardeleben Coal Company participated in a mass meeting at the small mining town of Sipsey. This rally produced a remarkable set of resolutions supposedly signed by the miners. Because only a typescript of the resolutions and the miners' names has survived, it is impossible to reach any definitive conclusions as to this document's origins and authenticity.

Nevertheless, according to the Sipsey Resolutions, the coal company operators provided "kindness and fair treatment" and "good wages" and "assisted us in time of trouble, nursed our sick and buried our dead." The resolutions also included the obligatory loyalty pledge: "We are Americans first, last and always, and . . . 'to make the world safe for democracy' it is our duty as coal miners to labor unceasingly to produce coal so that ships can move across the waters, munitions can be manufactured, and the wheels of industry kept turning."

However, four of the seven resolutions focused on "certain labor agitators" who were attempting to unionize Alabama coal miners for the United Mine Workers (UMW). Neither the coal company operators nor state political officials would have objected to the language of these four resolutions: "We as Negroes . . . profit by the unfortunate experience of our forefathers and refuse to be misled by 'carpetbaggers' from the North . . . with the same promise of '40 acres and a mule' put to us in another form. . . . We condemn any movement which seeks to fraternize white man and black in one organization, and . . . we believe that the white man can best serve his ends and the Negro further his purposes by going about their duties in their own spheres."[47]

Regardless of who actually wrote the Sipsey Resolutions, the DeBardeleben Coal Company operators likely played a significant role in the drafting process. By 1917 the UMW had organized about 25 percent of Alabama's coal miners. In so doing, the UMW and the state's coal operators became bitter enemies. The Sipsey Resolutions linked standard antiunion rhetoric with paternalistic racial themes—both of which Alabama's industrial bosses eagerly embraced during that era but which sound inauthentic when placed in the mouths of the miners themselves. Many who were not UMW members tacitly supported the union's efforts in the north Alabama coalfields. Even so, given the atmosphere of fear, paranoia, and racism during World War I, the coal company operators could have coerced the Sipsey miners into ratifying the resolutions.[48]

While African Americans pledged their fealty to the nation, white officials debated the details of mobilizing and training blacks for military service. White southerners generally opposed training and arming black troops anywhere, particularly in the South. Assign black recruits to labor battalions, insisted Senator John Sharp Williams of Mississippi, and send them to camps in Cuba if they required any specialized training.[49] James E. McCall, the black editor of the *Montgomery Emancipator,* disagreed. He excoriated white southerners for hypocritically opposing black training camps in the region while bemoaning the loss of blacks to the Great Migration, writing, "In the present war crisis is not the life of a trained Negro soldier as valuable to the Nation as that of an untrained Negro laborer from the South?"[50] The *Montgomery Advertiser* supported McCall's argument: "If the Negro soldier is worthy to carry a rifle in France, he is worthy to be trained in the use of the rifle in America."[51] This viewpoint was rare in the white South. Although this emotional debate initially delayed the training of black troops, the pressures of mobilization forced the War Department to assign recruits of both races to rigidly segregated camps across the nation. With the exception of twenty thousand African Americans then serving in the regular army and the National Guard, most black inductees were destined for training in labor battalions in the Midwest and North. Many southern blacks, including hundreds of Alabamians, were apportioned among these cantonments, such as Camp Dodge, Iowa.[52]

In the midst of this fearful, racially charged atmosphere, the actual mechanics of conscription had to be devised and implemented. After a lengthy debate, Congress passed the Selective Service Act, which the president signed on May 18, 1917. This act empowered the governors of each state to appoint "boards of responsible citizens" to administer conscription of all males between the ages of twenty-one and thirty-one. The president set June 5, 1917, as national registration day, and on July 20, a "great national lottery" at the War Department determined the order in which the local draft boards would call up inductees, also known as "selectmen."[53]

Virtually overnight the Selective Service Act created a bureaucratic nightmare for the nation's governors, including Alabama's Charles Henderson, who frequently became mired in administrative details and refused to exert his executive authority without specific directives from Congress or the White House. Shortly before the president signed the act, Henderson received a letter from Ernest T. Attwell, Tuskegee Institute's purchasing agent, raising questions about the conscription of blacks. "I have some fear," Attwell wrote, "that we may not get our full enrollment in Alabama because . . . so many Negroes in the remote rural sections have very little idea of what draft or conscription of registration may mean, and in fact have never registered for anything on earth, and in some cases are on no record book, neither state, county, or otherwise."[54] Attwell encouraged the governor to issue a statewide call for black volunteers for a separate national guard regiment, or at least a battalion, because other states were aggressively recruiting "disciplined and respected colored men" from Alabama.[55] Attwell also asked Henderson to utilize African Americans like himself who were familiar with the state's black residents in performing "a little missionary work" on behalf of conscription and registration. Such "missionaries" could prevent "any misunderstandings and friction that might occur" in registering blacks for service, Attwell urged.[56]

Henderson rejected Attwell's request for a black national guard regiment: "When the present units are recruited to their war strength Alabama will have her full quota of national guardsmen." His terse response to Attwell seems to have revealed his reluctance to revive the black militia—a politically contentious issue in Alabama since the early 1900s. To educate blacks about conscription, Henderson said, he had considered "taking it up with Major Moton" and have him publish information in the state's newspapers. "Then it occurred to me," Henderson continued, "that this would not reach the very class that need to be informed, because they do not see the papers, did not go out to the meetings much, and lived in the back-country and are not very access[i]ble. I fear . . . that there are many through lack of information [who] will either be frightened or treat the matter with indifference. . . . I do not see how this can be overcome in so short a time."[57]

Henderson and Attwell recognized a potential problem in registering Alabama's isolated, rural African Americans. But other black leaders predicted that registration difficulties were not confined to rural Alabama. On May 26, 1917, G. T. Buford reminded blacks in Birmingham of "the duty of all our people to assist in the patriotic work of informing men" to register on June 5 "so that no man will have to suffer the severe penalties fixed by Congress. . . . Registration is . . . entirely new to our people, as it is new to all the people; but Uncle Sam does not allow ignorance of the law. Let everybody talk registration and all ministers preach it from now until June 6th."[58]

Ned Cobb, a poor black farmer rescued from historical obscurity under the pseudonym of "Nate Shaw" by Theodore Rosengarten in *All God's Dangers*, registered for the draft but later received an exemption because he had several dependents. Almost sixty years later, Cobb recalled, "I didn't definitely know who it was in war in them times. And it wasn't clear to me what that war was all about."[59] Like Ned Cobb, many black Alabamians did not think that the war directly affected them. In August 1917, a BI agent reported that blacks in Mobile believed that the war was "the white people's war and the negroes had nothing to do with it, that the white[s] elected Wilson, . . . he had got them in the war and now let the white[s] fight it out."[60] Despite the federal government's intense patriotic campaign and their own leaders' public loyalty pledges, black Alabamians clearly were not unified into "one white-hot mass" in support of the war.[61] In other words, Alabama's urban and rural working-class African Americans, who had borne the worst abuses of Jim Crow, were not convinced that patriotic displays at home or military service abroad would provide them with better postwar lives.

Nevertheless, blacks in Alabama dutifully registered for the draft on June 5, 1917, and for the subsequent registration dates in June and August 1918. Between 1917 and 1918, local draft boards inducted 25,874 blacks and 32,480 whites into the service, or about 46 percent of the total number of registrants of both races.[62] In Jefferson County white registration figures were 10 percent lower than for African Americans, prompting G. T. Buford to write: "This simply proves that the black race contains no slackers but does not say so much for our white brothers."[63] Black leaders later charged that local draft boards discriminated against blacks during registration by preferentially granting exemptions to whites.[64] In Macon County, however, large numbers of blacks and whites sought and received exemptions from the draft board on June 5, without any obvious evidence of racial discrimination.[65] Throughout the Jim Crow era in Alabama, the harshness of discriminatory practices varied from place to place. Not surprisingly, many blacks expected that because everything else in their lives was subject to the biased dictates of white officials, draft registration would be no different. Moreover, black Alabamians' conformance with registration may have been borne more out of fear of the legal consequences of noncompliance than from any patriotic zeal. Once again, Jim Crow's legacy cast a heavy shadow over the draft registration process.[66]

During the summer and fall of 1917, as Alabama's selectmen toiled through basic training, events outside the state had a dramatic impact on African Americans' attitudes toward the war. In early July a bloody race riot erupted in East St. Louis, Illinois, leaving thirty-nine blacks and eight whites dead.[67] Six weeks later, on August 23, 1917, black troops of the Twenty-fourth Infantry Regiment at Camp Logan, Texas, mutinied and engaged in a shooting spree in nearby Houston. At least sixteen whites and four blacks died in the affray. Despite sworn testimony that the black troops responded defensively to extreme provocations from white police and civilians, thirteen of the soldiers were executed in December, forty-one were given life sentences, and forty were imprisoned indefinitely while the investigation proceeded. Emmett J. Scott, formerly Booker T. Washington's private secretary and confidant, argued that the Houston mutiny and its aftermath "did not dampen the ardor of the colored men who went to the front for the Stars and Stripes."[68] Very few blacks shared Scott's optimistic assessment of the situation. By the time he issued that statement, Scott had been appointed as a special assistant to the secretary of war and privately shared the Wilson administration's concerns about this episode's effect on black support for the war.[69] With his background in business and journalism, the Texas-born, forty-four-year-old Scott became the War Department's chief spokesman for issues concerning "Negroes and the War." Throughout the war, he continued to deliver patriotic speeches to black troops before they shipped out to France. Scott renewed old ties with Tuskegee loyalists among black businessmen, educators, and editors. He also ruthlessly thwarted the efforts of any black leaders he regarded as possible rivals to his hegemony—a tactic he had perfected as Booker T. Washington's loyal lieutenant during the formative years of the "Tuskegee Machine."[70]

Two racial incidents in October 1917 involving the black Fifteenth New York Infantry also attracted national attention. At Camp Mills, New York, the 15th New York troops fought ferociously with white recruits of the 167th Alabama Infantry. In Spartanburg, South Carolina, another training site for the Fifteenth New York, a racial confrontation with local whites almost sparked another mutiny and shootings by the black troops. James R. Europe, the Fifteenth's bandmaster, born and raised in Mobile, helped disperse the angry soldiers. The War Department quickly sent Emmett Scott to the camp to investigate the incident and to pacify the troops. Scott asked them not to dishonor the regiment and "their race."[71] Because these incidents coincided with the emotional public debate over whether black troops should serve in combat infantry units or be confined to labor battalions, they contributed to the growing disillusionment among black soldiers and civilians. Furthermore, the paradoxical scenes of white public demonstrations, replete with Old South symbolism, in support of departing black regiments undoubtedly led to more disenchantment on the part of African Americans. The white press, without any apparent sense of irony, dutifully chronicled these events. For example, the *Birmingham News* reported in October 1917: "Camp Wilcox No. 782, United Confederate Veterans, will participate in the general demonstration to be given the Negro selectmen who are drafted for the army, and who are to leave Monday for Fort Dodge, Iowa."[72]

Similar patriotic send-offs occurred in Mobile and other Alabama cities and towns throughout the war. While cheering, flag-waving whites crowded the railroad stations to send the black troops off to war, in 1917 and 1918 at least seven African Americans died at the hands of Alabama lynch mobs. G. T. Buford expressed the disillusionment of many blacks in the state in 1917: "I am ready to give my life and all in defense of . . . our common country. . . . You may continue to offer me worse treatment than our alien enemies. . . . What will be our spoils[?] Will we get the ballot and all that goes with it, including equality before the law and an opportunity to compete with brothers in white along all lines[?]"[73]

The Wilson administration's initial reaction to evidence of growing black alienation was twofold: accelerate federal surveillance of suspected disloyal African Americans and recruit conciliatory "leaders of the race" in the mold of Tuskegeans Emmett Scott and Robert Moton. While Scott served as Secretary of War Newton Baker's special assistant, Moton performed his governmental duties without relinquishing his principal's position at Tuskegee. Wilson tapped both men as advisors in hopes that they would offset the influence of more radical black leaders, particularly DuBois, and minimize the impact of any black protests or demands for equality.

Moton, who turned fifty in August 1917, like Scott, wholeheartedly espoused Booker T. Washington's racial philosophy of accommodation, conciliation, self-help, and vocational education for blacks. Moton labored in relative obscurity during Washington's lifetime. Prior to 1915, Moton often undertook some of the most difficult, thankless tasks, as when he unsuccessfully attempted to mediate the bitter conflict between the NAACP and the Tuskegee Machine over who would speak for blacks—W. E .B. DuBois or Booker T. Washington. This national struggle among black leaders persisted long after Washington's death.[74] During World War I, Moton led Liberty Loan and War Savings Stamps campaigns and food conservation programs while Tuskegee Institute accelerated its extension activities among black farmers to encourage food production and support for the war. Moton also frequently visited black troops in their training camps and dealt with soldiers' problems that arose during the war. For example, in 1918, President Wilson asked him to investigate charges that the Ninety-second Infantry Division's troops had raped numerous French women and had displayed cowardice under fire. Moton conducted a thorough investigation of the rape charges with the Ninety-second's judge advocate staff and found that only two black soldiers out of seven originally charged with the crime had been convicted. Likewise, Moton's examination of the Ninety-second's cowardice charge revealed that the troops' failure in combat occurred in "a very small portion of a single battalion" in one regiment. General John J. Pershing told Moton that most officers would have failed under the extremely adverse conditions that the Ninety-second encountered.[75]

Moton also convinced the president to make a public statement condemning lynching. On July 26, 1918, Wilson issued a lengthy article on this topic to the press in which he strongly attacked lynch law within the context of the war, writing, "Every mob contributes to German lies about the United States."[76] Although Wilson rejected Moton's recommendation for an open letter to a governor of a state where a lynching had occurred recently, the president's public condemnation of mob violence as a "disgraceful evil" was a significant achievement given the racial tenor of that era.[77]

After the armistice in 1918, white southerners became obsessed with the nightmarish image of angry, armed black soldiers returning home with unrealistic expectations about social and political equality. African American editors agreed that their military experience had altered black veterans' perspective on their segregated existence in the South. For example, the *Montgomery Emancipator* printed an editorial cartoon on its front page, illustrating the victory of "racial equality and justice" over "prejudice," with a black soldier asking Uncle Sam: "I've done my duty—What are you going to do for me and mine?"[78] Governor Henderson hastily convened emergency meetings to address this issue with the Alabama Council of Defense and the American Protective League, a semiofficial auxiliary unit of the U.S. Justice Department. The Council of Defense officials frantically asked the War Department to delay mustering out any black troops until they were no longer considered to be a threat to white civilians in the United States.[79]

President Wilson again turned to Moton and Scott for assistance with this latest home-front racial crisis. In January 1919, Scott assured a large audience of blacks and whites in Tuskegee that returning African American veterans had profited mentally and physically from military service and had a "broader vision of American citizenship, with new ideas of what liberty and freedom (not license) mean; [but] he will not jeopardize or impair the honor and fame his race has won in this war by any thoughtless or unmanly word or deed."[80] After sailing to France, Moton delivered essentially the same message to black troops: "You will go back to America as heroes, as you really are. You will go back as you have carried yourselves here—in a straightforward, manly, and modest way. . . . Find a job as soon as possible and get to work. . . . I hope no one will do anything in peace to spoil the magnificent record you have made in war."[81]

While attempting to allay white fears, Moton and Scott counseled black troops that they should not expect at home the same degree of freedom and equality they had experienced in France and that they must be satisfied with the racial status quo. Both men conveyed the conciliatory message they had heard frequently from Booker T. Washington during his tenure at Tuskegee. Although the president and the secretary of war praised the efforts of Moton and Scott, other black leaders, including DuBois and New York editor Cyril Briggs, launched blistering attacks on the two Tuskegeans. Briggs reserved his bitterest invective for Moton, whom he described as a "spineless Judas Iscariot type of leader," "living in the wrong era," whose entreaties to the black troops were demeaned by "shameless treachery and disgusting servility." Briggs was confident that neither black veterans "nor the Negro women and men who stood by the country and backed up all its soldiers, are going to adopt the 'modest and unassuming' attitudes that Robby recommends. . . . No man can serve two masters and we commend Robby to his white 'massas.'"[82] Moton and Scott believed that they had played positive roles on behalf of blacks during World War I, but both men obviously paid a heavy price for their government service, especially in regard to their future historical legacies as African American leaders.

Black Alabamians responded in disparate ways to the Great War. In the absence of a single charismatic leader or even a unified group of leaders, they spoke with many different voices and seldom coalesced around a particular set of philosophical goals. Although black Alabamians did not enthusiastically support the war, they still regarded themselves as Americans and served tirelessly on the home front and bravely in the military. Perhaps most remarkable, they performed these tasks despite white reactions of indifference and hostility. As the Great Migration accelerated after the United States entered the war, black Alabamians by the thousands went north. Even if the North failed to meet their heightened expectations, they found jobs in the war industries, and eventually many voted for the first time in their lives. They also educated their children in schools that were far better than those in the segregated South.

Alabama's black army recruits also went north, primarily to training camps in the Midwest such as Camp Dodge, Iowa. Many of these men were assigned to "SOS" (Services of Supply) units such as the 528th Service Battalion. Other men trained with the 804th Pioneer Negro Infantry Regiment, a slightly different version of the SOS units, and with the 366th Infantry Regiment. Many of these troops were close enough to the front lines to be shelled, gassed, and grievously wounded. Of the approximately 660 black Alabamans who died in military service during World War I, the majority were victims of disease. Twenty-two perished in combat. Incidentally, ten of these twenty-two combat deaths occurred on November 11, 1918, as the war's last shots were fired.[83] In addition, the Spanish influenza, the deadly scourge of the Great War, fell heavily on black troops in labor battalions, many of whom were still in training camps in the United States. The flu randomly killed men of both races, but it was particularly virulent among blacks whose immunizations, nutrition, and overall health had been deficient prior to their induction. Because they served their country as they were asked to do, these troops believed they were entitled to certain basic rights and at least a suggestion of equality when they returned to Alabama. Yet they quickly discovered their long journey to freedom and full citizenship had just begun.

Scholars have experienced a similar lengthy sojourn in their quest to carve out a historical niche for blacks and World War I. Over the past thirty years, historians have labored arduously to document the African American struggle for equality during the post–World War II era, with an emphasis on the dramatic years of the "Second Reconstruction" of the 1960s. By focusing on the modern civil rights era, scholars have frequently failed to connect it to its World War I antecedents. But some have begun to expose those connections. Professors Mark Ellis and Theodore Kornweibel have shown through painstaking examination of federal records that the government's surveillance of African Americans who were suspected "radicals" originated during World War I, not during the civil rights struggle of the 1950s and 1960s.[84]

At least partially because of scholars' concentration on other topics and eras, to date a definitive history of black Alabamians has not been written. Only fragmentary files of the state's African American newspapers have survived the passage of time. For whatever reasons, historians have not utilized fully the extant correspondence and other papers of lettered black Alabamians, including such leaders as Robert Moton and Emmett Scott. Likewise, the records of the NAACP and various federal agencies, including the Justice Department, deposited respectively at the Library of Congress and the National Archives, remain virtually untapped though they are rich primary sources for students of black Alabamians during World War I.

Alabama's post–World War I racial climate also had a significant impact on that generation's historians and their initial interpretation of African Americans' roles during the recent conflict. After the armistice, Alabama's white public officials, civic boosters, and journalists generated effusive rhetoric that opposed mob violence but dismissed any northern criticism of southern race relations.[85] Alabama's political and business leaders fully understood that the state's commercial prosperity depended on northern investments. Rather than dwelling on "unpleasantries," such as postwar racial violence and labor strife, which could impede the influx of northern capital, these men advocated in the 1920s a wide dissemination of "success stories" about Alabama cities. Among these white boosters, social solidarity and maintenance of the racial status quo became more tightly interwoven priorities in Alabama after World War I.[86]

More important, academic historians have deliberately or inadvertently kept this interpretation of the era alive throughout the twentieth century. This trend began with Albert Burton Moore, who rose to prominence as an Alabama historian in the interwar years. A student of George Petrie's at the Alabama Polytechnic Institute before World War I, Moore served in the U.S. Navy and completed his Ph.D. at the University of Chicago after the armistice. His two closest friends at Chicago were also former Petrie students—Herman C. Nixon and Frank L. Owsley. Moore taught history at Iowa State University before accepting a professorship at the University of Alabama in the early 1920s.[87] After returning to his native state, he devoted much of his scholarly efforts to completing his *History of Alabama,* published in 1927. He included in this work a description of Alabamians' service in World War I, both overseas and on the home front, and also briefly summarized African Americans' contribution to the war effort: "The colored people emulated the whites in their devotion to the nation's cause. The War organizations and activities were extended to them and they were instructed by the whites and their own leaders upon their obligations and opportunities. They caught the spirit of the hour and talked glibly about what 'us Anglo-Saxons would do to dem Bosches.'"[88]

Moore's simplistic assessment of black Alabamians' role during World War I became the standard interpretation of this topic. His *History of Alabama* served as the state's basic college textbook for at least forty years after its initial publication. As recently as the late 1990s, Alabama historians recycled an only slightly modified version of Moore's viewpoint by implying that black cooperation with the war effort was evidence of their uncritical support for the war itself.[89] The problem with this interpretation is that it is based almost exclusively on white press accounts, that is, on how whites envisioned the role of blacks in the war effort. White urban boosters and editors such as the *Mobile Register*'s Erwin Craighead enthusiastically chronicled joyous patriotic send-offs for black draftees and other interracial public celebrations on behalf of Wilson's declaration of war, war bond sales, and, in 1918, the armistice. The mere existence of such public exhibitions, however, does not necessarily prove that blacks were actually happy to be drafted or that whites were not terrified about arming these troops. The harshness of Jim Crow since 1865 had taught blacks that they must behave "correctly" in public and speak soothingly in nonthreatening tones, lest they risk further inflaming whites who were already deeply suspicious of their actions and motives. For blacks their very survival depended on an artful ability to play by the rules of this game that were proscribed rigidly by the Jim Crow system. Only rarely did courageous blacks such as G. T. Buford and James E. McCall risk their lives by publicly expressing their honest views on the war and its relationship to other issues of concern to their readers. These editors also articulated the feelings of thousands of illiterate black Alabamians such as sharecropper Ned Cobb, who at best were ambivalent about the war.

Scholars have only begun to scratch the surface of the story of black Alabamians during the Great War. To produce incisive monographs on this complex topic, historians must dig deeply into surviving black primary sources and analyze what African Americans actually thought about the U.S. declaration of war in 1917 within the context of Jim Crow. Historians can then turn toward more specialized studies of black Alabamians on the home front and in uniform. Through such scholarship, a more accurate history of black Alabamians and World War I will emerge in the years to come.

6
From the Cotton Field to the Great Waterway
African Americans and the Muscle Shoals Project during World War I

Victoria E. Ott

On April 17, 1917, African American citizens of Alabama's "Tri-Cities"—Florence, Sheffield, and Tuscumbia—gathered to discuss America's participation in the First World War. Newspapers in the area heralded the gathering as "the largest assemblage of negroes that ever met in this section." Led by prominent local religious and educational figures, participants drafted a resolution pledging their loyalty to President Woodrow Wilson and the national government and reminded the public that "the American Negro has never wavered in his loyalty to the government of the United States in all its conflicts with other nations." They also proclaimed that black citizens would follow the exodus of African Americans out of the region and to northern industries "unless they can be assured that the conditions now existing can be bettered and that the many discriminations . . . be by law prevented and that better wages be given the colored laborers and wage earners of the South."[1] African Americans in the area, like those all over the nation, had come to view economic and social advancement as rewards for their service on the home front and, thus, believed the time had come to pressure local and state officials to change the status quo. Their hope for higher wages and a better life came closer to realization when the federal government chose the Tri-Cities as the site of the so-called Muscle Shoals Project, two plants that made nitrates, the oxidizing agent in gunpowder, and a dam to control flooding in the Tri-Cities' area of the Tennessee River.

Before the war, blacks in the Tri-Cities, like those in the rest of the South, often worked at low-wage jobs or as tenant farmers. Legally sanctioned discrimination and white supremacy relegated them to second-class citizenship. The government's decision to build the Muscle Shoals

Project meant new jobs and higher wages for African Americans as well as a chance to leave the cotton fields. But the racial attitudes and customs of local whites and project employers threatened black advancement. Rendered politically powerless by Alabama's 1901 constitution, African Americans found it difficult to fight the discrimination they faced. By relying on the resources of the local black community and by forging alliances with national reform movements, they protested discriminatory hiring practices and gross inequalities in black and white facilities, and in these protests they planted the seeds of the civil rights movement of the 1950s and 1960s that secured a federal commitment to righting the wrongs of Jim Crow. For the Muscle Shoals Project workers themselves, the promise of a better life faded as the war ended and national attention shifted to the returning soldiers and the financial costs of both the project and the war itself. Nevertheless, their calls to action demonstrated the willingness of African Americans in the area to demand protection of their economic and social rights, a movement that would gain momentum by the mid-twentieth century.

Historians have illustrated for some time that the push for civil rights within the African American community began long before the sit-ins and boycotts associated with the modern agitation for racial equality. Robert J. Norrell's examination of the civil rights movement in Tuskegee, Alabama, and John Egerton's study of activism between 1932 and 1954 place the beginning of the struggle for civil rights long before the landmark case of *Brown v. Board of Education of Topeka, Kansas* (1954), the traditional starting point of the civil rights narrative. In his study of Mississippi, Neil R. McMillen also suggests that black participation in World War I at home and abroad initiated the final stage in the battle for civil rights reforms. The efforts of African Americans to retain the advances made while serving in wartime industries and to claim the rights of citizenship as a reward for military service, according to McMillen, "fostered a spirit of social change" that gained momentum after the end of World War II and culminated in the mass protests of the modern civil rights movement.[2]

Norrell and McMillen, along with Samuel C. Hyde, Jr., in his recent edited volume of essays on the Gulf South states, have shifted attention from national leaders and organizations to the significant contributions of local people, churches, schools, and groups to the movement. This bottom-up approach reveals that activist individuals and groups concerned themselves more with their local African American community than they did with national issues. Thus it was with African Americans in the Tri-Cities, where they championed the fight against discrimination to sustain the economic opportunities offered by the Muscle Shoals Project. Black residents hoped that their improved economic status would lead to improved social status. Local community leaders and workers joined with national organizations to increase the national awareness of African Americans in the Tri-Cities in their effort to sustain such improvements and battle segregation.[3]

The towns of Sheffield, Tuscumbia, and Florence seemed an attractive candidate for a massive federal defense and energy project. Before America's involvement in the Great War, Congress feared that German submarines might cut off America's supply of nitrates coming from Chile, the nation's biggest supplier, or that Chile might raise its nitrate prices. In 1916 Congress passed the National Defense Act, which allowed for government-funded programs to increase the nation's military resources. Section 124 of the act appropriated twenty million dollars to build plants "for the production of nitrates and other products for munitions of war." Alabama senators Oscar W. Underwood and John H. Bankhead waged a successful campaign to secure two nitrate plants and a dam for the Tri-Cities, located astride the banks of the Tennessee River. In 1917 federal funds went to the J. G. White Engineering Corporation to construct nitrate plant number one and to the Air Nitrates Corporation to build nitrate plant number two. Construction of Wilson Dam began the following year, on April 14, 1918.[4]

Most of the area's white tenant farmers and rural laborers welcomed the project to relieve the economic uncertainty of the local cotton monoculture. In 1910 farms made up 59 percent of Colbert County and 77 percent of Lauderdale County. Almost half the farmers were tenants; in Colbert County alone, tenants labored on 65.4 percent of the farms. By the early 1900s, however, agriculture had suffered soil exhaustion and depletion, a downturn in market prices, and the boll weevil epidemic. Farmers tried to improve their situation by forming cooperatives and learning innovative agricultural methods. The local newspapers ran articles urging white farmers to join the Lauderdale County Farmers and Merchants' Cooperative Association, the program that taught crop diversification and new marketing procedures. Despite these efforts, the financial situation of farmers remained poor.[5]

The African American community was equally optimistic about the Muscle Shoals Project. Blacks made up 29.6 percent of the population in Lauderdale and Colbert counties combined and 32.4 percent of the total population in the Tri-Cities themselves. In Lauderdale and Colbert counties, 26.3 percent of African Americans toiled in the countryside as independent landowning farmers, sharecroppers, or laborers. Like their white counterparts, black farmers struggled to fight soil exhaustion and the boll weevil and joined community efforts to increase crop diversification and better farming methods. On May 18, 1917, the *Florence Times* reported that a countrywide campaign to improve the situation of the black farmer was making its way through the Tri-Cities, advocating "for every home a garden; for every boy a brood sow; for every girl a canning outfit." Implicit in the message was that agricultural labor provided African Americans with the only avenue for economic uplift. Life outside farming did, in fact, offer some opportunities for employment. Many African American women worked as domestic servants, and a small black middle class comprised mainly of teachers, religious leaders, and business owners existed in the region. Jesse Patton, who owned a successful livery, feed, and sales stable, was the most notable among this group of entrepreneurs. He began business in the 1890s and offered services to both black and white citizens. Yet most black citizens relied on the deteriorating cotton market for their income.[6]

The construction project not only brought the potential for economic uplift but also offered opportunities to improve the legal and social position of blacks in the Tri-Cities. After the Civil War, segregation was a matter of custom in the Tri-Cities. Still, a transition from de facto to de jure segregation occurred in the late nineteenth century with the Supreme Court's ruling in *Plessy v. Ferguson* (1896) that upheld racial segregation as long as equal accommodations were provided. But as time would prove, black facilities were often inferior to those provided to whites. In *Cumming v. County Board of Education* (1899), the court extended *Plessy* by validating separate schools for white and black children.[7]

Exclusion of blacks from the polls also became a matter of law by the late 1890s. The Supreme Court's determination in *William v. Mississippi* (1898) allowed states to impose literacy requirements on voters, paving the way for southern states to strip blacks of the voting rights gained by the Fifteenth Amendment. By 1901 Alabama disfranchised blacks and many poor whites under the new state constitution. Article VIII gave supervision of voter registration to county officials, which ensured local whites would conduct the process. Besides white registrars, voting qualifications through the poll tax, understanding clause, and literacy and property requirements systematically prevented blacks from voting in elections. As a result, the 181,315 blacks who qualified to vote in Alabama in 1900 declined to merely 2,980 by 1903. Changes in voting qualifications also reduced the number of poor whites eligible to vote but only slightly in comparison to the number of African American voters. Out of the 232,821 whites able to participate in elections in 1900, only 191,492 qualified to vote in 1903.[8]

Combined with the custom of disdain, disfranchisement left blacks with almost no voice by which to combat inequalities in the legal system. In many cases, black defendants received excessive jail terms and fines. Judges in the circuit courts of the Tri-Cities often rendered sentences based solely on the defendant's race. Judge Ed B. Almon of Florence provides an example. He suspended the sentences of three white men convicted of crimes that included murder and assault with intent to murder but jailed three black defendants whose respective crimes were robbery, grand larceny, and assault with intent to murder. The convict lease system applied disproportionately to blacks as well. Rather than being leased to farms or serving their sentences at the penitentiary, black convicts went to the coal mines or worked on the streets of the towns. In March 1901, for example, the circuit court of Florence sent James Fields, Pink Rose, and James Hamell to the mines. That same year the court convicted Jim Rand of bigamy and sentenced him to a year and ninety-nine days in the coal mines. In July 1903, a judge sentenced Jesse Hatcher to work on the streets for eight days for the crime of stealing a box of sweet crackers. The *Tuscumbia Dispatch* reported in 1900 that city authorities arrested Will Hollinsworth, a young black man who drove a beer wagon in the area, for carrying a concealed weapon. Earlier that day, a young white man attacked Hollinsworth, hitting him several times in the head. Hollinsworth returned to the location of the attack with a gun, and a police officer arrested him. The court fined Hollinsworth fifty dollars plus court costs and sentenced him to sixty days on street work. The police did not arrest the white provocateur.[9]

Blacks and whites in the Tri-Cities traditionally attended separate schools, but the 1901 constitution enshrined such segregation into the basic law. Article XIV mandated separate school districts and prohibited using white tax dollars to fund African American education. Each district raised school funds through taxes levied on its respective communities. White hostilities toward support for African American education in the Tri-Cities grew after passage of the new state constitution. In a letter to the *Florence Times,* one citizen urged the Tri-Cities to follow the constitutional guidelines and allow each race only to "get just what ever money they pay into the educational fund." Blacks, who had fewer economic resources than whites, became responsible for funding and maintaining their schools.[10]

In spite of these obstacles, Tri-City blacks provided buildings for schools and staffed classrooms with qualified teachers. After the Civil War, the federal government gave African Americans land in the Tri-Cities to build a separate school. The facility began as a two-story structure, which later burned. In 1897 Mary Corpier, graduate of Fisk University's teachers' education department, ran a school in Canaan, a suburb of Florence. The American Missionary Association helped support the school, and parents paid fifty cents a month to help with extra expenses. In 1899 blacks in Florence built the John F. Slater School, at which C. G. Gray, Sallie Gray, and Josephine Handy taught first through fourth grades and Principal Y. A. Wallace taught fifth through eighth grades. In 1903 the American Missionary Association gave five thousand dollars to build Burrell Normal School to provide blacks with industrial training and basic secondary education. Although the American Missionary Association continued to donate funds, the African American community shouldered a good portion of the school's financial burden.[11]

Schools were a treasure, but churches formed the core of the African American community. They were vital resources in combating the inequalities of the Jim Crow South because they provided social services and fostered a network of community activists. In addition to worship services, churches often held public gatherings that encouraged leadership training among members of the congregation. The African Methodist Episcopal Church in neighboring Wayne County, Tennessee, for example, held an anniversary celebration during which young women from the congregation delivered papers on its history. Florence's Jackson Freewill Baptist Church asked its female members to organize a Woman's Board of Missions, which raised funds and kept up the church. Members of the Christian Methodist Episcopal Church took it upon themselves to raise $450 over the course of a year to purchase a new building.[12]

Given their social, political, and economic conditions on the eve of the Great War, African Americans welcomed the Muscle Shoals Project. The economic benefits, for example, would open the door for social advancement, particularly financing better homes and providing additional funds for schools. A wave of optimism flowed over African Americans in the Tri-Cities and in the surrounding rural areas. As government officials and company engineers broke ground on the project, hundreds of black workers rushed to join the labor force.

The construction of wartime industries in southern towns and the subsequent migration of black citizens occurred across the South. Many African Americans moved from their farming communities into southern towns that housed new defense industries. Historian James Moore Hammond found in his study of Charleston, South Carolina, that African Americans' labor was much in demand during the war. Work at Charleston's Navy Yard and on various construction projects offered an attractive alternative to farming or low-wage labor for many blacks in South Carolina. Mississippi also witnessed an upsurge in the number of African Americans moving from cotton farming into wartime manufacturing. Attracted by wages that were higher than they earned previously, many were willing to remain in the state rather than follow the "Great Migration" of blacks to faraway northern industries.[13]

Signs of change in the Tri-Cities appeared soon after construction began on the nitrate plants and the dam. The population boomed overnight as workers from both South and North poured into the small rural community. The *Florence Times* reported that "what was a few weeks ago a barren cotton field is today a good sized town which has sprung up by magic." Tri-City officials rushed to find accommodations for workers while local newspapers urged citizens to provide available rooms. The local business community responded to the demand for housing by building apartments and houses for the workers. In addition, the area's transportation infrastructure could not handle the sudden influx of new residents. City and county officers hurried to pave streets for easier transportation to and from the work site. Court Street, the main street in Florence, became the first paved road in the area, which local officials improved to handle the increased traffic. Community leaders also converted the Florence-Sheffield trolley into a transportation source for labor to the sites. To prevent outbreaks of diseases usually associated with overcrowding, city commissioners improved the area's sanitation, and a U.S. Public Health Service representative traveled to the Tri-Cities to help develop a comprehensive sanitation system.[14]

The construction camp at Muscle Shoals became a city unto itself. Air Nitrates and J. G. White Engineering scrambled to erect a "tent city" on the grounds. H-shaped tent dormitories offering each resident three hundred square feet of space became the primary housing unit for both black and white single male laborers. Air Nitrates built a section known as "married row" for white workers and their families. In addition to housing, the tent city included barbershops, laundry services, twenty-three mess halls equipped to serve four thousand workers at once, a fire department, and the plant police department.[15]

Labor agents scoured the nation in search of able-bodied workers. A survey of 1,806 residents in the Wilson Dam precinct revealed that almost 90 percent migrated from other areas in the South (see table 1), particularly Tennessee, Mississippi, and Georgia. Most workers, however, moved from within Alabama. The figures regarding black migration to the Tri-Cities are especially significant. During the war, African Americans created the so-called Great Migration as they moved north in search of better wages and social conditions. Yet southern blacks also migrated to southern cities that were building industries for wartime production. The Wilson Dam precinct survey bears this out, noting that the largest portion of black labor at the dam came from within the South. Only a small percentage of African American workers migrated from northern states such as Pennsylvania, Illinois, and Ohio. More whites than blacks moved to the Tri-Cities from the Northeast and Midwest. Finally, European immigrants from countries such as Ireland, Scotland, and Greece made up only a small number of workers on the dam.[16]

An examination of their marital status reveals that most workers, black and white, expected to make a better wage if only for the duration of the war. Of the 1,806 residents sampled for this study, single men made up the largest number of white and black workers on the project. Unmarried males made up 530 of the 865 African Americans surveyed, as well as half of the white workforce (see table 2). The large number of single men on the project indicates that many workers perceived the Tri-Cities as a place of short-term opportunity. Yet many workers chose to move to the Tri-Cities with their families. Almost 20 percent of the black male population was married, and married males made up 24 percent of the white population in the precinct. White and black women, most of whom had migrated with their husbands, also made up a small portion of the Wilson Dam community. White families had almost three times the number of children living with them as had black families. One family, for example, listed nine children in its home. It is unclear from the census data whether these families intended to remain in the area permanently or emigrate once the work ended. A percentage of married men, on the other hand, came to the area without their families. This data implies that those workers intended

Table 1. Previous States of Residencies of Workers and Their Families

State	White	Black	Total
South	**814**	**806**	**1,620**
Alabama	359	402	761
Arkansas	1	5	6
Florida	7	19	26
Georgia	65	84	149
Kentucky	19	11	30
Louisiana	10	61	71
Mississippi	75	57	132
Missouri	3	29	32
NC	15	13	28
SC	13	30	43
Tennessee	243	90	333
Virginia	3	4	7
West Virginia	1	1	2
North	**94**	**24**	**118**
Connecticut	5	—	5
Illinois	32	2	34
Indiana	4	4	8
Iowa	3	4	7
Maryland	3	4	7
Massachusetts	2	—	2
Michigan	9	—	9
New Jersey	8	—	8
New York	6	1	7
Ohio	8	5	13
Pennsylvania	12	4	16
Rhode Island	2	—	2
West	**12**	**35**	**47**
California	2	5	7
Kansas	1	—	1
Oklahoma	—	12	12
Texas	9	18	27
Outside U.S.	**21**	—	**21**
Total	941	865	1,806

Source: Sample of 1,806 residents listed in the United States Fourteenth Census (1920), Lauderdale County, Population Schedules, Wilson Dam Precinct.

Table 2. Profile of Citizens Living in the Wilson Dam Precinct

	Number of Whites	Number of Blacks	Total
Single Males	419	530	949
Married Males	135	131	266
Women	137	114	251
Children	250	90	340
Total Number	941	865	1,806

Source: Sample of 1,806 residents listed in the United States Fourteenth Census (1920), Lauderdale County, Population Schedules, Wilson Dam Precinct.

to seize the opportunity for better wages and then return to their homes once their job was through.[17]

Similar to other southern wartime industries, the Muscle Shoals Project offered African Americans a better income than farming. Blacks at the Shipbuilding and Dry Dock Company in Newport News, Virginia, for example, received fifteen to thirty dollars per week as general laborers. Those at the Dupont Construction Company in Jacksonville, Tennessee, earned wages as high as ten dollars per day depending on their skills. Skilled labor hired to build barracks for military troops made between four and seven dollars per day. Compared to other southern industries, the Muscle Shoals Project provided reasonable wages for laborers, both skilled and unskilled. Recruiters brought in black carpenters, bricklayers, mechanics, and general laborers. Skilled or semiskilled labor received up to five dollars per day depending on their duties. The general laborers, black and white, received two dollars and seventy-five cents per day plus regular overtime regardless of marital status or duties on the project.[18]

Despite the economic benefits of working on the project, blacks faced persistent racial discrimination in the area and on the project itself. Residential segregation signaled that fact. Newspapers that advertised the newly erected apartments in the Tri-Cities and reported the city government's call for residents to open their homes to workers targeted whites only. Most whites found apartments or rented rooms in private homes; those who brought their families leased or bought four- to five-room cottages. City officials also acknowledged the need for housing for black workers. In response, the Tri-Cities developed separate residential sections for African Americans that local papers called "colored towns." Tyler

Realty Company announced the development of "Shoals City" near the construction site of nitrate plant number 2 and advertised lots beginning at $150. Blacks could purchase property from Tyler Realty, but they were responsible for building their home. Traditionally African American residential sections in the Tri-Cities also provided homes and apartments for workers in search of a place to rent.[19]

Both black and white laborers fell victim to profiteering during their search for housing in the Tri-Cities. Homeowners and realtors recognized the opportunity to profit from the large influx of workers. Although local newspapers urged citizens not to gouge newcomers, several proprietors raised their rates on property rented to workers and their families. One proprietor gave a local tenant $1,200 to leave an apartment that the owner then let to a worker for almost double the rent. Land prices also increased dramatically during the life of the project. Some realtors profited by $10,000 for ten acres of land. Several local business leaders attempted to curb excessive rents. They formed the Tri-Cities Business Committee to help workers find housing and expose profiteering homeowners and realtors. The committee's campaign to link prospective tenants with proprietors, however, excluded black residential areas. African Americans battled inflated rental and property costs without help from the Tri-Cities' business community.[20]

In the construction camps themselves, blacks and whites lived separately. Whites became apprehensive about the possibility of living near black laborers in the camp as workers strained the housing market. The local newspapers assured white citizens that the housing for African Americans was a considerable distance from that of white workers. The construction companies placed housing for blacks farther from the construction site than white housing and near the cotton fields that surrounded the project. One local paper resorted to the crudest stereotypes to justify the location, arguing that blacks "feel more at home beside their native cotton fields than they would if further transplanted."[21]

The companies in charge of workers' accommodations likewise segregated married and single workers within the black section of the camp. The construction companies built thirty-three barracks to house the large number of single men at the project. A village of small houses accommodated the workers who brought their families to the construction camp. This section of the camp became a source of pride for whites in the Tri-Cities. The *Florence Times,* for example, reported that "the temporary negro village where men of that race with their families now live, is one of the show places of the whole works . . . there is room enough; for the negro likes plenty of company." Yet in reality, the home for a married worker and his family consisted of a two-room frame structure sheeted with tar paper. The section for white married workers and their families provided larger homes, usually consisting of four to five rooms.[22]

Churches and schools were also segregated at the camp. Although the Tri-Cities had several black churches, the construction companies provided room for worship services in the camps' residential areas. For the most part, the maintenance and staffing of the churches fell to the black workers, who received little or no monetary support from the companies. The construction companies did furnish accommodations for schools; however, much like the churches, they left the responsibility of upkeep to black workers. Overcrowding posed the largest problem for educators. City officials taxed every resource to find room for the children of white workers in their schools. African American schools in the construction camps, and in the Tri-Cities, struggled to adapt to the increased number of students. The American Missionary Association continued providing financial aid to the Burrell Normal School, yet was unable to contribute more to account for the surge in attendance. Lack of tax dollars combined with overcrowding meant that African American educators relied even more on private donations to support the expanding schools. Educators from Burrell even ran an ad in the *Florence Times* asking for donations from black citizens.[23]

Segregated health care was another concern because supplying even rudimentary services to dual systems strained them both. The influenza epidemic that swept across the nation made its way to the Tri-Cities in early October 1918 and forced the company to house the ever-increasing number of patients in warehouses after both hospitals filled beyond capacity. Fearing negative publicity, local newspapers refused to run articles about the number of influenza deaths. Only after the epidemic had passed were newspapers willing to report the casualties. Officials at the nitrate plants also attempted to conceal the effects of the flu within the camps for fear that workers would leave if news of an epidemic spread. Testimony before the House Committee on Expenditures in the War Department revealed that plant managers misreported the number of flu cases in an effort to keep its workforce intact. J. W. Young, presiding manager of the Air Nitrates Corporation, informed the Ordnance Department that only 4 flu cases existed in the camp when in fact reports indicated that there were "1,500 men in the camp ill from this disease, some of them falling about in the mud."[24]

Gross inequalities existed in the provision of flu relief for black and white citizens. Anticipating the onset of the epidemic in their city, Florence commissioners passed an ordinance in May 1918 prohibiting citizens from working or living in an establishment without approval from health officials. The local Red Cross and the local public health services provided advice on improving sanitation in the home. These community organizations, however, focused their educational efforts predominantly on the white community. Much like their experience with the schools and churches, blacks found themselves responsible for taking care of their own health. They conducted flu relief efforts under the supervision of G. N. White, a local black teacher and leader in the African American community. He organized a relief fund to which blacks contributed money for their health care. Whether White's campaign provided the necessary aid to treat all those affected by the flu is uncertain, yet his willingness to champion the cause exemplifies the active role African American leaders played in assisting their community.[25]

In addition to creating a boom in demand for housing and health care, the growing population of workers created a demand for entertainment. City, business, and plant officials responded, but only within the confines of Jim Crow segregation. Prior to the war, Florence's white-only opera house was one of the few sources of entertainment in the area. Local business leaders seized the opportunity provided by the Muscle Shoals Project to build new recreational facilities in the towns. Plant officials also erected movie theaters and dance halls around the construction site and used profits from them to fund the mess hall. These facilities, like those in the Tri-Cities, were segregated by race, a move that demonstrated the government's willingness to work within the racial caste system. Recreational houses for both races, however, experienced problems remaining open throughout the project. Officials at plant number 2 in Sheffield, for example, hindered YMCA workers from offering leisure activities and took over recreation buildings to use as storage.[26]

Racial discrimination and white supremacy shaped the relationship between white and black workers on the job. Problems emerged when skilled white laborers refused to work alongside blacks during the construction project. Such racial animosity was not new to southern war industries. Historian Henry M. McKiven found the same tensions among skilled workers in the iron and steel industry in Birmingham, Alabama. He posits that "white skilled workers believed that their social and economic interests were inextricably linked to the maintenance of a rigid caste system."[27] Many white workers feared that skilled African American laborers would threaten their economic power in the workforce. L. A. Gabriel, president of the Key West, Florida, branch of the NAACP, reported cases of white carpenters refusing to work with nonunion African Americans. According to Gabriel, representatives from the union continuously denied blacks' application for membership or a charter for a separate local union chapter. Similar workplace discrimination occurred on the Muscle Shoals Project. On one occasion, the J. G. White Engineering Corporation summarily discharged five black bricklayers who had traveled from Cleveland, Ohio, after their white coworkers refused to work with them because of their race.[28]

Nowhere else was the color line more apparent than in the actions of the plant police. The Air Nitrates Corporation organized its own police force and during their recruitment campaigns in the region hired men from northern states as officers. In testimony before the House Subcommittee on War Expenditures, Air Nitrates attorney J. W. Andrews testified that the plant police had a stellar record in dealing with workers. But in private correspondence to the corporate manager, Andrews wrote that "the entire police force and the entire force of guards, and the organization by and through which they operate . . . should be fired off the job." He described the officers as a "very undesirable, unreliable, and incompetent lot." Plant police tended to arrest large numbers of laborers, sometimes resulting in "a whole truck load of men being carried and dumped into county jail at one time." Although Andrews included white workers in his description of police depredations, he noted that the treatment of African Americans was extreme. "The best element of Negroes coming to Muscle Shoals," Andrews contended, "are driven away from the plant by the harsh treatment accorded them by the Air Nitrates police." His solution was to hire a force "made up very largely of local people who command a like respect from the local public, and who know and understand the Negro and the southern white man."[29] Despite complaints about the behavior of plant police, corporate officials took no action, and the officers served throughout the remainder of the war.

Relations between workers and local law enforcement outside the construction site reflected similar racial tensions. Many members of the white community feared that the growing number of black workers would increase crime in the Tri-Cities and suggested forming a home guard to subject young men, particularly blacks, to military supervision. This notion was not unique to the Great War era. During the Civil War, white male citizens created home guards to police their community as well as enforce white supremacy as the slave system crumbled. These guards eventually evolved into local Ku Klux Klan organizations in the Reconstruction era. During World War I, some southern communities revised the efforts of home guards to thwart possible subversive activities of Germans in their communities. Soon after their formation, however, guards directed their activities toward African Americans, believing that blacks were so disaffected that they would cooperate with the enemy if approached. One local citizen, thinking the "home guards" would control crime, placed an ad in the newspaper asking, "Are we [Tri-Cities] waiting to have the experience of some of our other Alabama towns, before organizing [the home guards]?" Florence city commissioners responded by organizing an all-white auxiliary police force with the same "privileges" and "responsibilities" of the regular police. Auxiliary officers patrolled the streets, made arrests, and supported the regular police in their duties.[30]

Tensions between blacks and whites mounted as city officials implemented discriminatory "work-or-fight" ordinances. Many southern towns used such laws to slow the migration of black workers toward war industries. In Mississippi, for example, community leaders forced blacks to work in service jobs for the city and on the local farms if they could not show proof of employment. These same laws also existed in the Tri-Cities. As more of the Tri-Cities' workforce joined the Muscle Shoals Project for better wages, local businesses and farms experienced a labor shortage. The Florence mayor contended that a vigorous vagrancy law would not only make the city safe but also provide "a good step toward recruiting men for the farm, the army, and other necessary enterprises." In response, commissioners in the Tri-Cities passed ordinances requiring people to present adequate proof that they either enlisted in the military or worked. Those without documentation were arrested and sentenced to work for five days or pay five dollars.[31]

Politically stifled by the 1901 constitution and with no voice in the courts, blacks in the Tri-Cities and at the Muscle Shoals Project turned to national race reform organizations for help. In 1918, the NAACP broadened its agenda to include the issue of black labor in war industries. After receiving complaints from all over the South, the NAACP joined other organizations to improve conditions for black workers. It fought racial discrimination in labor practices by mediating between the complainants and the government industry in question. The bricklayers from Cleveland dismissed by J. G. White Engineering at Muscle Shoals, for example, appealed to the NAACP. Activists from the organization tried to have the men reinstated, taking the case to the employers and to the executive council of the American Federation of Labor. They did not succeed, and the bricklayers never returned. The NAACP also received complaints regarding the discriminatory work-or-fight laws. Several African American citizens contested the laws through the courts with help from the NAACP, though the outcome of their cases is uncertain.[32]

The National Urban League also responded to the situation of black workers in the South. Created in 1911, the Urban League concentrated on improving conditions for African Americans in cities through social work and community organizing. Members, primarily black professionals, touted the group as the "advocate of economic and social advancement."[33]

Working together, the NAACP and the Urban League pressured the U.S. Department of Labor to appoint more black representatives to the new bureaus organized under the National Emergency Labor Program and to create a bureau specifically concerned with African American labor. The continued migration of African Americans out of the region and into northern industries, a trend that had begun in the 1910s and was accelerated by the war, also concerned white employers in the South who were losing their workforce. They too believed that the government should step in to help alleviate the problems with labor. Eventually, the Department of Labor formed the Division of Negro Economics under the direction of Fisk University professor George Haynes. Haynes identified the fundamental problems affecting African Americans in war industries and the primary cause of outward migration. "Racial prejudices and antagonisms," he contended, "are ever present facts, making more delicate and difficult what, in any case, would be difficult labor problems." He also pointed to the arduousness of African Americans adjusting to the transition "from rural life and agricultural work to town residence and industrial work." He believed the solution lay in "greater cooperation between Negro wage earners, white employers, and white workers in agriculture and industry."[34]

Haynes and his staff launched an impressive program of biracial cooperation on the state and local levels. He began efforts to rouse support of the African American population by embarking on a patriotic speaking tour, encouraging black workers to do their part to ensure victory. He created committees consisting of both white and black citizens, developed a publicity campaign for the program, and appointed African American staff workers to promote the division's agenda. Within his first six weeks, Haynes boasted of holding informal conferences and interviews with black and white citizens in North Carolina, Mississippi, Virginia, and Florida to spread "good feeling and information" about the division and its work. By the end of the gatherings, participants in their respective states created a State Negro Workers' Advisory Committee that worked closely with white-led organizations such as the state Council of Defense and United States Employment Services. Haynes appointed supervisors for the division in five southern states.[35]

Efforts to organize a cooperative movement also occurred in Alabama but with less success. Informal meetings, such as that hosted by black citizens of the Tri-Cities, and interviews took place in Alabama within the first six weeks of the division's program. Walter S. Buchanan, president of Alabama A&M College in Normal wrote Assistant Secretary of Labor Louis Post asking for more work to be done in Alabama to mobilize black workers and address their concerns. Post responded that the division had begun organizing a statewide movement. Yet by the end of October, just days away from the armistice, the division had not appointed a supervisor for Alabama. The division did receive cooperation from organizations in Alabama. The state Council of Defense appointed an auxiliary council of African Americans to help with its war work, and a representative from Tuskegee Institute helped the division promote its program in the state.[36]

Haynes and supporters of the division identified the problems specific to black workers in the state. Research into the conditions of workers revealed racial tensions between African American and white workers. Moreover, staffers found that the working environment for black laborers was less than adequate. Pointing to problems ranging from sanitation and health care to living quarters and entertainment facilities, the division exposed the harsh circumstances under which most African Americans labored for the war. Haynes also found that the compulsory work-or-fight laws worsened tensions between blacks and white employers and played a large role in the African American exodus from the South. Their hope was that through the cooperative efforts of black and white organizations, along with the support of the Department of Labor, the division could eventually improve working conditions and, at the same time, stem the migration of African American workers to the North.[37]

The end of the war eclipsed efforts to improve the conditions of black workers on the Muscle Shoals Project. A few months before the armistice, the federal government suspended construction on Wilson Dam for the duration of the war. Although the nitrate plants became functional just before the war ended, they never contributed to the war effort. After the armistice, the debate in the federal government over what to do with the nitrate plants and the partially constructed dam, as well as overall high costs and the misuse of government money, overshadowed any discussion regarding race relations or discriminatory practices. The only attempt Congress made to address issues concerning black workers was in reference to the incompetence of Air Nitrates in handling a large labor supply. The House hearings on war expenditures failed to address issues of racial discrimination and inequalities between white and black workers. The findings of the Division of Negro Economics on labor conditions, generated from its conferences and interviews, fell on deaf ears.[38]

The size of the Muscle Shoals Project and its labor force diminished considerably as the nation quickly demobilized. The nitrate plants retained only a skeleton crew until they closed in January 1919. Work resumed on Wilson Dam, but the government no longer viewed it as important to national defense. It was only 35 percent completed by the time money and supplies ran out in 1921. Construction resumed again in 1922 but merely limped along as the war expenditures debate in Congress continued.[39]

The reduced number of workers in the nitrate plants and on the construction of Wilson Dam contributed to a postwar economic decline in the area. Many workers left the area and took their business with them. The government's downsizing of the Muscle Shoals Project also curtailed federal dollars coming into the Tri-Cities. Unemployment rose as laborers sought local jobs outside the project. Many whites directed their frustrations toward African Americans, who they blamed for their own limited job opportunities. The animosity of white citizens toward black workers in the area led to a rise in area lynchings. Only a few days after the armistice, mob violence claimed the lives of two black men in Sheffield—William Byrd, whom the mob accused of "creating a disturbance," and Henry Whiteside, who authorities believed killed a police officer.[40]

Heightened racial tensions in the Tri-Cities drew renewed attention from the NAACP. The organization notified Alabama governor Charles Henderson of the lynchings and requested he act against those suspected of participating. Henderson had the attorney general conduct an investigation, and in December the state handed down twenty-four indictments. Only eighteen of those twenty-four stood trial. The outcome of the trial proved a disappointment to the association. For the lynching of William Byrd, "the jury took only twenty minutes to find the defendants innocent." In the second case, the judge dismissed all charges.[41]

Haynes's Division of Negro Economics also attempted to address the problems associated with the postwar readjustment of the labor force and the attendant racial tensions. In the wake of race riots during the summer of 1919 in cities such as Chicago and Knoxville, Tennessee, Haynes began an investigation of postwar industrial conditions. Although his initial research excluded a survey of circumstances in Muscle Shoals, Haynes and his staffers did recognize that areas of Alabama, in particular Birmingham and Montgomery, were undergoing similar conflicts among workers. He concluded that the government had to intervene to offer some assistance in mediating between black and white laborers in an effort to avoid future violence. Specifically, Haynes concluded that a "large, national, constructive program for bettering the living and working conditions of Negro workers and improving their relations with white workers and white employers may be . . . put into operation." But the fate of the division precluded putting its plan into action. Dominated by southern Democrats, Congress ignored Haynes's pleas to continue funding the division, and by 1921 it disappeared.[42]

The Muscle Shoals Project not only brought economic and social opportunities but also ushered in a new era of social activism among African Americans in the Tri-Cities. Construction of the dam and nitrate plants offered new jobs and better wages for those once tied to the cotton fields. Yet workers who came to the Tri-Cities in hope of a better life soon realized the limits to which their lives could change. Segregation in housing, education, leisure activities, and health care undermined any possibility that conditions would improve. Work-or-fight laws and police brutality subverted attempts to ameliorate tensions between white and blacks in the area. Project employers likewise gave little attention to the complaints of black workers. Rather than succumb to discrimination and bigotry, local blacks turned to national black reform groups and the federal government for help. The NAACP and Urban League, along with the U.S. Department of Labor's Division of Negro Economics, took notice of the conditions facing African Americans in the Tri-Cities, and it was clear that a relationship between local citizens and national race reformers had begun. But as the lynchings of Byrd and Whiteside—as well as subsequent deterioration of race relations—showed, it was only when the civil rights movement of the 1950s and 1960s swept across the South that the seeds of reform planted in the Great War would bear the fruit of social, economic, and legal freedom.

7
Mobile in World War I

Michael V. R. Thomason

World War I began the modernization of Mobile. Many of the issues of gender, race, and economic transformation associated with World War II had their origins in the city's experience in the Great War. That war gave the old city a modern shipbuilding industry and provided the infusion of capital that helped to fund unprecedented economic growth in the twenties. Indeed, the war brought Mobile into the economy and mentalité of the twentieth century. But the war and its changes came slowly. August 1914 was hot and sultry in Mobile, as Augusts always are. Those who could took refuge in cottages or hotels along Mobile Bay or along the rivers that flowed into it. Those who could not, whether because of financial status, race, or business commitments, endured the seasonal discomfort, perhaps escaping briefly on a bay boat across the bay and back, on a trolley to Monroe Park, or in a car for a leisurely drive down the Bay Shell Road. African Americans' opportunities for relief, circumscribed by the laws and customs of segregation then in full flower, were few. They went to Dixie Park or the bay front east of their "Down the Bay" neighborhood south of the city center, the riverbanks, or Mon Louis Island. Many men and women in service to affluent white families accompanied them on their escape from the oppressive heat of the city, but their work limited their opportunities to enjoy the change of scene. Indeed, the overwhelming majority of the city's fifty-one thousand inhabitants simply coped with the weather, as they had always done.[1]

The trouble in the always-troubled Balkans that August did not arouse much notice in Mobile, even among the commercial elite. But, as the month wore on, the news from Europe grew more and more ominous until Mobile's greatest foreign customers were at war with one another.

The unthinkable had happened, and with it the price of cotton, which had crested at over fourteen cents a pound, collapsed almost overnight. The South was enjoying record production of its famous crop and record prices. Now war ended that, as no one knew whether the product could be shipped to European markets or paid for in wartime.[2] Cotton exchanges, including Mobile's, closed down, and prices fell to less than five cents a pound, the lowest since the Panic of 1893. A better demonstration of Mobile's involvement in the world's trade can hardly be imagined. Merchants hurried back to their offices despite the weather to try to make sense out of the sudden commercial collapse. The season's harvest would normally be coming down the rivers and by rail to the port in sixty days. Where would it be stored if it could not be shipped, and who would finance the European trade that had depended largely on the British banking community that was now otherwise involved?[3]

The effect of war in Europe on the cotton trade or other commerce leaving the port for that continent would be largely beyond Mobile's control. Such issues would be resolved, if at all, at a higher level. Nevertheless, Mobile, Alabama, and the South had loyally supported the Democratic Party and Woodrow Wilson in the 1916 presidential election. Indeed, the "solid South" was his most dependable ally. So the plight of the cotton states hardly went unnoticed in Washington . . . or in London. Neither capital wanted to alienate King Cotton, though the British had more pressing concerns as summer turned to fall in 1914. After the Miracle of the Marne halted the German advance virtually at the suburbs of Paris, and the enemies began digging in for winter in a trench system that would instead endure for four years, Britain's foreign secretary, Earl Grey, addressed the South's concerns. His country needed the cotton, and it needed American friendship. Later in the war the British government concluded that America was "an absolutely irreplaceable source of supply" of essential war materiel. Anticipating the importance of even a neutral America, Grey declared that cotton would not be categorized as war contraband, so it could be shipped to the Central powers as well as to England. With the assistance of Wilson's government, Grey arranged to restore British financing for the commodity shipped to its ports. The result was a gradual stabilization of cotton prices, and by the following spring, business had recovered somewhat, though prices remained low well into 1915.[4]

Throughout the first months of war Mobile's principal newspaper, the *Mobile Register*, opposed American involvement in the European quarrel. Since 1910 the paper had been owned by F. I. Thompson, a native of

Mississippi but well connected in Mobile. Thompson was a staunch supporter of Wilson, a foe of legalized vice, and a supporter of Prohibition. He was politically ambitious and had little respect for many of the city's political leaders. His editorials were hardly subtle.[5] Instead, the *Register* called on the federal government to protect the South's commercial interests by negotiations, certainly not by force.[6] Only later did Mobile and America learn to fear the impact of the new naval tool, the German U-boat, which the war saw develop into a practical weapon. By Christmas 1914, Mobilians, like most Americans, were probably glad not to be involved in the distant conflict. The "Christmas Tree for the Poor" event, the largest since it had begun in 1911, provided a clear demonstration of the war's initial impact on the city's economy and the fervor with which some Americans tried to ignore the war. The *Register*'s account of the celebration contrasted sharply with the headlines describing battles on Europe's western front. The party for more than two thousand children of the "deserving poor," sponsored by the Elks, the Ladies of Charity, the *Register*, and others, filled downtown Mobile's Lyric Theatre to overflowing. Although organizers did not invite African American children or orphans of any race, they made provisions for white orphans separately.[7]

Regardless of how Mobilians felt about war in 1914, its effects relentlessly altered Alabama's economy and infrastructure. Since the mid-1890s, Mobilians, working with long-serving Alabama senator John Hollis Bankhead and business leaders from the mineral district around the "Magic City," had cooperated to get federal funding for a monumental project of seventeen locks and dams on the Black Warrior River that would allow iron ore and coal to be shipped by barge from Birmingham to Mobile.[8] The project was completed in 1915 and, had there been peace, would have brought greatly increased traffic in these essential industrial commodities through Mobile. The shortage of shipping that accompanied the war, however, prevented this result until America entered the war and Mobile was transformed into a shipbuilding center.

Most of Mobile's business and political leaders and the *Mobile Register* believed the city's docking and warehouse facilities very much needed modernizing, especially after the completion of the Black Warrior waterway. The majority of dock space was in private hands, primarily those of the railroads that served the city—the Louisville and Nashville; the Mobile and Ohio; the Alabama, Tennessee and Northern; and the Southern. None was equipped to unload barges coming down from Birmingham.[9] Adding further to the demand for modern docks, oceangoing steamers were able to travel to the Gulf and the world beyond down Mobile Bay's thirty-five-mile-long ship channel. Once again, the federal government, prodded by Alabama's senators and congressmen since Reconstruction days, had invested millions of dollars in rivers and harbors. By 1917 Mobile Bay's ship channel was twenty-seven feet deep, which meant that the antiquated harbor facilities were the impediment to further progress. Led by city commissioner Harry Pillans, an influential group of citizens wanted a municipally owned dock constructed south of the city along Garrow's Bend at the mouth of the Mobile River. The project's expense was so daunting that other citizens proposed that the State of Alabama build and operate a facility located north of the city or on Blakely Island. Railroad executives were cool to both plans as challenges to their control of the waterfront.[10]

Dock and warehouse schemes advanced against a perverse slowdown of Mobile's economy. Although orders for war material from France and England increased monthly and business was brisk in the ports of the northeastern United States, Mobile's trade declined precipitously in 1915–16. Because the British and the French depended on ocean-borne ships to supply them with men and materials, their increased demands used up most of the world's available vessels, the overwhelming majority of which flew a Union Jack. Much of the cotton and timber trade that had gone through Mobile before the war moved to New Orleans. With the severe shipping shortage, the few ships that did call found New Orleans a more profitable stop. Business became so bad in Mobile that people of all classes economized any way they could, and houses went vacant even in the most desirable part of town, Government Street. This housing surplus stood in sharp contrast to what came after 1917.[11] The docks were idle much of the time, the local economy was largely stagnant, and workers, especially African Americans, left the city for jobs in the North and Midwest. Things began to change once the port city became a shipbuilding center after the United States entered the war, but first it would have to recover from the major devastation of the 1916 hurricane.[12]

Like people in many parts of the South after the Civil War, Mobilians had not celebrated Independence Day until the Spanish-American conflict made national patriotism respectable again. On July 4, 1916, the city had an especially elaborate parade with a long, bunting-like American flag carried by dozens of marchers down Government Street. The parade's theme was "Preparedness," and the people lined the street to watch. Unfortunately, while Mobilians were demonstrating their support for President Wilson's policy, a hurricane bore down on the city, and not having any warning beyond dropping barometric pressure, Mobile was unprepared. By evening the storm had reached the city, wrecking warehouses, washing cotton into the streets and the bay, and devastating the waterfront. Utilities failed, the streetcars did not run, and telephones and telegraphs were inoperable. On the bay at Garrow's Bend, Monroe Park was so badly damaged that it would never quite recover its earlier glory. For some time, war news from Europe took a backseat to rebuilding from the storm. The damage to property was very considerable, but few lives were lost, a far cry from the area's experience a decade earlier. In time, life returned to normal, and by the fall the worst of the effects of the storm had been put right. War-related economic news once again rose to the forefront.[13]

After carefully weighing its options during the fall and early winter of 1916–17, on February 1, 1917, Germany resumed unrestricted submarine warfare. When it did, the *Register* demanded the United States declare war.[14] A month later, the British government released the Zimmermann telegram, which outlined a German policy to intervene in and destabilize Mexico and Central America. Mobile had a long history of interest in the region. It had supported the construction of the Panama Canal, and for more than twenty years before the outbreak of the Great War it conducted a thriving banana trade with Central America.[15] Mobile's commercial connections in Central America had prompted President Wilson to declare at the Southern Commercial Congress held in the city on October 27, 1913, that the United States had no intention of adding to the territory it controlled in Latin America.[16] But in April 1914, Wilson sent the Marines into Vera Cruz in a vain attempt to stop German arms from reaching General Huerta. Although the United States claimed no territory, it had intervened in the internal affairs of a neighbor to the south. Afterward, Mexico fell into the grip of civil war, which further destabilized that republic. Against this background, the Zimmermann telegram appeared particularly ominous to Mobilians.[17]

On April 6, 1917, the United States finally declared war on Germany and its allies. That evening more than ten thousand people crowded into Mobile's Bienville Square to demonstrate their support at the request of the city government.[18] On April 16 black Mobilians gathered at the State Street Zion Church to pledge their support for the war. One of the speakers that day asked the packed audience, "If this is not our country, tell me where is our country?" The *Register* reported favorably on the sentiments expressed.[19] This coverage contrasted sharply with editor Thompson's suspicion of Americans of German extraction. "All Germans here and elsewhere should watch their steps and their speech," he wrote.[20] In the months before the declaration of war, the newspaper had run powerful daily editorial cartoons depicting the Germans as malevolent war lovers who had to be stopped before they conquered the world. Now that America was in the war, the paper showed no restraint in castigating the nation's enemies at home or abroad, and the anti-German cartoons by Rollin Kirby and J. H. Cassel were an almost daily feature.[21]

Beyond the walls of the *Register* building on St. Joseph Street, progressive Mobilians—and few would refuse that label however they defined it—saw the war as an opportunity to expand the port and its facilities, deepen the ship channel to at least thirty feet, and become a major shipbuilding center. Almost all of this effort would require federal money, and the federal government had its own agenda. Washington had been pressuring ports around the country to create publicly owned docking facilities and not rely solely on those owned by railroads. Successful pleas for federal harbor-improvement funds increasingly depended on taking such steps.

Discussion and debate about the Mobile port's future was spurred by the outbreak of war in Europe and the shortage of merchant shipping that resulted. In the 1915 state legislative session, two Mobile factions had pressed for two different projects that each proposed would help the port cope and lay the foundations for future growth. On one side, editor F. I. Thompson and his protégé, state senator Harry Hartwell, wanted Alabama to create a State Harbor Commission with authority to run and develop all aspects of the port of Mobile. On the other side, city commissioners Harry Pillans and Pat Lyons wished to develop a municipally owned facility on the sand islands at the mouth of the Mobile River adjacent to what was referred to as the Arlington property. The state constitution prohibited the state or its instrumentalities from borrowing money for any port development, and Lyons and Pillans were convinced that the state would not act. Nevertheless, after much wrangling, the legislature created the State Harbor Commission in 1915, giving it sweeping powers but little or no money. Throughout 1915 and 1916 the Harbor Commission struggled to give effect to its great theoretical powers to determine a course for the growth of public wharfs and warehouses, but without much success.

As often happened, F. I. Thompson, annoyed by the delay, publicly and loudly blamed the railroads, their allies, Lyons and Pillans, and almost anyone else he could think of. When the United States entered the war, what had been a local turf battle became an impediment to the war effort.[22] Exploiting the outpouring of patriotic emotions in April 1917, Mayor Pillans broke the impasse by proposing the city make a $600,000 bond issue to build a mile-long pier on the Arlington property. The amount of money was too little to do the project, especially as the war inflated prices, but it was all the city could borrow. That August, after various delays, the city's voters approved the proposed pier, 1,054 to 31, but the project would be dogged by delays and never finished. Nevertheless, the effort did demonstrate Mobile's willingness to expand the 1,250 feet of publicly owned docks at the foot of Government Street at a critical time early in the war. The decision to build the Arlington project was by no means the last word in Mobile's struggle over locating, controlling, and funding a modern, publicly owned docking facility. As subsequent events showed, the city of Mobile alone simply did not have the money to develop a modern port. Thanks to the creation of the State Harbor Commission, the eventual decision was not Mobile's to make. The State of Alabama became the leading power in port development, but it did not exercise that power until well after the war in Europe was over.[23]

The United States was woefully unprepared for the war it declared in 1917. The federal government created the Emergency Fleet Corporation (EFC) of the United States Shipping Board to build up the virtually nonexistent merchant marine, but bureaucratic wrangling prevented the letting of any shipbuilding contacts until Edward N. Hurley became EFC chairman. Finally, in August 1917, the first such contracts in Mobile were signed.[24] Since Germany resumed unrestricted submarine warfare, its U-boats had sunk more shipping than Allied shipyards could build. Only the U.S. Navy's insistence on using the convoy system—in which U.S. Navy warships accompanied compact formations of merchantmen to guard against U-boats—prevented the collapse of the shipping lifeline England depended on to stay in the war.[25] The wasted months in getting American shipbuilding geared up were costly, and few ships were completed in Mobile before the war's end. Nonetheless, the federal government's intention to use the wartime emergency to build a large peacetime merchant fleet meant that Mobile built ships long after Armistice Day 1918.[26]

The first shipbuilding contracts—for 3,500-ton steam-powered wooden freighters called Ferris-class ships—went to locally owned Alabama Dry Dock and Shipbuilding Company (ADDSCO), the Murnan Corporation, and the Chicago-based Kelly-Atkinson Corporation. ADDSCO and Murnan had to expand their facilities, and Kelly-Atkinson had to construct theirs, before they could even start building the ships. ADDSCO, formed by an amalgamation of four older shipyards in January 1917, was the first to launch a ship, the *Banago*, but this event did not occur until July 4, 1918. The *Banago* was completed and delivered to the EFC on September 10, 1918, the only cargo vessel to be turned over to the EFC by a Mobile shipyard during the war.[27] The yards delivered smaller ships for wartime service, but the lead time necessary to turn undeveloped waterfront into productive shipyards was an inescapable fact of life. Also all the shipyards had to recruit and train workers and obtain supplies.[28] The severe shortage of rolling stock on the nation's railways rendered the latter problem more serious. Fortunately for Mobile's shipyards, the first contracts were for wooden cargo vessels, and there was no shortage of wood thanks to the vast forestlands of the South and entrepreneurs such as Frank Boykin, whose business interests ranged from real estate to lumber to shipbuilding. Even after being nationalized "for the duration," however, the railroads' ability to move war material remained a problem throughout the war.[29]

In the late summer of 1917, rumors began to circulate that a new player was entering Mobile's shipbuilding game: U.S. Steel. Indeed, the company bought up thousands of acres north of Mobile.[30] Finally, on November 25, 1917, George Gordon Crawford made the official announcement: the steel giant was going to spend $15,000,000 to develop fourteen thousand acres of swampy land into a modern shipbuilding facility. This "Chickasaw plant," which took its name from the Chickasabogue Creek on which it was built, would have a steel mill, power-generating plant, twelve modern shipways, and, for its more than 3,500 workers, company housing adjoining the facility.[31] In its long history, Mobile had never seen such a large investment. Since 1915, coal, iron, and steel could be transported by barge from Birmingham to Mobile for $0.40 per ton rather than the prevailing rail rate of $2.80 thanks to a series of federally funded locks and dams on the Black Warrior River.[32] Birmingham's Tennessee Coal, Iron and Railroad Company (TCI), a subsidiary of U.S. Steel, could supply the new shipyard's material needs directly, cheaply, and quickly. U.S. Steel hired an army of laborers of both races and sexes to build the facility immediately. African American women in overalls worked alongside men moving bricks and doing other construction work there. "For the first time [such mixed race/gender activity had occurred] in the history of Mobile," the *Register* noted on September 15. The workers had to build everything from scratch, so although the yard had begun to take shape before the war's end, not a single ship had been started when the armistice was signed. Eventually the yard produced fourteen steel freighters displacing 9,600 to 10,000 tons, launching the last on September 11, 1921. The yard's two villages, one for each race and totaling 1,600 homes, were linked by then to Mobile via Telegraph Road and an interurban trolley line. They continued to be occupied between the closing of the yard in 1921 and its reopening on the eve of World War II.[33]

U.S. Steel was the only wartime employer to build houses for its workers in Mobile. As government contracts showered down on the city's shipyards, workers found housing increasingly difficult to afford or even obtain. The federal government did not build any housing, and by 1918 there were eight thousand to ten thousand workers at the yards that lined both sides of the Mobile River. The shipyards blamed the shortage on local real estate interests, saying that they were unwilling to invest in new construction but were all too willing to overcharge shipyard workers.[34] On May 2, 1918, the Mobile Chamber of Commerce Housing Committee decried the poor state of rental housing available to either race and called for vacant buildings to be converted into dormitories for the steady stream of new workers. The next day, the *Register* castigated "unoccupied shacks" being offered to workers. Except for U.S. Steel, however, neither the shipyards nor local real estate interests invested in building housing for workers during the war, and the chamber of commerce did nothing to implement its committee's recommendations.[35]

As if the housing shortage were not enough, workers were unable to get back and forth to work. The streetcar line was simply overwhelmed. It had so little rolling stock available that people rode on the roofs of packed cars during rush hours. There was a shortage of material to build new cars, and many trainmen and conductors had left their jobs for various reasons, including better-paying shipyard employment.[36]

Despite problems with housing and transport, the contracts kept coming, and new companies entered the business. In May 1918, the F. T. Ley Company announced it would erect a new shipyard just north of the Arlington pier project to build a 7,500-ton concrete ship every ninety days. It would work four shipways and hire up to four thousand employees.[37] A month later, Mobile Shipbuilding Company, a subsidiary of Kelly-Atkinson headed by the irrepressible Frank Boykin, who later served for decades in the U.S. Congress, announced it had secured a contract to build twelve 7,500-ton steel ships at one million dollars each.[38] Monthly shipyard payrolls were staggering. ADDSCO paid its 3,600 employees nearly $500,000 per month, equaling the Chickasaw payroll of 3,500 to 5,000 workers. F. T. Ley paid out $30,000 to $40,000 each week. Mobile had never seen such payrolls, which would continue for nearly two years after the war's end while the shipyards completed their government contracts.[39]

Benefiting from such unprecedented investment in the local economy, Mobilians found it easy to lend the government money for the war effort. Local participation in the Liberty Loan drives and purchase of War Stamps surpassed all expectations. There were four Liberty Loans during the war, and in each case Mobile exceeded its quota, raising a total of $8,264,700 when the government had asked for only $6,741,910. The city's contribution was one of the best in the South, and with each loan the amount subscribed and the percentage by which the city exceeded its goal grew.[40] Scouts, newsboys, and all sorts of other groups participated in the drives. The city government issued proclamations urging people to take part, and the newspaper ran banner headlines and frequent editorials reminding everyone of their patriotic duty to loan the government money. On April 26, 1918, the *Register* took a different tack. It editorialized that anyone who did not support the third Liberty Loan was a "parasite."[41] Still, the Liberty Loan parades and rallies seemed to be more effective. The greatest of all the parades was scheduled for April 6, 1918, for the third Liberty Loan drive. As happens often in Mobile, it rained that day, and the parade was postponed to April 12, when Secretary of the Treasury William McAdoo was to visit. That day the parade went off without a hitch and took an hour and a half to pass the reviewing stand. The *Register* estimated that twenty thousand people participated, with representatives from all the shipyards, the Red Cross, the Mothers' Army and Navy League, and other groups. Black fraternal and service organizations marched with their white counterparts alongside elaborate floats, and everyone waved flags.[42] McAdoo was very impressed. He reportedly said, among other things, "It was bully." Mayor Pat Lyons declared the parade to be the finest he had ever seen in thirty years of watching parades in the city and that April 12 would thereafter be known in Mobile as "McAdoo Day."[43] Just over a month later, on May 17, an only slightly smaller parade wound through the city streets, this one in support of the Red Cross. Black and white Red Cross volunteers marched together, accompanied by black and white bands and 277 white draftees, or selectmen as they were called, who were about to leave for basic training. The Red Cross goal was $50,000. When the campaign ended later in the month, Mobile had contributed $120,000.[44]

Bienville Square was always the focal point of parades and rallies. The Labor Day parade of 1918 showcased thirty-eight labor unions, black and white, and featured models of ships under construction. That parade took forty-five minutes to pass a single point. After it was over, the crowd moved to the Arlington fairgrounds, which had been converted into a shipyard workers' park. Streetcars to Arlington were full to overflowing from 11:00 a.m. to 7:00 p.m., when festivities finally wound down.[45] On September 13, women selling War Stamps used the square as the site for raising a fire truck's ladder straight into the air and climbing it. The event was so graphic that the *Register* ran a picture of it the next day, at a time when few photographs were printed.[46]

But the largest rally held before Armistice Day itself was organized by the tireless Frank Boykin and sponsored by the Mobile Loyalty League. This "Labor Efficiency Rally" was similar to those planned in cities across the country, but few could have matched the show Boykin put together the evening of September 14. The program consisted of speeches by Governors Charles Henderson of Alabama and Theodore Bilbo of Mississippi, along with remarks by local civic and economic leaders. After each speaker talked, a five-hundred-voice African American choir arrayed on the stage behind the dignitaries sang patriotic songs and spirituals. Two blacks spoke about the need for racial harmony, greater job opportunities for African American women, and an "even balance on the scales of justice" for all. The crowd of ten thousand was composed of blacks and whites, which was remarkable, as Bienville Square was traditionally reserved for whites. The rally went off without any problems. As the *Register* wrote the next day, it was "the first rally in Mobile where white and colored patriots stood together."[47] September 1918 was quite a month, but parades and rallies happened all through the war.

Not all the public events were as exuberant as Boykin's rally or the Labor Day festivities. For the Fourth of July 1918, the Wilson administration urged U.S. shipyards to launch one hundred ships and asked all naturalized American citizens to march in local parades as a show of loyalty to their adopted country.[48] The nation's shipyards did not quite meet Wilson's goal, though Mobile did its bit by launching two vessels.[49] The city did have a parade for one thousand naturalized Americans. The two largest contingents were the Germans and English, each with approximately two hundred members.[50] The next day the *Register* admitted the parade had gone well, but proclaimed, "There is disloyalty in the land" and repeated its demand that foreign-born people continually prove their allegiance to America. The fact that the *Register* never found any evidence of disloyalty by Mobile's large German-born population did not make any difference. Its nativist editorials continued throughout the war. Anti-German sentiment expressed itself in Mobile, as it did across the country, by calling sauerkraut "liberty cabbage," harassing dachshund dogs and their owners, and calling on Germans to anglicize their names.[51] The *Register* reflected the feelings of some Mobilians who took their own action. On April 25, 1918, the German Relief Society, an old and well-respected club in Mobile, received a letter threatening it with arson and mob action if it did not change its name and cease to allow German to be spoken by its members. On April 30 the organization changed its name to the Mobile Relief Society and ceased using the German language. Authorities never identified the author of the threat.[52]

The unease caused by the city's rapid growth and the wartime shortages and uncertainties were also reflected in race relations. African Americans accounted for just over 40 percent of Mobile's population. They suffered under the social, political, and economic discrimination that lay at the heart of racial segregation.[53] Blacks proclaimed their loyalty to America at every opportunity, and their support for the war effort was acknowledged, albeit without enthusiasm. Blacks held patriotic gatherings in the larger churches or at Dixie Park, the one municipal park facility available to them. Perhaps the most dramatic demonstration of their patriotism came late in July 1918 when 501 African American selectmen were to report for service. On Sunday, July 28, the State Street Zion Church held services for the men and their families, followed later in the day by a dinner provided by the black Red Cross women at Dixie Park. Reverend C. First Johnson presided over the occasion, and leaders of the black community, including Professor W. A. Caldwell, Dr. E. T. Belsaw, and Dr. Roger Williams, addressed the crowd. It was one of the rare occasions that the *Register* covered an event in the black community, and it reported that four thousand to five thousand people were at the park.[54] Two days later the selectmen reported to the county courthouse to be sworn in and then made their way two blocks to the Louisville and Nashville Railway station. So many families and friends came to see them off that the two-block journey took a half hour. The draft board praised the people for their support, and though the white inductees did not get such a send-off, thereafter the black community followed a similar pattern as its young men were drafted.[55] Also, black men and women bought Liberty Bonds and War Stamps and served in various ways to help the war effort. Despite their support, their efforts did not arouse sympathy for advancing the race. The *Register*, for example, vocally opposed training African American troops in the South, characterizing them as "hundreds of armed black men."[56]

Perhaps reflecting the heightened wartime racial tensions, on June 2, 1918, a fight at ADDSCO between black and white workers broke out following the drowning death of Marshall Madison, a young black worker at the Pinto Island facility. Upset at the accident, Daniel Stevens allegedly shoved a white man in the pay line later that day, thereby triggering a donnybrook. Police made fourteen arrests, all of black men. ADDSCO itself seems to have been more racially tolerant than the *Register*. The ADDSCO employee magazine, *Fore and Aft*, began publication on August 10, 1918, so it did not comment on the June 2 altercation. But its rhetoric was less racist than that of the *Register*. It reported in its first issue that fifty ADDSCO workers were part of the eight hundred Mobile "colored citizens" drafted into the national army. Its tone contrasted markedly with that of the *Register*, which never described African Americans as "citizens."[57]

Fore and Aft and the *Register* were both more racially tolerant than the revived Ku Klux Klan, which made its presence felt after the ADDSCO brawl. That same evening, June 2, Klansmen wearing their robes and masks drove cars around the city. On June 6, Joseph C. Rich, chair of the Mobile County Council of Defense, denounced the Klan, saying that people "should work in the open."[58] Ten days later the Klan stopped policemen who had arrested a black labor leader, Rafe Clemmons, on Davis Avenue in the heart of the African American community. The Klansmen took Clemmons and went down Cedar Point Road. Efforts by officials and friends to find him were unsuccessful for several days. Eventually the story emerged that the KKK had beaten him severely and that he subsequently fled to New Orleans.[59] The city commission reviewed the event, and Commissioner Pillans declared it was a "serious problem." To break the anonymity of Klansmen, the commission passed an antimasking ordinance and reminded the police chief that there were already ordinances prohibiting parades without a permit and cars being driven without clearly visible licenses. The *Register* also decried the events and blamed the problem on Mayor Lyons, whom it accused of encouraging the Klan activity in the first place. The *Register* offered no proof to support the charge, and the police arrested no Klansmen, but no further Klan activity was reported during the war.[60]

Mobile's black community continued to render loyal service to the war effort, but without any hope of change in the Jim Crow world in which they lived. It is hardly surprising that in April 1919 a local group of nearly fifty petitioned the NAACP to organize a Mobile chapter. The petitioners were not the elite of their community; instead, they were manual laborers, domestics, and similar workers.[61] Despite their wartime loyalty and efforts to found a local NAACP branch, blacks in Mobile had to endure two more generations of legal discrimination after the armistice in 1918.

Another large segment of Mobile also supported the war efforts with little reward. Women played key roles in Mobile's war effort and often crossed the racial divide to organize war work.[62] Lura Harris Craighead, wife of the *Register*'s associate editor, chaired the Mobile chapter of the Women's Committee of the Council of National Defense, coordinating its committees to parallel those of the very effective Mobile County Council of Defense. She not only was active among white clubwomen in this work but also recruited black women for war service, including the Red Cross. For their part, black women organized themselves under the leadership of Mrs. Lillie Williamson, principal of the Mayesville School.[63] The war work itself changed according to the most pressing need, as the activities of the Mothers' Army and Navy League demonstrated. The league raised funds to send comfort packages to the "Sammies," as Americans called their soldiers throughout most of the war. In the influenza epidemic in October 1918, the league and other female volunteers took food to victims and worked as hospital volunteers at great risk to their own lives. Recognizing their many contributions to the war effort, the *Register* strongly supported the suffrage amendment that became law after the war.[64]

One of the most controversial issues involving women before and during the war was legalized prostitution. Mobile had a red-light district when America entered the war; the port city had had one for most of the previous century.[65] Reformers decried the city's toleration of the district, which they saw as an encouragement to vice. The *Register* was particularly vocal, and it led the fight against sexual vice and the sale of alcohol, which it saw as closely allied evils.[66] The city outlawed the district in January 1918, though subsequent enforcement of this new state of affairs was sporadic at best.[67] The official end to legalized prostitution was intended to make Mobile more attractive to the federal government as a site for a military base, but in the end no base was forthcoming.[68]

In June the respectable men of the city created their own project to eradicate vice. With the financial support of the local Rotary club, the U.S. Army Medical Corps rounded up 475 women and put them in the county jail, where it was discovered that 90 percent needed medical treatment. By September thirty-two white and eighty-five black women from this group had gotten married, and another thirty-two of the white women had gotten jobs. Medical Corps captain J. O. Rush praised the project but noted that the low wages paid to women was the principal impediment to the program's success. Women could not find work at a living wage. His clear implication was that the women were prostitutes, though none were so charged. Perhaps reflecting the mores of the era, no further public discussion of the matter survives.[69]

Although women served in the Red Cross and various auxiliary services in the United States and Europe, none were drafted. All males were subject to the Selective Service law, however, and throughout the war many Mobilians of both races were registered and inducted, and many more volunteered. Still others had served in the Fourth Alabama Infantry on the Mexican frontier and went to Europe in the summer of 1917 in the Rainbow Division. Although the initial federal efforts to create a massive national army in the summer and fall of 1917 was plagued with difficulties, by the end of that year the system was functional. Mobile city and county registered 19,835 men for the Selective Service System, of which 2,503 were inducted. Another 387 enlisted, and approximately 300 served in the National Guard, for a total of 3,190 Mobilians who wore their county's uniform during the war. Of the draftees, 1,600 were black and 903 were white, despite the fact that the city and county were predominantly white. Similar ratios are found in other Alabama cities and counties and probably reflect the deferments available to skilled white workers.[70] With fewer opportunities to learn and practice a skill, blacks qualified for fewer deferments. Of the soldiers, airmen, and sailors from Mobile, only a half a dozen were killed in action; a similar number died in accidents in Europe or at sea. Mobile's first fatality was Charles E. Bromberg, Jr., who was killed in an accident in France on April 13, 1918. On July 22, the *Register* reported that Leo Chastang was the first Mobilian to be killed in action. Both men were veterans of the Mexican campaign and served in the Rainbow Division.[71] When the final figures were tabulated, sixty-three men from Mobile died while in service, many from influenza.[72] In addition to supplying infantrymen and laborers, Mobile had its own air ace. Lieutenant Frank Baer was first credited with three confirmed kills in mid-April and seven by the end of the month, only to go down behind enemy lines on May 22. On June 18, he was reported to be alive in a German POW camp, where he remained for the rest of the war.[73]

The most famous Mobile native to serve in combat was rarely identified as a Mobilian at all until recently. James Reese Europe served with the "Harlem Hell Cats" of the Fifteenth New York Infantry. He was born in

Mobile in 1881, but his parents moved to Washington, D.C., when he was ten years old. Both parents were musicians. At the age of twenty-two, Europe moved to New York to make his living playing jazz. When America entered the war, he joined a unit being raised in Harlem and recruited a jazz band from the best African American musicians he knew. That band led the Harlem unit into France, where it became an overnight sensation, as it delighted audiences with American jazz music Frenchmen had never heard before. Then the Harlem Hell Cats were assigned to fight as a unit attached to the French army. American Expeditionary Force commander General John "Black Jack" Pershing resisted doing this with his other AEF units, but it was the only way he would allow black soldiers to see combat. For 161 days the Hell Cats were on the front line, the longest such service by Americans in the entire war. Europe was an officer in charge of machine guns and was wounded and gassed, but he survived the war and led his band in a great victory parade through New York to Harlem on February 17, 1919. He did not return to Mobile, and he was not generally identified with the port city at the time or for many years thereafter, perhaps because of his race. Today he is remembered in the Museum of Mobile and elsewhere as one of the city's own.[74]

Even though the United States participated in the war for only nineteen months, Americans began to tire of it in 1918. From mid-September on, newspapers across the nation reported the impending collapse of the Central powers.[75] As the month wore on, it was clear that there was a chance for the conflict to end before winter. Ironically, Mobile's shipyards were just then approaching full production. Every train brought in new workers, but the housing shortage was so serious that many were turned away despite the need for them all along the waterfront.[76] Also, Mobile faced the daunting task of raising twice as much money in the fourth Liberty Loan drive as it had in the third just months earlier—$3,400,000. City leaders initially feared that Mobilians, thinking the war would soon be over, would not buy bonds, so they developed elaborate plans for parades and rallies to encourage the necessary enthusiasm.[77] Frank Boykin proposed building a seventy-five-foot-long model ship in Bienville Square at a pace matching the Liberty Loan's progress. He christened his brainchild the "Liberty Ship" and began work. Mobile responded with great enthusiasm. On November 3 the *Register* reported that loan subscriptions exceeded the quota by $544,650.[78]

This response is remarkable considering that in October the city fell victim to the global Spanish influenza pandemic. The infection spread like wildfire. Mobile saw its first case on October 2, and within the week doctors reported that 608 people had fallen ill. By October 13, 1,607 cases had occurred, with 25 deaths, and the worst was yet to come. After some confusion the city government closed all schools, theaters, pool halls, and churches on October 7, and they did not reopen them until November 5, when the epidemic began to abate.[79] Hospitals quickly filled to capacity, and the Red Cross opened a 150-bed emergency hospital in the Mobile Relief Hall. It, too, filled quickly. The Mothers' Army and Navy League took food to homebound victims. Mobilians died in such great numbers that undertakers could not keep supplied with enough caskets to bury them. Of course, the epidemic affected war work. The shipyards reported absence rates of 50 percent and more.[80] Mobile Shipbuilding was perhaps the hardest hit. It had 952 men working and 1,175 absent, but other facilities were not much better off.[81] People living in crowded, substandard housing were most likely to get the disease and die of it, so it was no surprise that more African Americans died than whites. Still, the suffering was very nearly universal in the city and the county.

The *Register* claimed this epidemic was the worst in the city's history, yellow fever included. In 1918, 504 people died of influenza and pneumonia. In 1919, 265 more succumbed, for a total of 769 deaths. In all, doctors reported that 6,090 people caught influenza in the county in those two years, with most cases occurring in October 1918 and February 1919. Though it had supported his recent election, the *Register* blamed the rapid spread of the epidemic on Mayor George Crawford and the city medical officer, Dr. Charles Mohr, accusing them of not acting forcefully enough to save the city.[82]

On November 7, after the first wave of influenza subsided, United Press Association wires prematurely announced an armistice. It quickly corrected its error, but celebrations based on the news began across America. Rumors ran wild in Mobile, and people stood outside the *Register* office waiting for more news.[83] On November 11, the *Register* reported the armistice in giant headlines, "World War Is Ended." Across the city, church bells rang, and shop whistles blew. Celebration began before dawn and lasted well into the night. People packed the downtown streets, where a hastily organized parade featured floats calling for revenge and demanding that the victors "Hang the Kaiser." The *Register,* in what could only be described as an understatement, noted that "Mobile went patriotically and joyously wild yesterday."[84]

With the armistice all draft calls and inductions were suspended, but work in the shipyards went on at its wartime pace.[85] Chairman Hurley of the EFC asserted that the United States still needed ships, and the *Reg-*

ister agreed, saying there would be "no reduction for years to come" in shipbuilding in Mobile.[86] Despite such assurances, which were repeated by government officials and the press, there were no new orders or contracts. Nationally, the EFC had 721 ships under construction as of November 1918: 321 wood freighters of 3,500 tons and 400 steel ships of 7,000 tons or more. American shipyards would finish all these ships.[87] In 1921, because the wooden vessels were not commercially viable in peacetime, the federal government sold a group of 205 for less than it had paid to build one. The government considered itself fortunate to dispose of them at any price.[88] On September 11 of that year, the last of Mobile's wartime-era ships, the *City of Chattanooga,* was launched from Chickasaw. Part of the day's festivities included a boat ride around nearby Twelve Mile Island in the Mobile River where the EFC moored sixty surplus ships. The *Register* assured readers all were in good condition, but despite efforts to build a peacetime merchant marine, the supply of ships far outstripped demand.[89]

In 1920 President Wilson appointed the *Register*'s F. I. Thompson to the United States Shipping Board, which controlled all the ships constructed in wartime.[90] Thompson used his position to help Mobile businessman John Waterman lease many of the ships cheaply and secure federal mail contracts, which were effectively subsidies, for the steamship company Waterman built after the war. By the end of World War II, the Waterman Steamship Corporation would be "the largest dry cargo fleet in the American Merchant Marine."[91]

The Great War was a turning point in the history of the old city. From July 4, 1918, to September 9, 1921, Mobile's shipyards launched forty-six oceangoing vessels: twenty-four steel, twelve wood, and two concrete freighters; one steel barge; and an assortment of submarine chasers and minesweepers. As these ships were finished the major shipyards closed except locally owned ADDSCO and Henderson Shipbuilding, both of which shifted to ship repair.[92] Because of the wartime shipbuilding boom, Mobile had enjoyed the largest investment of capital in its history as well as several years of unprecedented payrolls.

Many workers left as the ships were completed, but overall the city and county experienced a net growth of nearly ten thousand and twenty thousand people, respectively, in the decade of 1910–20.[93] But the city's ethnic diversity was a casualty of war. The African American population increased very little, and its proportion of the city's total fell from 44 percent to 39 percent. The percentage of foreign-born Mobilians also fell, from 4.3 percent to 3.3 percent. In 1910 Germans made up the largest foreign-born nationality in the city (567), followed by the Irish (385) and the English (339). A decade later there were 251 Germans, 229 English, and 197 Irish.[94]

Nevertheless, the changing demographic picture was overshadowed by a postwar economic boom. During the war the number and aggregate tonnage of merchant vessels calling at the port fell sharply. In 1914, 894 ships totaling 1,033,284 tons called at Mobile. In 1917 and 1918 the figures were little more than half that, reflecting the wartime merchant shipping shortage. By 1920, however, dockings and tonnage surpassed prewar levels, fueling demands for port expansion.[95] The partially completed Arlington pier project, which had been virtually abandoned, was not thought adequate for a variety of reasons, and Mobile turned to the State of Alabama to build a modern, publicly owned facility. It did so only after years of political struggle.[96] In the end, Mobile's success in securing its state docks was due to the support of U.S. Steel's George Gordon Crawford, who had built the Chickasaw shipyard and saw a modern port in Mobile as a definite advantage for his company. Thanks to the state docks and various local initiatives such as the construction of the Cochrane Bridge across Mobile Bay, new factories, and tourist initiatives, the twenties would be a very prosperous decade for the city. The millions invested in the war were available for a variety of peacetime uses, and the port's prosperity created many jobs that endured though the decade.[97]

The impact of the war and its aftermath would be overshadowed by the following world war, but the 1914–18 conflict certainly changed the old town.[98] The First World War would certainly have brought more change if the Germans had continued fighting into 1919. Even with the war's abrupt end in November 1918, the city saw its port transformed with new shipyards built where virtually nothing had existed before, fueled by millions of dollars in investment. U.S. Steel invested $15,000,000 in Chickasaw, and a similar amount was spent expanding and amalgamating the small prewar yards along the Mobile River, such as Henderson and ADDSCO, and building wholly new ones, such as Mobile Shipbuilding and the F. T. Ley Company. The federal government honored its contracts, worth $20,000,000 when the war ended, in the years that followed.[99] Payrolls had never been so high as in the war's immediate aftermath, nor would they be again until World War II. Although shipbuilding was largely over after 1922, some of the yards were converted to ship repair facilities and continued to employ many skilled workers thereafter.[100] The State Harbor Commission, established in 1915, was not able to achieve the goals its supporters desired, but it did signal the entry of the state of Alabama into the life of the port. The Arlington pier project demonstrated that the city acting alone lacked the financial resources to build the public docks the port needed and the federal government required if the Army Corps of Engineers was to continue to deepen the ship channel. If the corps did not do so, the port of Mobile could not compete with rivals in the Gulf and elsewhere. The net result of all this was a state-financed dock system that might never have happened had not the war shown its necessity.[101]

Other developments were less obvious at the time. The war's abrupt conclusion capped the city's growth just before a housing crisis exploded. There were few dwellings available or under construction in November 1918, but demand was growing rapidly. The armistice saved Mobile as it stopped further growth that would have continued as long as the war raged. Housing shortages did not worsen, and gradually the anticipated crisis evaporated. The end of the war also meant that demands for relaxation in racial or gender discrimination were not heard or, if heard, were not acted on. Both the issue of race and the issue of gender would assert themselves more forcefully in the subsequent world war, which lasted almost three times longer for America. As it was, African Americans continued to endure segregation, and women saw little change in their status, except for those few who could afford to pay the poll tax once they were granted the vote. Neither group saw its economic or social opportunities improve, despite their war service, for many years to come.

At the war's end there was one piece of unfinished business. On November 22, 1918, the Mothers' Army and Navy League announced plans to raise money for a memorial to the men who had died while in the service of their country. They planned to begin fund-raising after the holidays that year, and they did, but it would be eight long years before the memorial was built. The group was denied funding by the city government and eventually raised more than $20,000 from private contributions. On March 21, 1926, the memorial, located on Government at Houston Street, then in the city's western suburbs, was dedicated. The names of the sixty-three residents of Mobile County who had given their lives were inscribed on a bronze plaque on one side of the simple marble monument, executed in the classical style.[102] The monument still stands, a silent tribute to a forgotten war. Even if largely forgotten nearly a century later, however, the Great War nonetheless began the modernization process that would change Mobile forever.

"The Incoming Tide" of racial equality and justice, an effect of black participation in World War I. From the *Montgomery Examiner*, July 26, 1919. Courtesy of the Alabama Department of Archives and History, Montgomery.

Robert Russo Moton, principal of Tuskegee Institute during World War I and leader of the African American community in Alabama. Courtesy of the Eufaula Athenaeum.

Governor Charles Henderson and pilot after governor's first air flight, Aerodrome No. 3, Maxwell Field, 1918. Courtesy of the Alabama Department of Archives and History, Montgomery.

Mrs. Hundley "Bossie" O'Brien, chair of the Alabama Four Minute Women. Courtesy of the Birmingham Public Library Archives.

Second Lieutenant F. Scott Fitzgerald, Camp Sheridan, Montgomery, 1918. Courtesy of the Alabama Department of Archives and History, Montgomery.

Grounds of the U.S. nitrate plant no. 2 in 1919. Courtesy of the Bill Scott Archives, Florence-Lauderdale Public Library, Florence, Alabama.

Cyanamid plant, view of Block D in 1918. Courtesy of the Bill Scott Archives, Florence-Lauderdale Public Library, Florence, Alabama.

Richard M. Hobbie, U.S. food administrator for Alabama. Hobbie was an original member of the Alabama Council for Defense and also served on the advisory committee for the Montgomery Cooperative Canning Club. Courtesy of the Alabama Department of Archives and History, Montgomery.

Annie Dimmick Jones, chair of the Montgomery Cooperative Canning Club Executive Committee, 1918. Jones went on to serve as president of the Alabama Federation of Women's Clubs, 1920–21, and opened the first United Service Organizations in Montgomery in 1942. Courtesy of the Alabama Federation of Women's Clubs.

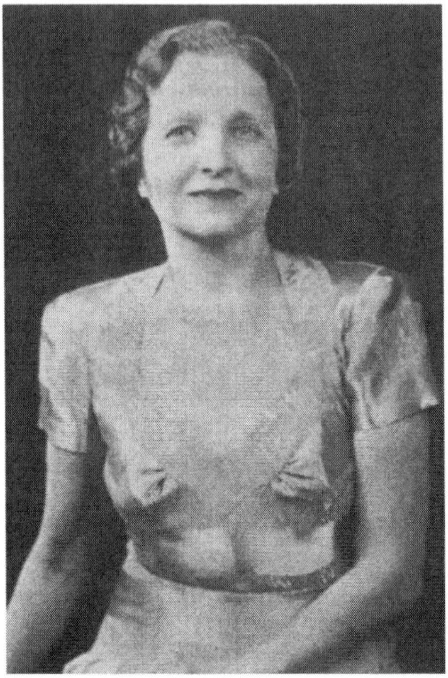

Vera Quinn, first operations manager for the Montgomery Cooperative Canning Club, 1917. This photograph dates from Mrs. Quinn's tenure as president of the Alabama Federation of Women's Clubs in 1930–31, when she instructed women's clubs in the state to create canning clubs to supply food for Depression-ravaged citizens. Courtesy of the Alabama Federation of Women's Clubs.

Red Cross nurses in a 1918 Liberty Bond Parade on Government Street in Mobile. Courtesy of the Erik Overbey Collection, University of South Alabama Archives.

Launching of the USS *Swan* from Alabama Dry Dock and Shipbuilding Company, July 4, 1916. The *Swan* was the first ship launched in Mobile during the Great War. Courtesy of the University of South Alabama Archives.

Associated Trades Labor Day Parade, September 1918. The float commemorates a concrete ship being constructed by the F. T. Ley Company. Courtesy of the Erik Overbey Collection, University of South Alabama Archives.

The F. T. Ley Company closed almost immediately after it launched this concrete ship, the SS *Latham*, on August 9, 1919. Other shipyards in Mobile built ships until the fall of 1922. Courtesy of the Museum of Mobile.

Marie Bankhead Owen in 1913. She was a prominent leader among Alabama's Progressive women, state archivist from 1920 to 1955, and securer of the Alabama War Memorial Building in 1940. Courtesy of the Alabama Department of Archives and History, Montgomery.

Governor Thomas Kilby, 1919–1923, shown authorizing the Alabama War Memorial. He ran for office and won on a Progressive platform. Courtesy of the Alabama Department of Archives and History, Montgomery.

Dr. Samuel Welch, state public health officer following World War I. Courtesy of the Alabama Department of Archives and History, Montgomery.

General Robert Steiner shown later in his life. He commanded the mobilization camp in Montgomery during the months after April 1917. Courtesy of the Alabama Department of Archives and History, Montgomery.

Colonel William P. Screws, circa 1918, commander of the 4th Alabama, which became the 167th Infantry Regiment of the 42nd Division. Courtesy of the Alabama Department of Archives and History, Montgomery.

Dr. Thomas M. Owen, first Alabama archivist and member of the Alabama Council of Defense, at work in the capitol archives room, circa 1910. Courtesy of the Alabama Department of Archives and History, Montgomery.

8
The Alabama Council of Defense, 1917–1918

Dowe Littleton

In reaction to the European war that had raged for nearly two years, Congress created the Council of National Defense (CND) on August 29, 1916, as a component of the Army Appropriations Act. Congress granted the CND a broad mandate, including being charged with "the coordination of industries and resources for national security and welfare and with the creation of relations which will render possible in time of need the immediate concentration and utilization of the resources of the nation." The council thus became the framework on which the nation constructed its mobilization for war.[1]

The CND consisted of six cabinet members—the secretaries of war, navy, interior, labor, agriculture, and commerce—assisted by an unpaid advisory commission made up of experts in the fields of utilities, manufacturing, and related professions. An appropriation from Congress of two hundred thousand dollars provided for a director and clerical staff as well as for financing of the CND's war-related projects. Although the council was slow to get started, within a year more than four hundred people were involved in its work. Once it was established, rapid developments in the council's work led to refinement and specialization. The table of contents of the CND's first annual report listed no less than twenty-five committees, boards, councils, and sections.[2]

In early 1917, this emerging bureaucracy focused its efforts on preparing the nation's economy for supplying the needs of the military. To bolster and sustain popular support for the war and direct sundry and often-confusing mobilization activities, the CND needed to erect some type of organization within the forty-eight states themselves. It sent a letter to the governors of the states and asked them to appoint state councils of defense. Soon after, the CND invited governors or their representatives to attend a National Defense Conference, which would be held in May in Washington, D.C. All this activity was directed by the CND's Section on Cooperation with States. That name was later changed to the State Councils Section.[3] Early in April 1917, Alabama governor Charles Henderson began to develop plans for a state affiliate of the CND. On May 17, he officially established the Alabama Council of Defense in a proclamation that touched on several themes and issues at the center of his state's mobilization effort.[4] Henderson charged the council with overseeing production of "food and other commodities upon which the war makes a special drain," and he stressed the overall need for protection of public health, increased efficiency, elimination of waste, and proper distribution of the labor force.[5] In the proclamation he asked the citizens of the state to support the work of the state and local councils of defense throughout the war, specifically emphasizing the need for volunteerism. Indeed, the successes of the mobilization rested on volunteer activity.[6]

Its membership wholly appointed by the governor, the Alabama Council of Defense underwent several administrative changes throughout its three-year tenure. Initially, Henderson appointed an executive committee composed of himself, Richard M. Hobbie and Ray Rushton of Montgomery, L. M. Bashinsky of Troy, Albert P. Bush of Mobile, Oscar Wells of Birmingham, and J. F. Duggar of Auburn. Interestingly, Bashinsky was a cashier in the Troy Farmers and Merchants National Bank where Henderson had been a director. The governor also appointed his private secretary and cousin, William E. Henderson, as executive secretary of the council. Richard Hobbie, the chairman of the executive committee, resigned in August when he accepted the position of federal food administrator for Alabama offered to him by Herbert Hoover, director of the United States Food Administration. Lloyd M. Hooper, a Selma businessman, took Hobbie's place and served for the duration of the council's existence.[7]

The state Council of Defense organized itself into twelve committees that corresponded to the plan recommended by George Porter at the National Defense Conference that met on May 2 and 3 in Washington. This meeting was the first opportunity for the federal government to discuss mobilization with state leaders. The conference intended to explore "the relationship of state and federal activities in the prosecution of the war, and the methods of organization of state and local defense committees and of their cooperation with the Council of National Defense," but the states wanted to discuss agricultural and industrial labor shortages, the establishment of home guard or militia organizations, agricultural surveys, and the need for the previously discouraged industrial and manpower censuses. The federal response to these concerns was tentative and noncommittal. George Porter attempted to define the relationship with the states by proposing a "Clearinghouse of information" through which state councils could share their successes and failures in mobilization activities. Porter also distributed a recommended plan of organization for each state's Council of Defense; the plan was useful to many of the states that had not fully organized. Soon after the conference, Governor Henderson notified members by letter of their appointment and called an organizational meeting for June 1 at the state capitol. Alabama's organized mobilization began at this meeting.[8]

The *Montgomery Advertiser* ran the governor's proclamation letter on May 19. It provided more information about the several committees of the council. Henderson charged the Executive Committee with general supervisory responsibilities and asked it to act in an advisory capacity. It handled all matters addressed to the state as a whole without reference to any particular committee.[9]

Other committees took care of specific council tasks. Tom Smith and Louis Pizitz of Birmingham, A. G. Parrish of Selma, and N. P. Renfroe of Opelika were among the Finance Committee's members.[10] Tom Smith was the vice president of the Birmingham Trust and Savings Company, and Louis Pizitz was a Birmingham businessman. A. G. Parrish served as director of the Selma Gas Light Company and as president of the Selma Fire and Marine Insurance Company, and N. P. Renfroe was a banker and former state legislator. The Finance Committee presided over all matters related to ways and means of revenue and administered any appropriated funds. Gathering funds was complicated because the council was established between the quadrennial sessions of the Alabama legislature. Its last session adjourned in 1915, and by the time it met again in 1919, the war was over, and the work of the council was nearly finished. The council thus had to rely on voluntary contributions and limited funds from the governor's office.

The Coordination of Societies Committee sought to prevent duplication of war work at both the local and state levels. A large part of this committee's work dealt with the women's clubs in the state. The Food Production and Conservation Committee, chaired by Commissioner of Agriculture and Industry James Wade, and the Animal Industry Committee, chaired by Dr. Charles A. Cary, veterinary professor at Alabama Polytechnic Institute in Auburn, were concerned with agricultural issues. They would bear a large part of the mobilization's burden.[11] The state health officer, Dr. Samuel W. Welch of Montgomery, served as chairman of the Health Committee, the work of which involved several projects related to public hygiene, health, and sanitation.[12]

Workplace mobilization fell to the Industrial Committee and the Labor Committee. Governor Henderson wanted the former committee to conduct a survey of the state's industries to provide reliable data to the government, but much of this committee's work was absorbed by other federal agencies established later in the war.[13] The Labor Committee oversaw problems associated with the supply, distribution, and welfare of labor, an issue of great concern to many people, particularly farmers, who saw their labor force either being subject to the Selective Service System or moving to the northern states in pursuit of higher wages. Judge H. T. Benton of Seale served as its chairman.[14]

The Transportation Committee also dealt with new problems brought on by the war. The governor stated that the committee members "should be familiar with highways and railroads so that they can render service if needed."[15] That need arose early. Alabama relied heavily on the railroads to ship coal and other goods, but in late 1917 local needs conflicted with federal intervention to unsnarl the rail traffic jam that stretched from the ports of New York and Boston to the Great Lakes. United States railroad administrator William McAdoo, who also served as secretary of the treasury, demanded that the federal government receive priority rail service, thus causing temporary coal shortages in Alabama.[16] Samuel P. Kennedy chaired the Transportation Committee. A businessman from Anniston who had railroad and other business interests, Kennedy was a longtime associate of Governor Henderson. He and Henderson had served on Alabama's Railroad Commission together, and Henderson had appointed Kennedy president of the Alabama Public Utilities Commission in 1915.[17]

The state council had three additional committees. The Legal Committee, chaired by state senator T. L. Bulger of Dadeville, provided both advice on legal questions that came before the state Council of Defense and administrative expertise. The Military Committee, chaired by General G. J. Hubbard of Troy, assisted in selecting campsites and other facilities needed by the government and advised local communities on the establishment and maintenance of the popular home guard units.[18] The council's Publicity Committee, chaired by Captain William T. Sheehan, editor of the *Montgomery Advertiser*, "control[ed] and disseminate[ed] all information and . . . [carried] on the propaganda work of the Council of Defense," including the council's educational activities. The posters and publications produced by the federal Committee on Public Information (CPI) supported the Alabama Publicity Committee's work. These CPI publications illustrated the state and national home-front efforts.[19]

In addition to creating the state's Council of Defense, Governor Henderson also organized its counterparts in each of Alabama's sixty-seven counties. The rural character of the state and the scarcity of large communities made the counties the primary local governmental jurisdiction. Each county was divided into beats, which provided a geographical designation particularly useful for voting, mail delivery, road maintenance, census enumeration, and other purposes. The counties and their beats provided Henderson with a convenient and familiar schematic for command and control of the home front in Alabama.

For leadership at the county level, the governor appointed a single chairman, who then appointed additional members from each beat of the county. Governor Henderson addressed a letter in mid-April to individuals in each county eliciting their support for his proposed county councils. He emphasized that the focus of the county councils' work would be on increased food production.[20]

The governor's targets were predominantly bankers, most of whom had ties to the state through the deposit of state funds in their banks; they generally pledged their support. Frank S. Moody of the First National Bank in Tuscaloosa responded on April 18, saying, "It will give me pleasure to help you in organizing Tuscaloosa County."[21] The president of the Talladega National Bank also accepted and went on to recommend that "the urgent necessity for us now is a market" and help from the farm extension agents in marketing crops.[22] From St. Clair County came word that McClane Tilton, Jr., president of the First National Bank in Pell City, would organize the county and had been doing similar work "for years [and] I have written about it [food production] in my newspaper and preached it from the stump."[23] The president of the First National Bank in Dothan accepted the task of organizing Houston County, but indicated that "it is rather late for this section to do more towards increasing the planting of food crops."[24] Although the vice president of the Farmers National Bank in Opelika declined because of illness, he related that the farmers are "well awake to the needs of the times."[25]

Some counties had already formed mobilizing organizations. In Marengo County, "a patriotic meeting" had elected a Public Safety Committee of fifteen.[26] The governor simply accepted it as that county's Council of Defense. In Limestone County the county demonstration agent, R. H. Richardson, had organized the farmers before the governor could. Richardson wrote to Henderson, "The food producers are manifesting much interest, are volunteering there *[sic]* services for better conditions and seem unusually interested in this welfare work."[27]

Governor Henderson's initial success in establishing the county councils of defense did not guarantee their sustained activity. As the summer of 1917 passed, the ability of the councils to influence food production waned, at least for the year, and the governor's office issued no new orders or instructions. Consequently, the county councils became less active. The governor's executive secretary, John Moffat, perhaps summed up the county councils' status best when he wrote to a Clarke County resident in early 1918 regarding the vacancy of the local chairmanship: "There is not very much work to be done in connection with the chairmanship," he offered. "What we are after is to get a complete organization so that if something should come up everything would move along smoothly."[28] This lack of direction hampered the ability of the county councils to become more effective partners in the home front in Alabama. Their inactivity remained a problem throughout the war.

Concerted efforts to revitalize the county councils of defense began in the winter of 1917–18 when Lloyd Hooper, the chairman of the state Council of Defense, took over the day-to-day leadership of the council's work. Hooper recognized the lethargy in the county council system and pointed out another problem to the governor, writing in February, "The particularly weak feature in the work of the State Council of Defense is the inactivity of the County Chairmen."[29] He gave three examples of elderly chairmen who were unable to travel in their counties because of personal health reasons and the weather. Hooper had written the governor previously about two other ineffective chairmen—one had "defective hearing and sight," and the other had been dead for more than two years. Hooper advised the governor to appoint "much younger men" who lived in the county seat or the largest town in the county as chairmen.[30] In all, the governor replaced twenty-one county chairmen for various reasons in 1918.[31]

Not all county chairmen were inactive. The Cullman County chairman sought to resign in February 1918 because his previous year's activities had been so "strenuous."[32] He had worked with the YMCA fund-raising campaign, the Red Cross, and the County Fuel Administration in addition to the county Council of Defense. His case was not unique. A number of war-related programs competed for time and resources with various counties' councils of defense work.

Many states experienced problems with their county councils of defense. By June 1918, Virginia, Florida, and Kansas employed paid executive secretaries to reorganize the states' inefficient county councils. Texas, Oklahoma, Mississippi, Ohio, South Carolina, Wisconsin, California, Colorado, and Maryland resorted to hiring field agents to strengthen the work of their county councils of defense. To organize its local councils better, the state of Tennessee divided its territory into five management districts. The state Council of Defense in Arkansas had done the same in January 1918 and assigned state council members to each district to learn about local needs and problems.[33]

Alabama attempted to bolster the efficiency of its councils beyond appointing more energetic chairmen. In June 1918, the county chairmen of war activities banded together into one group in an effort to reduce the amount of duplication and to improve efficiency.[34] Recognizing that competing for limited human resources sapped the strength of every organization involved in home-front activities, the state Council of Defense joined the Four Minute Men (discussed in more detail below), the War Savings Committee, the Women's Committee of the Council of National Defense, the Alabama Food Administration, the Alabama Fuel Administration, the Agricultural Extension Service, the Red Cross, the Department of Labor, the Liberty Loan Organization, and the Public Service Reserve to make a unified body of home-front organizations. The Alabama state Council of Defense employed six field agents to aid in the transition to the new organizational scheme. By June 1918, according to a council estimate, seven thousand people worked in these various programs. Although this very effective and efficient organization was in full operation by the summer of 1918, by the end of the next season the war was over.

Governor Henderson had created a mechanism to contend with the demands of mobilization. The state Council of Defense and the county Council of Defense network was, theoretically, well suited to carry out any home-front measures ordered by the federal or state authorities. The plan for the state Council of Defense followed the organizational structure used by thirty-six states, including all of the southern states except Mississippi. The new experiences of home-front management that World War I brought, however, demanded changes in the councils of defense as the war progressed. Early organizational schemes and methods were altered to improve efficiency; the result was the 1918 reorganization of the state and county councils of defense.

In Alabama this reorganization and revitalization portended the broad expansion of programs and interests assigned to the state and county councils. In addition, a measure of refinement led to the improvement and increased efficiency of other existing programs. By the end of 1918, the scope of the council's work in Alabama was vastly greater than that of the preceding year, and its ability to carry out its charges significantly improved.

Much of the council's success during its second year was due to its greatly expanded fund-raising and publicity programs. In addition, the council undertook a number of programs that, though diverse and often unrelated to one another, illustrate the rich complexity of the American home front and the role of the state Council of Defense in managing it.

The state council raised funds for the war effort since its beginning. It participated in the "remembrance fund" for the Alabama troops overseas and was active in promoting the four Liberty Loan campaigns within the state that raised millions of dollars for the war effort.[35] The council also raised $25,000 to fund its own work. In the absence of a legislated appropriation, the Alabama council was left to its own means for obtaining financial support until 1919 when the legislature convened for its quadrennial session. Many other state legislatures had appropriated between $25,000 and $50,000 for their Council of Defense's work, with Michigan granting the most—$5 million—and Mississippi the least—a mere $1,500.

Tom Smith, state treasurer and chairman of the council's Finance Committee, headed the Alabama council's drive for operational funds. He wrote to the governor in June 1917 about the dearth of available money and the gloomy prospects for raising more, saying, "This town has been gleaned by so many different organizations I fear it will be an uphill job to raise money for this work in time to do any good."[36] Smith was correct; the drive met with only limited success. He was still trying to reach his goal in February 1918 when he again wrote the governor and suggested that one problem was with the people appointed by Henderson to raise the money—frequently the same person served as the local representative of many organizations that competed with each other for scarce contributions. Smith closed by saying, "I want a victory." The fund drive garnered enough support to provide the state Council of Defense with a budget, and by the close of 1918, a total of $17,847.75 was collected to fund its work. Many of these donations came from Mobile and Birmingham, with smaller amounts given by citizens in Troy, Pell City, Gadsden, Carollton, Wetumpka, and Marion.

Of the council's fund-raising activities that met with success, the most important were the four Liberty Loan drives. Since the start of the war in 1914, the United States government had incurred massive debt obligations through financial loans to the Allies. When the United Stated entered the war in 1917, the Treasury Department borrowed more money to mobilize the army and navy. These obligations required the acquisition of significant amounts of new capital from revenue sources other than the traditional federal ones of taxes, fees, and duties. On April 24, 1917, Congress authorized Secretary of the Treasury William G. McAdoo to meet the costs of the war by issuing bonds that totaled five billion dollars. The act also set interest rates for the bonds and gave the secretary related revenue-raising authority. These bonds became known as Liberty Bonds and were sold to the public in four separate campaigns called Liberty Loan drives.[37]

Alabama leaders contributed to the Liberty Loan drives in various ways. Louis Pizitz, who, as mentioned earlier, was a Birmingham businessman and member of the state council's Finance Committee, offered an opportunity for his employees to subscribe voluntarily to the bond drive through salary deduction. Pizitz paid the total amount of the bond to the government up front, essentially allowing interest-free purchases for his employees.[38] The *Alexander City Outlook* beseeched its readers to "sing my country 'tis of thee" on their way to the bank to buy U.S. Liberty Bonds. In the same paper, the editor implored all citizens to buy at least a $50 bond so as to receive a button from the government: "A U.S. Liberty Bond Button is your badge of honor."[39] Emmett Scott, the former private secretary of Booker T. Washington, urged black Alabamians to buy bonds as an act of accepting "the duties and responsibilities of citizenship,"[40] and Montgomery postmaster C. T. Fitzpatrick enlisted black ministers, teachers, and other leaders to help sell bonds and war-savings stamps, a less-expensive variation of the Liberty Bonds, to that city's black residents.[41] In addition, several ministers delivered Sunday sermons about the bond drive.

The second Liberty Loan drive occurred in October 1917, the third in April and May of 1918, and the fourth in September and October of 1918. With each bond drive, the promotional tactics became more refined. For each drive, one day was designated as "Liberty Day" to emphasize the importance of the drive. In the third Liberty Loan campaign, Liberty Day coincided with Confederate Memorial Day. It was celebrated in Dadeville with speeches and a bond auction. A dance and reception were held in the evening for the Camp Sheridan Band, which had played earlier in the day. Other Liberty Day events in Dadeville included a parade of the white draft registrants and publication of all Liberty Bond holders who, it was proclaimed, "are helping to whip the Kaiser."[42]

Cullman County also marked the third Liberty Loan drive with special events, most notably the arrival of the "war relics train." This train was sponsored by the federal government and made stops at towns throughout the country in an effort to promote Liberty Bond sales. It featured captured weapons and equipment such as machine guns, helmets, and airplane parts from the battlefields of Europe. In Cullman, churches cancelled services so citizens could visit the displays on the train. A big crowd listened in the rain to four speeches from local dignitaries who urged the purchase of Liberty Bonds. The town also sought to win the distinction of an honor flag for doubling its subscription rate in the third Liberty Loan drive.[43]

The state Council of Defense provided publicity and event coordination that helped in the overall success of the campaigns. Alabamians bought more than $78 million of Liberty Bonds by the end of the war. The level of response increased over time, with subscriptions rising from approximately $6 million in the first drive in 1917 to more than $36 million in the final drive in 1918.[44] The Council of Defense assisted other financial drives in 1918, most notably those of the Red Cross and United War Work, but these efforts were overshadowed by the magnitude and success of the work accomplished by the Liberty Loan drives.

The state Council of Defense also excelled in disseminating war publicity. The need for an organized and efficient means of issuing government news to the press became obvious to President Wilson and members of his cabinet in the days before the United States entered World War I. There was no central clearinghouse for government information, so government officials and press representatives were constantly at odds over the release of information. To alleviate the problem, Wilson created the Committee on Public Information by executive order twelve days after he had delivered his war message to Congress.[45]

The CPI consisted of the secretaries of state, navy, and war and was directed by a private citizen. Wilson named George Creel, a journalist and longtime political supporter, to the position.[46] Creel had been the editor of the *Rocky Mountain News* in Denver, Colorado, when Wilson was elected in 1912. He had written a number of campaign brochures and editorials favorable to Wilson's administration. In 1917 Creel expressed his concern over a repressive censorship law and urged Wilson to oppose it. The ideas of the Colorado editor concerning voluntary censorship and free flow of government information to the press intrigued Wilson and he called Creel to Washington.[47]

From the outset, the CPI concerned itself not only with its primary duty of releasing government news but also with generating and disseminating publicity—which people of that day called "propaganda" without the opprobrium that word now engenders. Creel considered this work to be of major importance because of the need to boost public morale and to rally support for the war.[48] To accomplish this second duty, Creel divided the CPI into two main sections: foreign and domestic. The domestic section influenced the American public on war-related issues and programs. Creel subdivided the domestic section of the CPI into, among others, the Division of News and the Speaking Division. These two units developed products and programs that the state councils of defense emulated and used in their own activities.[49]

The publication of the *Official U.S. Bulletin* was perhaps the most important means the CPI's Division of News used to release information to the press. Created in May 1917, the *Bulletin,* which was published daily, was the official source of government news. It provided the American press with information about the war and relieved the government of the burden of added correspondence. The *Bulletin* printed communiqués from the military, executive orders, speeches of the president, notices of awarded contracts, and casualty lists. Distributed without charge to war-work administrators rather than to the general public, the *Bulletin* reached its peak circulation of more than 118,000 copies in August 1918.[50]

The Alabama Council of Defense published its own version of the *Bulletin.* Titled the *Alabama Defense Record,* it began publication on May 16, 1918, and was circulated on a semimonthly basis. The *Record* provided Alabamians with a complete description of war activities around the state. It reported news from government agencies, particularly the council, the state Military Department, the Alabama Extension Service, and the Food Administration, as well as the activities of nongovernmental members of the reorganized council such as the Red Cross, the YMCA, and the Advisory War Council of the Alabama Education Association. Fred Gormley, a journalist from Montgomery and charter member of the state Council of

Defense Publicity Committee, served as the *Record* editor throughout its life.[51] Six thousand copies of the newspaper went to the council's county chairmen, local draft boards, Women's Committee members, U.S. Food Administration employees, sheriffs, probate judges, libraries, and newspapers. The *Record* served as a vital link between the state and counties in the Council of Defense system.[52]

Another important means of communicating war news and extolling patriotism to the American public was the Speaking Division of Creel's Committee on Public Information. Its "Four Minute Men" (and later, women) carried the burden of this activity across the nation. On April 15, 1917, less than two weeks after the United States entered the war, Donald Ryerson made the first Four Minute speech for the CPI in Chicago.[53] Ryerson, a Chicago native, devised the plan by which local speakers would deliver informative, patriotic talks to captive audiences nationwide. The name for the new group was a reference to both the Minutemen of the American Revolutionary War and the brief time allotted for the speakers' messages.[54] George Creel approved the program and appointed Ryerson to be its director.

The Four Minute Men generally spoke in movie theaters during intermissions, enabling them to reach millions of American with their homefront patriotic messages. They were held to a maximum of four minutes and focused on topics selected by the CPI. Each topic issued by the Washington office came with an information sheet, but the speaker had some latitude in the presentation of the material. The number of topics reached forty-seven and included appeals for binoculars, food conservation, the Liberty Loan drives, and fire prevention.[55]

In Alabama, the Four Minute Men first became active late in 1917, but until the reorganization of the Council of Defense in June 1918 and the appointment of Thomas Crittenden as state director, they accomplished little.[56] By the end of the war, however, there were more than 3,500 Four Minute Men in the state saturating movie and other audiences with patriotic, mobilization-minded presentations.[57] The Four Minute Men network expanded in 1918 to include women and blacks, two sizable segments of the Alabama population. Because gender and racial segregation prevailed in war work as it did in every other social institution in the state, patriotic women and African Americans who wanted to reach their distinct audiences had to form their own organizations separate from those of white men.

Mrs. Bossie Hundley of Birmingham directed the women's division of the state's Four Minute Men. Like many wartime leaders, Hundley had a long history of community involvement. She was an early leader of the Alabama Equal Suffrage Association, chairing its legislative committee in the 1915 suffrage campaign. In addition, she was a member of the Women's Advisory Committee of the National Republican Party, the United Daughters of the Confederacy, and various music clubs. She used her connections to establish Four Minute women in most Alabama towns. Local members spoke at movie matinees, women's clubs, and in the workplace. Like the men, women speakers had a great deal of autonomy in their presentations; the Birmingham chapter, for example, outfitted its forty speakers in special uniforms. By war's end, Hundley's women's division included ninety-five chairpersons and more than nine hundred speakers.[58]

Black Alabamians were well led by Oscar W. Adams and Mrs. A. W. Harney, chairpersons of the "colored" men's and women's divisions, respectively, of the Four Minute Men. Adams, the editor of the *Birmingham Reporter* and a prosperous businessman, supervised 120 speakers. Harney was responsible for fifty speakers. Although segregated by race and gender, these speakers delivered the same four-minute speeches as were delivered across the nation. It is illustrative that very little documentation of either the women's division or the black Four Minute Men can be found outside of the council's report.[59]

Two other branches of the Four Minute Men were the junior speakers, recruited from the public schools, and the choral division. The Junior Four Minute Men, who enrolled more than two thousand speakers from the state's school districts, gave patriotic talks to their schoolmates. The Choral Division numbered seventy-two singers, who performed renditions of patriotic songs at public rallies and meetings.[60]

The Alabama Council of Defense also organized a related state Speakers Bureau. Distinct from the Four Minute Men, this organization consisted of more than 120 locally prominent politicians, businessmen, attorneys, and other professional men. The Speakers Bureau reached its apogee on July 4, 1918, when it provided speakers to public celebrations in each of Alabama's sixty-seven counties. The bureau also participated in the Liberty Loan drives, Red Cross drives, and other campaigns.[61] Together with the Four Minute Men, these speakers helped to educate and influence the Alabama home front during 1918. They provided a mechanism for support of the new state Council of Defense that had been lacking in 1917 and created a higher degree of success for its initiatives.

The broader responsibility for home-front activities that the new member organizations brought to the state Council of Defense in 1918 meant that many projects the council carried out were unrelated to its original mandate of spring 1917. On the other hand, adding the Four Minute Men, the Red Cross, and others enabled the council to strengthen its activities by providing additional manpower and financial resources.

The council supported several important new programs in 1918, foremost among which was the campaign to reduce the illiteracy rate among Alabama draftees and those from other states who were stationed in Alabama camps. The State of Alabama had recognized the problem of illiteracy long before the war. In 1915 the legislature established the Alabama Illiteracy Commission, which was composed of "five persons, both men and women, including the state superintendent of education who shall be an ex-officio member." All members were appointed by the governor. The commission's purpose was to study the illiteracy problem in the state and make recommendations to the governor.[62]

The problem of illiteracy among the drafted men was demonstrated by the failure of many to complete properly their draft registration cards.[63] Some eight thousand to ten thousand men lacked basic reading and writing skills. In response, Spright Dowell, state superintendent of education and secretary of the Alabama Illiteracy Commission, formulated a plan in February 1918 to educate these men through a network of volunteers located by county committees. Each county committee consisted of the probate judge, the county superintendent of education, the county high school principal, a representative from both the Federation of Women's Clubs and the county medical association, and the president of the county school improvement association. The Illiteracy Commission planned a volunteer drive for March and April, but that effort met with limited success. Only in the counties of Covington, Jefferson, Barbour, Madison, and Conecuh was any measure of work accomplished.[64]

The Illiteracy Commission planned to overcome the earlier problems of limited funding and the inactivity of the counties in a second education project during the summer. The state Council of Defense contributed funds to the effort, as did the state's Federation of Women's Clubs. The funds also served to publicize the governor's designation of June 22 as Illiteracy Day. These funds paid for textbooks and for staff; most of the workers involved were volunteers. The state Council of Defense provided publicity in the *Alabama Defense Record* and through press releases to the state's newspapers. In an effort to improve the involvement of the counties, the chairman of the county Council of Defense was appointed to several central committees.

The results of the second Illiteracy Commission drive were much better. Every county in the state reported activity in providing instruction to the draftees. Some counties, such as St. Clair, Clay, Conecuh, Cullman, and Henry, reported teaching more than 80 percent of their illiterate drafted men. Many others claimed teaching more than 50 percent. Statewide, nearly half (45 percent) of the illiterate drafted men received instruction. The total number taught was 3,636 and reflects only instructional services provided to white draftees.[65] The program was extended to black draftees in a limited way, especially in Jefferson and Montgomery counties, but the numbers were not reported. This program proved to be extremely effective in preparing draftees for military life and indicated the state council's ability to mount successful statewide projects in the months following its reorganization.

In addition to the Illiteracy Commission, the council also supported the Red Cross, which, as noted earlier, had joined with the council in the 1918 reorganization. The two groups worked so closely together that it became difficult to distinguish the activities of the Red Cross from those of the council itself. Although the Red Cross had been an important player in the home front from the outset of the war, its programs and contributions were a vital and highly visible component of the state council's achievements.

The war work of the Red Cross in Alabama began in the summer of 1917 when W. J. Leppert of the district office in New Orleans began establishing local chapters. The state later joined Mississippi and Louisiana in forming the Gulf Division, and Leigh Carroll was appointed to direct the work.[66]

In Alabama the Red Cross established chapters in every county by the end of 1917 and started auxiliaries in nearly every town by war's end. Primarily, women staffed the chapters and were the source of much of the volunteer work. The Red Cross chapter in Montgomery was organized in early May 1917 and set members to work in knitting and sewing projects.[67] The group sent more than thirteen hundred bandages per week to France by September and also made woolen socks, mufflers, and sweaters for the troops.[68] Schoolchildren raised money for the Red Cross by staging backyard shows for their neighbors. One Montgomery show raised seven dollars by presenting songs, speeches, and living pictures depicting a nurse giving aid to a wounded soldier. The Negro Red Cross Auxiliary mailed a Christmas contribution of sweaters, mufflers, socks, candy, nuts, and cigars to the troops overseas.[69]

Early in the war the same problem that stymied the state Council of Defense—competition for capital and volunteers—handicapped the Red Cross. In spite of its accomplishments, the Red Cross chapter in Montgomery appealed almost constantly to the public for more help.[70] The local paper in Dadeville noted that the town failed to meet its "Red Cross responsibilities" and editorialized about the importance of the work.[71] The situation improved in 1918. By joining with the state Council of Defense in June, the Red Cross found new avenues of promotion and support opened to it. By the end of the war, it had formed a well-established network of chapters and worked more efficiently.

The east Alabama communities of Lanett, Fairfax, Shawmut, Langdale, and Riverview are exemplars of the Red Cross's accomplishments. These towns shared a common economic bond—they all hosted the textile mills of the West Point Manufacturing Company and the Lanett Cotton Mills.[72] Each town established a war service center as a base of operations for Red Cross activities.[73] These centers provided workrooms for sewing and knitting activities, the mainstay of the Red Cross's work in 1917. But the war service centers also provided a place for local citizens to find war news and fellowship. There, people wrote thousands of letters to local men in the military service and updated news on their soldiers from casualty lists and other available sources. The centers also served as the headquarters for the Red Cross's major fund drives of June 1917 and May 1918, as well as other community fund-raising efforts. Textile mill managers and local business leaders supported the Red Cross and other home-front activities. This support was important to the success of the Red Cross in these towns, and the types of work engaged in were typical of other Alabama communities.

Because the Alabama Council of Defense reorganized its structure so thoroughly in June 1918, which made each member organization more effective in contributing to the overall war effort, the council could take at least some credit for the successes of the Red Cross in the Great War's final months. But the council's early history did not signal its later success. It had appeared quickly in 1917 in response to the U.S. entry into World War I and, like its counterparts in many other states, slowly developed its ability to carry out its mandate. By the war's end it had become increasingly well organized and capable of initiating and implementing effective mobilization programs on a statewide basis. The reorganization of the council in 1918 transformed it from an uncoordinated group of volunteers who gave individual effort and money to a modern association of organizations that provided more money, better coordination, and higher focus. The Red Cross, the Four Minute Men, the Federation of Women's Clubs, and others were all better directed toward the accomplishment of specific goals that led to the success of the council's activities in 1918.

As in the rest of the country, the opportunity to respond to the government's war needs in Alabama required a high level of volunteer activity. Never before had this type of endeavor been undertaken. The war programs affected many aspects of Alabama society. Alabama's women for the first time were able to contribute their time and energy to projects outside of their traditional duties in the home and church. Black Alabamians also found themselves in a new environment. They had never been called on to contribute their personal and financial resources in an inclusive national enterprise. The state's local business and political leaders enthusiastically embraced volunteer activity as well. The success of the home-front mobilization would not have been possible without the strong reliance on volunteerism.

The Alabama Council of Defense, and its organizational system, though brought about by the exigency of war, was the precursor of an enhanced and enlarged federal role in the states that came with the Depression and World War II. Even so, the example it set for those later emergencies was limited. In World War I, the council depended on part-time volunteer labor for support and success, but in later years the role of volunteers was usurped and replaced by a larger, professionalized federal bureaucracy and increased reliance on the private sector for contracted services.

9
"Can All We Can, and Can the Kaiser, Too"
The Montgomery Cooperative Canning Club

Martin T. Olliff

Since ancient times, marauding armies have spread famine in their paths and privation in those markets directly served by the farmlands they ravaged. Only the relatively small scale of early campaigns limited their impact on food supplies.[1] The worldwide scale of war in the twentieth century changed that. Mass national armies fighting across huge battlefields ruined thousands of square miles of farmland and took millions of agricultural laborers from their work, for year on year. Privation of varying intensity rippled across the Western world. Famine engulfed those close to the front lines, hunger enveloped countries actively engaged in war, and food price inflation besieged farther-flung nations that tried to supply the combatants.

World War I embodied this nightmare, though neither the Allies nor Central powers imagined paying such a price. The French thought their élan and 75-mm howitzers would drive the enemy from the field, and the Russians thought their giant army could defend the motherland at her borders. For their part the Germans had planned to sweep quickly through Belgium, subjugate France, then wheel east to help the Austrians smash the slow-mobilizing Russians. But the French stymied that plan at the Marne, bogging down the German Army in murderous trench warfare that destroyed the countryside from Flanders fields to the Swiss border. The western front stalemate allowed the eastern front to sprawl back and forth across the fabled "breadbasket of Europe"—the Ukraine—disrupting food supplies there just as much as did the fighting in northern France.[2]

The military machines arrayed on both sides of the continent were remarkable for their destructive efficiency and size. Europe's armies concentrated millions of soldiers into veritable cities of death. These armies were too large to live off the neighboring land, so they demanded ever-increasing amounts of food be shipped from an ever-growing circle of suppliers.[3]

Problems in feeding not only the troops but also the civilian populations created famine in the immediate proximity of the war and produced hardship across the continent. The Entente powers averted outright starvation in Belgium, for example, only through the heroic efforts of Herbert Hoover's Committee for Relief of Belgium. To the east, the Russian czar and his successor government under Alexander Kerensky both fell to demands for "Peace and Bread." Germany implemented severe food rationing, which the Americans later called "Prussianization." England seemed so close to starvation that the German high command resumed unrestricted submarine warfare in 1917 though the generals knew this would bring the United States into the war.

The Great War's scale and scope disrupted food markets only slightly less dramatically in the nations of the New World. North and South America tried to supply northern Europe with enough to eat, but doing so strained their economies to the breaking point. Poor harvests in mid-decade made the situation worse. In the United States itself, poor weather caused the wheat harvest to fall by 40 percent. At the same time, demand spiked—Europeans doubled their prewar imports from the United States—and serious food price inflation ensued. Historian Tom G. Hall notes that "between July 1916 and April 1917 the cost of food [in the United States] increased 46 percent, and rose another 45 percent by December."[4] Americans rightly feared the return of inflation propelled hunger for the first time since the Civil War.

President Wilson understood that food was as important to the war effort as tanks, machine guns, troops, ships, and airplanes. Before the end of April 1917, he called Herbert Hoover from Europe to become head of the United States Food Administration. Although Congress took until August to pass the Food and Fuel Control Act, which made his position official, Hoover began agitating in May and June to promote food production; enlist women to conserve fat, sugar, and wheat; and put the nation on a patriotic diet of "meatless Tuesdays," "wheatless Wednesdays," and "porkless Saturdays."[5]

Americans recognized that this new war required them to pull together in unaccustomed ways, but most still favored local, nongovernmental control of their activities over directives from Washington, D.C. Thus it was with the white women's clubs in Alabama's capital city. In 1917 they created the Montgomery Cooperative Canning Club, a food factory, well before Herbert Hoover began his tenure as "food czar" or the Women's Committee of the Council of National Defense issued its first directive. The Canning Club flourished for only two seasons, but its history shows how at least one group of Americans negotiated the tension between traditional localism and the emerging nationalistic mentalité of the twentieth century. It also speaks to the way Alabama's Progressive women moved from their deeply rooted world of family and friends into the public arena of politics and commerce.[6]

Women's clubs were one mechanism by which elite women defined their roles during the Progressive Era. Originally the clubs were highly selective, only slightly larger than an intimate circle of friends, dedicated to cultural study and members' self-improvement. For example, the No-Name Club, a charter member of the Alabama Federation of Women's Clubs in 1895, was "devoted to music and art" and required unanimous consent to install new members.[7] Another, the Tintagil Club, began in 1896. Named for King Arthur's legendary castle in Cornwall, its members studied literature, cultural geography, world religions, and similar subjects. Its rules supported a very definite role for women in the larger society; for example, it limited membership to twenty young women who agreed to resign if they married. The Tintagil Club did not want to divert married women to something other than family. This rule became moot, however, when Olive Pierce married Richard Arrington in 1906 and simply refused to resign. By 1917, nine of twenty Tintagil members were married. Also, the Tintagil membership was remarkably stable. Six members from 1901 and nine from 1910 appear on the its 1916 roster.[8] In addition to the No-Name Club and Tintagil Club, an incomplete list of white women's literary clubs in Montgomery includes the Magazine Club (founded in 1896), the Ionian Club (1898), the Twentieth Century Club (1908), and the Sesame Club. The last-mentioned self-described mission was "promotion of mental culture and the furtherance of educational philanthropies."[9]

Other women's clubs organized around shared experiences, such as the Alabama University Women, and still others engaged in social service work. In 1897, fourteen women organized a capital city section of the National Council of Jewish Women. Though originally dedicated to "spreading a more thorough knowledge of our religion and history," the Montgomery Council embraced community service the following year.[10] Of all the service groups, the Mother's Circle, one of three mothers' clubs in

Montgomery, had the most prominent public profile. It formed in 1900 "to make a study of all subjects beneficial to parents in their relations to children," and its standing committees included child hygiene, child welfare, home economics, playgrounds, and juvenile court. Rather than have members read research papers or lead discussions of cultural topics as was common in the literary clubs, the Mother's Circle listened (in 1916 and 1917) to lectures on teacher training, the father as parent, safe foods, and Mother's Day.[11] For the Mother's Circle, the leap from prewar service to the Canning Club was short.

The idea for erecting a cannery was not original to the capital's clubwomen. County home demonstration agents had blazed the trail by establishing rural girls' tomato-canning clubs after 1911. The Smith-Lever Act of 1917 funded the spread of this canning work into every Alabama county by February 1918. As war fever—and fear of food shortages—gripped the state, small communities built common-use canneries. In mid-April 1917, the agricultural teacher at the State Normal School for Negroes, Harry Simms, announced that "the school will install a cannery for the benefit of the patrons and others living in that vicinity" after a student survey revealed 79 percent of African-American families in Montgomery cultivated gardens. In addition, farmers in the Pinedale community five miles south of Montgomery opened their own cannery in mid-May.[12]

Commercial entrepreneurs made food canning a speculative business venture in wartime Alabama. By the end of 1917, they had built approximately forty commercial canneries and produced five million containers of food valued at $750,000 ($11.8 million in 2006 terms). The Alabama Marketing and Canning Company was the largest of these enterprises, with thirty for-profit canneries operating in farm communities across north Alabama. Headquartered in Birmingham, Alabama Marketing and Canning was the ambitious brainchild of Charles F. Bell, who had extensive wholesale grocery experience as president of Bell-Rogers Produce Company. Although Bell created a network of canneries that implied permanence, Alabama Marketing and Canning disappeared from the Birmingham city directory by 1920. Bell himself seems to have moved to Mentone in northeast Alabama after the war before returning to Birmingham to resume grocery wholesaling.[13]

Neither the small community canneries nor the Bell business provided much of a direct model for the Cooperative Canning Club of Montgomery. That came from the Prattville Sanitary Canning Company created by the newly organized Prattville Commercial Club in April 1917. Initially capitalized at $5,000 ($78,600 in 2006 terms), all of which was subscribed within a week, the Prattville cannery employed as many as fifty workers who produced ten thousand cans of fruits and vegetables between late May and August. Company officers were crafty speculators. They laid in a stock of 250,000 tin cans, the price of which rose so rapidly that the business declared a profit before it opened.[14]

Men with access to capital, such as Bell and the Prattville investors, made money from canning, but the Mother's Circle of Montgomery pursued a different end. The circle met during the week of April 30 to discuss how its members could best help the community during the war. According to the *Montgomery Advertiser*, one idea became a "movement"—to erect a cooperative canning plant "devoted towards fulfilling the government injunction to conserve the food supply."[15] Such a plant would preserve "the surplus growth of the thousands of city and suburban gardeners, the only cost being the price of the cans or glass jars used."[16]

This was a significant undertaking, for large-scale canning was not easy. A water bath canner sufficed for acidic tomatoes, vegetables preserved in vinegar, or fruits preserved in sugar, but garden vegetables required canning temperatures over 240°F to prevent botulism. Knowing this, the Mother's Circle decided to invest in a steam canner. Even so, the factory still had much to do. Cannery workers washed and pared, peeled, or husked vegetables and cut them into satisfactory sizes. Next, they packed the produce into No. 2 (pint) or No. 3 (quart) cans and "tipped" the lids—sealed them with a soldering iron to the cans. They loaded the cookers with up to sixty cans, processed those in live steam, then moved and unloaded the cookers. When the cans cooled, workers attached labels and stored the finished product.[17] Coordinating this project required manufacturing experience.

On May 5, 1917, the same day Herbert Hoover arrived in Washington, D.C., to meet with President Wilson about the as-yet unorganized U.S. Food Administration, ten members from the Mother's Circle, the City Federation of Women's Clubs, and the Women's League for Service met with Mrs. Birdie Doster at Montgomery's Exchange Hotel for guidance about creating the proposed cooperative cannery. As the wife of Howard S. Doster, well-known editor of the *Prattville Progress* newspaper and former state senator, Mrs. Doster possessed the social power to legitimize her advice. But more important, she possessed expertise in canning and in women's issues of the day. She had worked closely with the Prattville Commercial Club to open its cannery, was a longtime advocate of girls' tomato canning clubs, and served as both the assistant chair for food conservation in Autauga County in 1917 and president of the Alabama Mother's Circle in 1918.[18]

At that May 5 meeting, Mrs. Doster urged the Montgomery women to coordinate their project with their city chamber of commerce. As luck would have it, the chamber's Public Welfare Committee was meeting in the Exchange Hotel at the same time as the women, but had decided it was too late in the season to build a commercial cannery. The women believed they could not succeed without the support of the men of the chamber, so led by Frances Nimmo Greene, they barged into the chamber meeting and announced they had formed themselves into the Montgomery Cooperative Canning Club. It was obvious they expected the men's assistance. The *Montgomery Advertiser* reported that "this evidence of feminine activity was received with genuine delight by the men present," but how much help the men gave is not apparent. The newspaper also reported that the chamber committee "relapsed into a discussion of the subjective side of farming," especially the state of food crops after a spate of rain.[19]

With or without the chamber's help, the new Canning Club forged ahead. It formed a temporary executive committee the members of which were of such social standing that they could secure cooperation from the women's clubs as well as operate legitimately in the public world of politics and business. They came from powerful families, had college educations in an era when the state's white male illiteracy rate topped 25 percent, and married prominent husbands or had independent careers. Committee member Frances Nimmo Greene was a well-known author and journalist who created the first free public library in Birmingham before moving to Montgomery. She was related to state archivist Thomas M. Owen and University of Alabama president Richard C. Foster. In April 1917, as home demonstration agent for Montgomery, Greene had secured a fifty-acre plot of city land for use as community gardens. Adele Weil's father was a partner in one of the largest grocery wholesalers in Montgomery, and her husband was his biggest competitor. Henrietta Gardner attended Troy Normal School in Alabama and Pratt Institute in New York. Her husband was an Alabama Supreme Court justice. Mary Houghton's husband was a director of the Alabama National Bank. Annie May Dimmick Jones, who emerged as a leader of the club, graduated from Wellesley College in Massachusetts and subsequently held offices in a dozen local and state organizations. She was president of the Alabama Federation of Women's Clubs (AFWC) in 1920–21, served on the boards of both the Partlow Home for Children in Tuscaloosa and the Alabama College for Women in Montevallo, and later organized the state's first United Service Organization in 1942. Her father was a bank president who once served as clerk of the U.S. Circuit Court of Alabama; her husband was both the tax agent for the Louisville and Nashville Railroad and a relative of former governor Thomas Goode Jones. The club's first operations manager, Vera Quinn, attended the University of Alabama and Judson College. She, too, served as AFWC president, though in 1931–33. Her husband was a well-regarded Montgomery county extension agent who later served as fish and game commissioner in both Alabama and Virginia.[20]

This committee originally set two goals for the Canning Club: to operate as a nonprofit cooperative supported by the existing network of local women's clubs and to make canned goods readily available to keep down the cost of living. A short time later it added a third goal: "educate the women of the city, as farm demonstration agents are educating the women of the country, in how to can their surplus product."[21] Within days of the May 5 meeting, the Executive Committee prepared a business plan that called for selling 1,500 shares of stock worth $1 each to the city's clubwomen. It sold one-third of the shares within the first week. With that money the club bought a supply of containers and an $800 ($12,580 in 2006 terms) steam canning boiler capable of turning out "several thousand" cans or jars of vegetables per day. Demonstrating how much even elite white Alabama women relied on men in order to participate in the public sphere, the Canning Club appointed an "advisory committee" of prominent men, including Annie Dimmick Jones's husband and the soon-to-be-appointed Alabama food administrator, Richard Hobbie, to operate parallel to its own Executive Committee. It also appointed *Montgomery Advertiser* managing editor R. F. Hudson as its fiscal agent. These moves were both clever and wise. The Canning Club was the first women-run enterprise of its type in the state, and there was great danger that it would be reviled, ignored, or worse—mocked—if it failed. The advisory committee endorsed the club's business plan and its financial health on May 19. The *Montgomery Advertiser* report of that endorsement on May 20 added gravitas to the club's endeavors.[22]

Organizing the Canning Club and gaining publicity was one thing; building a functional factory in a convenient place within a budget was a bit more problematic. The women worked quickly. On May 9, 1917, the Montgomery City Council rejected the club's request to place the cannery in the basement of the city auditorium and refused to appropriate $100 to offset utility costs. Unbowed by this setback, the club had secured by May 17 a site at 10 S. Perry St., less than three blocks south of city hall and a half block from the Dexter Avenue streetcar line in a neighborhood of title research offices, haberdasheries, and restaurants. Things moved quickly after that. On Friday, May 18, contracted workmen installed shelves, office equipment, and a flue. The following Monday they put in the furnace with gas and electric connections and installed the canner that had arrived from Chattanooga by rail, probably from the Royal Canner Company. On Wednesday, May 23, the factory opened.[23]

The Canning Club had pushed hard to open as soon as possible, fearing any delay might frustrate small gardeners who would find other avenues to sell their surplus produce. The strategy paid off. W. B. Crockett of Carter Hill Road expressed his happiness with this "unexpected cash market . . . for his surplus products" when he delivered the first cartful of freshly picked beans that Wednesday morning. But haste brought problems, and opening day was bedlam. While Operations Manager Vera Quinn, canning consultant Mrs. R. L. Head, and their small staff of volunteers received vegetables, prepared them, canned them, and handled financial transactions, carpenters continued to finish the plant's interior with saw and hammer. At the same time, so many excited visitors poured into the factory that the club decided to schedule a demonstration day the following week after the carpenters had finished. As if this chaos was not enough, the Operations Committee met at the cannery to finalize sales policy. It decided that those gardeners who did not have enough cash to buy the finished products could can on half shares or on one-third share plus five cents per can. At that meeting the committee also rejected an offer from a Montgomery wholesaler to buy the entire output of the cannery, deciding instead to retail its surplus at the lowest possible price "to assist in keeping down the high cost of living."[24]

The cannery ran full-time for the following weeks while managers coped with the public attention it garnered. Because of the press of business, the Operations Committee hired more women to run the actual canning boiler while volunteers still did most of the preparation work. The *Montgomery Times* wrote of these volunteers that "women who formerly played bridge or attended places of amusement are busy as ants, giving their time gratis, many trying their hand for the first time at stringing beans."[25] Mrs. Quinn led the promised canning demonstration on May 29, showing the overflow crowd all the steps required to preserve beans. She invited the Elmore County home demonstration agent, Miss Leo Ziegler, who was in the audience, to join in the demonstration, much to the delight of the women present. The audience was so large that the Executive Committee decided to hold a demonstration every week, inviting women from different parts of town to different sessions. On June 2, Governor and Mrs. Charles Henderson visited the plant, where they both spoke of the great contribution to the overall war effort made by the Canning Club.[26]

The excitement generated by the club's first weeks was contagious. On the same day as Governor Henderson's visit, club women from Tuscaloosa met with Mrs. Quinn to gather data on labor and supplies so they could open their own cannery. By year's end the Tuscaloosa club had produced thirty thousand cans valued at $6,900. Montgomerians themselves began making plans to build a more elaborate plant to open in autumn. Although these plans were just excited fantasies, they were big, calling for capitalization at $15,000, ten times the size of the Canning Club factory. The club chairwoman, Helen Cadden, generated a little excitement of her own about the cannery. She sent a friend in Norwich, Connecticut, a letter about the Canning Club complete with *Advertiser* clippings, much of which the *Norwich Bulletin* reprinted. Norwich women set up their own "Housewives Committee" in hopes of imitating Montgomery's work.[27]

The club had a good first month, overcoming the original skepticism of local producers who subsequently pledged their crops for canning on shares. In its first three days, the cannery produced 400 containers of beans, berries, and English peas, followed by 1,380 more the next week. By the end of the month it had produced more than three thousand cans with only eight hundred on shares. Surplus product filled the shelves. Besides rejecting an earlier offer from a grocery wholesaler to buy the cannery's products, the club refused two offers from agents of the U.S. government to buy the entire output for the American Expeditionary Force headed to the western front. Instead, it sold its products directly to local customers. The club originally set aside only one day per month for such sales, but its first sales day on June 9 was so successful it decided to sell anything it canned any time it was open. Working both the supply and the demand side, Mrs. Quinn advertised her willingness to receive "pledges for acres of tomatoes, okra, corn, etc." to sell alongside beans and berries (15 cents per quart), squash (12.5 cents), and pickled beets (twenty cents). Such prices adhered to the club's stated mission. A Federal Trade Commission survey of five hundred canneries in June revealed the average price for a can of corn was seventeen cents, for peas eighteen cents, and for tomatoes twenty cents, all slightly higher than Canning Club prices.[28]

The club's success was fickle, however. Production ebbed as drought slowed the harvest, but good rain on June 25 allowed Mrs. Quinn and her crew to produce 246 cans of squash and beets. Two weeks later they preserved eight hundred quarts of peaches and tomatoes. The club's educational work also reduced the number of customers as "War Gardeners" learned to can at home. In response, Quinn reorganized the cannery's production staff and schedule. She continued to employ up to five paid workers, supplementing them by assigning women's clubs and high school home economics students to help on a once-per-week rotation. When the workload was heavy, Quinn and her volunteers pressed into service visitors who dropped by to see the plant. Nevertheless, the cannery closed during the week of August 26, victim of its success in educating home canners, the drought, the end of harvest, and, most important, Mrs. Quinn's exhaustion. "Her strength," bemoaned the *Montgomery Advertiser,* "is not equal to her energy."[29]

Local newspapers make no mention of the cannery until the spring of 1918, when great plans resulted in many headlines but little action. The *Montgomery Advertiser* announced on April 28, 1918, that the "Montgomery Canning Club To Be Operated on Elaborate Scale," but on May 12 it proclaimed, "Plans for Canning Club Are Progressing." Mrs. Quinn could not resume her supervisory duties at the cannery, and it appeared that the second season might flounder.[30]

But the canning club's 1917 success had drawn the attention of Ralph Quisenberry, president of the Southern Syrup Company of Montgomery, head of the Baking and Ice Division of the Alabama Food Administration, and food administrator for Montgomery County. He became very interested in reinvigorating and expanding the club because, he reported, the federal government planned to buy the entire output of the nation's commercial canneries in 1918. If citizens wanted canned goods for the winter, therefore, they would have to can them locally. Quisenberry's clout persuaded the city commission to locate the revived factory beneath the city auditorium on North Perry Street, in the spot originally refused to the women in 1917, and to provide free electricity. He hired Billy Nunn, an expert from Prattville who was running for sheriff of Autauga County, to set up and begin operating the cannery. J. C. Fischesser of Alabama Machinery and Supply Company installed equipment with three times the capacity of the 1917 canner, leading the *Montgomery Times* to crow that the new factory would "provide regular work for twenty people."[31]

The women reorganized the Cooperative Canning Club to run the new factory after it opened on May 27. The club elected Annie Dimmick Jones as president and retained Helen Cadden as first vice president. Three other officers and twenty-one directors oversaw five committees appointed to coordinate various Canning Club duties: publicity, finance, organization, store management and supply, and labor. The officers sent a letter to area farmers announcing the cannery's grand opening and soliciting their excess crops of string beans, okra, peaches, blackberries, tomatoes, and squash. Jones instructed the new plant manager, a Mr. Moore of Prattville who had replaced Billy Nunn, to order a stock of twenty thousand cans.[32]

The club's Finance Committee raised funds as it had the year before, by offering stock to the women's clubs. But it refined its quest for operating cash by dividing the city into districts and then selling club stock in focused, concentrated campaigns. While fund-raising proceeded, the Labor Committee secured a workforce through the moral economy of volunteerism and the women's clubs' organizational network. President Annie Jones, who also chaired the Labor Committee, enforced a rotating schedule by which each women's club provided workers for the cannery every ten days. She and other Labor Committee members recruited help from home economics classes at Lanier High School, Decatur Street School, Bellinger Hill School, Lawrence Street School, and West End High School. So many students, both girls and boys, volunteered that the committee divided each school's contingent into two teams and placed them into the rotating schedule to assist the women's club members. Each week's schedule appeared in the Sunday *Advertiser*'s "Women and Society Section."[33]

In 1918 the Canning Club was more thoroughly integrated into other wartime service projects run by Montgomery women. The previous year, the club had set up its own demonstration classes to teach local women how to preserve food. In 1918 it conducted classes in close coordination with the Montgomery War Kitchen, a systematic county extension program that used federal and state funds to teach women how to preserve food by drying and canning. The only War Kitchen in Alabama to find a permanent home was Birmingham's. Montgomery's was nomadic, and the Canning Club played host to it frequently beginning in early April even before relocating to the city auditorium.[34]

In spite of the cannery's late May opening, June provided a bounty, particularly in peaches. Shelves again bulged with product, so Adele Weil, Mrs. Joseph Baker, and one Mrs. Holloway organized a sale for July 16–18. They sold quarts of peaches for $0.20 each and also offered bulk rates—six cans for $1.00 and cases of twenty-four for $3.60. But business at the cannery had dropped off precipitously by then. Drought stifled vegetable production while the War Kitchen's numerous springtime demonstrations once again taught gardeners to can for themselves. But the club women and home economics students soldiered on, showing up for work even when no produce arrived to be canned. In late July the Executive Committee set aside Mondays to provide demonstrations and to can specifically for home gardeners—a response to the plant's rapidly diminishing business. In 1917 the club had established regular demonstration days to control the large crowds of visitors to the plant, but the 1918 schedule was a promise it would open the cannery at least one day per week. But the club could not keep that promise because of the dearth of produce, so it closed the cannery after only one Monday demonstration. The *Advertiser* reported on August 4 that "[the club] will reopen at some later date if farm produce becomes more plentiful. . . . In that case they will be glad to serve the home-gardener as heretofore."[35]

From then through mid-September, as American soldiers got a real taste of trench warfare, the Canning Club retailed the ten thousand quarts of fruits, beans, berries, beets, okra, tomatoes, and squash it had produced. But with the coming of autumn, the club women wanted to stop "keeping store." This put them in a bind. If Ralph Quisenberry was correct and the government was buying up all available canned goods, the club could sell to the army, but doing so would leave Montgomerians without canned foods for the winter. On the other hand, selling to local wholesalers violated the club's goal of keeping prices down because the jobbers tacked on a 10 percent surcharge to groceries for retail. The club had rejected this option before it opened in 1917. To make matters worse, existing grocery stores made home deliveries, not only doubling the price of food but also using scarce gasoline and tires needed for the war effort.

One grocery retailer offered the club a viable option. Piggly Wiggly was an entirely new, cost-effective concept in grocery stores. In fact, it initiated the modern self-service supermarket. Other groceries operated like department stores, employing large numbers of clerks who filled shopper's orders from shelves and cabinets and delivered orders to those who called. Piggly Wiggly did not make deliveries and even had shoppers fetch their own goods from the shelves, reducing store staffs to one cashier and one stocker. This method made it possible for Piggly Wiggly to sell goods at lower prices than competitors while maintaining excellent profits. Although many shoppers resented having to serve themselves, Piggly Wiggly's business model became the industry standard. Piggly Wiggly did not break with all grocery traditions, however. Its central office forbade buying goods from local wholesalers, but it allowed its franchisees to continue buying products for resale from individuals. Consequently, its two local franchised stores, each within a few blocks of the city hall cannery, served all the needs of the club. In September 1918, Piggly Wiggly bought all the club's remaining product to retail to local customers at a low price.[36]

Drought and home canning were not the only reasons the Montgomery Cooperative Canning Club closed with a whimper in 1918. By midsummer, the public was not panicked about the food supply, and food prices seemed to have stabilized. As a result, the club's retail sales were sluggish. Furthermore, the women's clubs could not keep up the level of enthusiasm they originally had shown for the Canning Club. Men had taken over its early stages of renewal in 1918, and the efficiency of the club's new Executive Committee channeled and regularized the women's enthusiasm. With the cannery under good control, Montgomery's women could ignore it until it was time for them to work there. Most women's clubs returned to their study programs and other organizational work during the year. For example, the Tintagil Club closed its 1917–18 season in May with members reciting their favorite war poetry and eating "dainty refreshments."[37]

Other local welfare projects diverted women's attention from the cannery, too. Rejection rates from the Selective Service exposed embarrassing levels of illiteracy among Alabama men of military age. Having incorporated public service, at least in education and child welfare, into its mission, the Alabama Federation of Women's Clubs turned its members' attention to fighting illiteracy. The AFWC asked the Montgomery City Federation to take charge of the campaign in central Alabama, a more exciting project for well-educated women than sweating over a commercial canning boiler. Another diversion was the Alabama Children's Home Society. Canning Club president Annie Jones and other club women had worked with area businessmen since 1915 to address the plight of "dependent and delinquent children," those whom the county would have incarcerated with adult inmates at the county jail. In 1917 the society paid for such children to receive foster care in private homes. "Boarding out" failed almost immediately because wartime inflation made it difficult for families to accept more members. The society changed its goals, and in August 1918, it rented the "Stern Place" on Upper Wetumpka Road for use as a group home for twelve children "under the superintendence of a competent woman who understands . . . the helpless child."[38] The campaigns to secure the house and raise operating funds absorbed the attention of some of the most prominent leaders of the Canning Club at exactly the same time as the club was struggling to stay open.

The national war effort was even more important in distracting Montgomery women from the cannery. The War Department built Taylor Field to train pilots and, more important, Camp Sheridan for infantrymen near town in 1917. Montgomery lacked the social and physical infrastructure to accommodate the newly arriving troops from Ohio's Thirty-seventh Division, so club women volunteered to help in ways that paralleled the activities of national groups but that addressed local problems. Club women joined the Motor Division of the Women's League for Service to ferry soldiers and ordinary citizens around town; worked with the Red Cross to run camp canteens, roll bandages, and make comfort kits for the troops at the front; and opened their homes to give southern hospitality to the soldiers in hopes of luring them away from the so-called camp followers and the city's red-light district. Extensive socializing led some soldiers and airmen to return to Montgomery. Others successfully courted local girls, as Lieutenant F. Scott Fitzgerald did with the young belle Zelda Sayre.[39]

With the armistice of November 1918, Americans rapidly demobilized. The Canning Club faded away—the last *Advertiser* article on it had appeared on September 22, 1918. But there is an epilogue, a final act consistent with the spirit that originally animated the club. In 1923, its Executive Committee asked stockholders to allow it to turn over the cannery's assets to the Montgomery Children's Home. The only source for this request is the minutes of the Montgomery Section of the National Council of Jewish Women, so it is unclear how other stockholders voted. Nevertheless, the council's favorable vote hints at the resolution of this matter.[40]

The women's clubs did not forget their experience with providing local solutions to national problems. Vera Quinn, who, as noted earlier, served as the Canning Club's operations manager in 1917, was president of the Alabama Federation of Women's Clubs in 1931, at the height of another national emergency, the Great Depression. She directed every AFWC district to establish canneries modeled on her wartime experience. Local clubs responded with enthusiasm, particularly those in Montgomery, where former Canning Club leader Adele Weil took charge. Using funds provided by the Reconstruction Finance Corporation, Weil erected a new Cooperative Canning Club in Montgomery's Bibb Street warehouse district. The Red Cross provided money to buy a canning plant, and the new club geared up to provide "up to 50,000 cans of foodstuffs." Unlike its retail operations of 1917 and 1918, the 1931 cannery distributed its products through the Red Cross.[41]

The history of the Montgomery Cooperative Canning Club demonstrates how at least one group of Americans viewed the changing relationship between their community and the nation during the Great War. The Mother's Circle of Montgomery feared that rapidly rising prices and a threatened food shortage would cause actual hunger among its neighbors. Without direction from the Alabama Council of Defense, the Women's Committee of the Council of National Defense, or the U.S. Food Administration but following the model of other local initiatives, the Mother's Circle created a cooperative canning club that erected successful factories during the Great War. Because the Canning Club was the first such endeavor run by Alabama women, it relied on the existing network of Montgomery's white women's clubs to finance, build, and operate its business. The Cooperative Canning Club accepted only local produce and sold its canned products as cheaply as it could to Montgomery families. In fact, the club rejected offers to make a profit by selling its products to wholesale grocers and it privileged local citizens over the national army by rejecting federal offers to buy the cannery's entire output. When the club ceased business in September 1918, it sold its products to Piggly Wiggly, a low-overhead grocery that resold to local citizens at the lowest possible price.

Furthermore, the history of the Canning Club shows how limited a role women—even elite women—could play in the public sphere. Women in the Progressive Era of the early twentieth century had carved out a public space for activities that were akin to their duties in their private sphere: caregiving, education, and spiritual uplift. The Mother's Circle was on the cutting edge of these activities in Montgomery. It led the way in humanitarian services, concerning itself with child labor, the plight of juvenile prisoners, educational finance reform, public libraries, and the care of unwed mothers. Such concerns gave the Mother's Circle and its allies a public presence, so no one objected when it sponsored the Canning Club. Other organizations, such as the Tintagil, No-Name, Twentieth Century, Sesame, and Magazine clubs, had interested themselves in cultural, artistic, literary, and musical study rather than public service, but the world war changed that, at least for a while. The women's clubs of Montgomery bought stock to finance the cannery, stringed and blanched beans, and sweated over the steam canner for the good of the community.

Regardless of their good intentions and the social space that was open to their service work, the club women were not able to access the world of finance, management, or local politics without allying with men. In 1917 the Cooperative Canning Club appointed an "advisory committee" of well-connected men to legitimize its work. Even then, the 1917 club could not secure cooperation from the Montgomery City Commission. Although there is no direct evidence indicating how commissioners actually thought about the woman-run cannery, their actions the following year suggest that gender was a significant issue. In 1917, the commission refused to help the Canning Club with space or fiscal support, but in 1918, with a cabal of men in charge of the cannery, the city commission provided the exact city-owned site it had denied the women and abated all utility costs.

The Canning Club closed as other community and national needs took attention away from it, as the harvest ended, and, eventually, as the war itself ended and Americans sought to return to normalcy. The Canning Club served its purpose—to provide a way of preserving garden products that might have gone to waste, to give low-cost sustenance to the citizens of the city, to educate the women of the city in preservation techniques, and to give the elite white women's clubs of Montgomery a way to participate in the war effort. The same philanthropy and desire to contribute to the common good that animated the original cannery project survived the war. A few years later, the club turned over its assets to another altruistic project, and women's club leaders in the Great Depression resurrected the cannery idea. Though it faded away, the Montgomery Cooperative Canning Club of World War I provides a demonstration of how women during the Progressive Era negotiated not only the crisis of the war but also the change from local to national concerns and their emerging place in the public world of commerce and politics.

10
World War I
Catalyst for Social Change in Alabama

Robert Saunders, Jr.

It is understandable but nonetheless unfortunate that Alabama's experiences during the First World War have been eclipsed by World War II and the civil rights movement. The story of the modernization of Alabama—such as it has been—cannot be appreciated thoroughly without understanding the fundamental changes wrought by the Great War. The winds of socially progressive reform had been swirling about the state for much of the two decades previous to the war, but the movement in Alabama had been limited largely to private organizations, religious groups touting the social gospel, and associations such as the Alabama Child Labor Committee, the Alabama Federation of Women's Clubs, the Alabama Women's Christian Temperance Union, the Alabama Medical Association, and a number of others.[1] Nationally, Progressives sought to make government more directly responsible for people's welfare, whether their poor working and living conditions were by-products of industrialization, alcohol abuse, ignorance born of pathetic educational systems, or, as was then the most commonly cited culprit, government indifference to social inequities or intransigence founded on preserving laissez-faire doctrines that had dominated much of the previous half century. Progressivism was complex—sometimes even contradictory—and the movement defied clear definition. But in a general sense Progressives sought both political and social reforms they believed necessary to rejuvenate American values and traditions.

In Alabama most prewar Progressive reforms seriously considered by lawmakers centered on political changes; the social justice component of Progressivism hardly resonated within a state that had so little experience with the concept of government serving as the steward of the citizenry's welfare. The notion of proactive government, in fact, diametrically contradicted New South doctrines that promoted economic development through inducements to northern investors and manufacturers. Southern apostles of the New South creed promised investors a "friendly" business environment unencumbered by government regulations or property taxes. Likewise, manufacturers relocating to Alabama would enjoy a completely pliable labor force—which included thousands of children—that would not dare travel the dangerous and disruptive road toward unionization. As one leading Alabama historian has explained, Social Progressivism in the state during the prewar years was little more than a "chimerical impulse" hopelessly strangled by conservative ideologues, concerns over racial equality, and political battles involving prohibition and unionism.[2]

Social Progressivism, with its emphasis on eradicating child labor, promoting unionization, educating the laboring classes, gaining equal political and economic rights for women, and ensuring a more egalitarian society, was in so many respects far too radical and disruptive of the social status quo for most Alabama legislators. The result was that by the World War I era Alabama lagged pitifully far behind virtually every other state in terms of child welfare programs, public education, and public health. Such dereliction and the resultant social decay had been perfectly acceptable to the ruling elite before the war. Several factors, however, manifested themselves during the war era to prompt a rather dramatic paradigm shift in the state: federal investments in war production and ports brought unprecedented prosperity to an economy that had been nearly destroyed by the European conflict, and federal mobilization and conscription indirectly—but nonetheless dramatically—lent considerable impetus to socially progressive reforms. Whereas the Progressive movement faded from the national agenda with the end of World War I, in Alabama several social justice campaigns—particularly in the interest of promoting public health, education, and child welfare—gained enough momentum between 1917 and 1919 to drive much-needed attitudinal changes respecting what Alabamians considered the proper role of government in society.

Mobilization for and prosecution of the war, claimed the state and federal governments, required unprecedented centralization of authority, and throughout the conflict both the federal government and state leaders called on all citizens to do their patriotic duty to the utmost. Alabamians were barraged almost daily by speakers, poets, writers, journalists, and politicians proclaiming that the war could be won only through the collective efforts of all patriotic Americans. Thousands of young men throughout the state answered the call for enlistments and draft registration. It was simply expected that Alabamians would support the war in every conceivable way and that Alabama males would perform heroically on the battlefield—just as their forebears had done during the Civil War.

Nevertheless, one of the starkest realities of the war era appeared during the registration periods that belied commonly held beliefs about Alabamians' fighting prowess. The need to induct millions of Americans into the armed services meant that Alabamians would be measured against potential inductees from across the nation. No matter how such measurements were made, Alabamians fared poorly in their health and basic intelligence. To the state's great embarrassment, the U.S. Army ingloriously rejected thousands of Alabama's young men. Heart-sinking revelations emerged when local draft boards told Alabama's "selectmen" to go home because they did not meet the minimum physical, emotional, or mental standards—even for basic infantry soldiers.[3]

The draft registration statistics—numbers that reasonably can be extrapolated to reflect overall population health—presented immutable evidence that Alabama's population fared poorly when compared to other states. Of the 438,657 Alabama males between the ages of eighteen and forty-six who registered for Selective Service during 1917 and 1918, only 58,368 (13.3 percent of total registrants) were inducted. The remaining 380,289 (86.6 percent) were rejected for not meeting health requirements, for failing intelligence examinations, or by gaining exemptions on the basis of family and/or economic considerations.[4] The military rejected more men from Alabama during the first half of 1918 than from any other state in the nation.[5] Likewise embarrassing were reports that 60 percent of the men of the Alabama National Guards were infected with hookworm. This parasite "lowered vitality" and rendered the host far more susceptible to pneumonia, which in turn led to "abnormally high mortality rates" among Alabama soldiers.[6] Such unusually high rejection rates cut deeply in a culture that had long revered manliness, militarism, and the attainment of personal honor on the battlefield.[7] But the fact was that many young males in the state simply did not measure up.[8]

Yet hookworm infestation, pellagra, and other preventable diseases, the leading culprits behind Alabama's high rejection rates, were not the only sorrowful health problems in the state. Other and more-serious illnesses, such as typhoid, hepatitis, tuberculosis, malaria, and smallpox, plagued Alabamians at abnormally high levels. Though there was still much to learn about all of these common maladies, the medical community and the Alabama Board of Health well understood that clean, uncontaminated water supplies were essential for maintaining public health. Alabamians also knew that various communicable diseases were spread by mosquitoes. It was reasonable to believe, therefore, that many common diseases suffered in the state could be avoided through proper nutrition programs, cleaner living and working environments, proper sanitation and sewage systems, and more proactive state efforts to inform the citizenry of how to live cleaner, safer lives. But the state had never invested in the public health of its citizens. Annual budgets for such matters—generally about $25,000—were nugatory and usually only partially funded. Alabama's great embarrassment during draft registration might have been lessened had the state taken more initiative in promoting public health.[9]

Loraine Bedsole Bush, a prominent social reformer and a tireless promoter of health reforms and child welfare in Alabama, wrote that after reports of social conditions in Alabama appeared in 1918 and 1919, many Alabamians were "chagrined" when these reports, despite being "taken in our best Sunday clothes," showed that Alabamians lagged far behind virtually all other states in public health and education. "They [the reports] had the effect of saying, like Uncle Mose preaching the gospel of his faith: 'I ain't a-arguin' with you, I'm a-tellin' you.'"[10] It became clear, in other words, that the state government needed to become far more active in improving social conditions.

A joint investigation into health conditions in Alabama, cosponsored by the National Child Labor Committee and the University of Alabama and published in early 1918, shed considerable light on why Alabamians suffered such poor health and explained why far too many common maladies of the day seemed to be more widespread than in any other state. The verdict by this investigatory panel was quite simple: in even a rudimentary sense the state government had long neglected its obligation to promote public health and improve social conditions. Dr. J. H. McCormick, a faculty member with the university's school of medicine, contributed an essay to the overall report titled "Public Health." "It is a truism," McCormick wrote, "that public health is public wealth." It was a "striking fact," he continued, "that for the most part, especially in rural sections, the people possess no true appraisal of community health as a supreme value."[11] McCormick stressed that public health—the "intangible asset," he called it—was as important as economic or industrial well-being and that the state had a fundamental obligation to improve overall public health conditions in Alabama. The government in Montgomery, he insisted, "has no duty paramount to that of protecting the health and lives and of aiding in the increase of physical efficiency among its citizens." Private organizations that in the past had assumed some responsibility for promoting public health were simply ill-equipped and insufficiently funded to carry out such enormously important functions. McCormick warned Alabama politicians that they ignored public health issues at their peril: "The public is slowly but surely realizing this truth and is beginning to demand from the state a greater degree of protection against preventable diseases than formerly."[12] McCormick maintained that the state had to accept a far broader role with respect to improving Alabama's society and that the winds of Social Progressivism had blown away old concepts of laissez faire. Concerns about government impeding individual liberty increasingly rang hollow during an era when faith in government's ability to improve people's lives increased dramatically.

By early 1918 a consensus built among the state's leading health care professionals that immediate and progressive reforms at the state government level were essential. Echoing McCormick's sentiments in "Public Health," Dr. Samuel W. Welch, the state health officer, wrote in his 1918 annual report that the overall health picture in the state was bleak and that the government should aggressively address such intolerable conditions.[13] Welch proposed that the Alabama Board of Health, which was in reality little more than a glorified version of the Medical Association of the State and not a functioning department of the state government, be recognized through proper legislation as an official department, charged to promote public health, oversee sanitation facilities, and manage all county boards of health to coordinate efforts to combat various communicable diseases. Welch and other state health officers wanted both statutory authority and sufficient funding to manage municipal and county health departments. Welch would have enthusiastically agreed that it was no longer acceptable for the government simply to react to recurring outbreaks of seasonal diseases or to ignore altogether easily preventable, chronic illnesses such as pellagra and hookworm infestation.[14]

Welch expressed gratitude to the U.S. Public Health Service for providing the majority of the funds used in Alabama to promote public health, writing, "It would have been impossible, with our meager means, to have accomplished anything along some lines without this aid." The U.S. Public Health Service provided 130,000 typhoid fever inoculations and 30,000 smallpox vaccinations. In 1918 alone it funded digging more than two hundred miles of drainage ditches and implementing several successful drainage programs. Nevertheless, Welch reported, because local officials neglected to maintain the ditches, a number of them subsequently refilled and thus reverted to breeding grounds for disease-carrying mosquitoes. Nowhere in Welch's report does he thank the Alabama state government for providing adequate funding in the interest of promoting public health. The omission was well warranted.[15]

Reflecting the mounting pressures for government activity along Progressive lines, Welch suggested that a properly created state Department of Public Health should be run as "a business organization with the unit of operation corresponding with the political unit, the county." Welch thought it prudent "to express the conviction that any public health work undertaken without a stable business organization to carry it on is a mistake and should not be done." "Sentiment and gush," he counseled, "are not good foundations on which to construct a superstructure." Welch was concerned that Progressive appeals to legitimize and empower the proposed Department of Public Health would bear little fruit because of the fundamental conservatism of Alabama's political power brokers. By insisting that a greatly enhanced Health Department strictly function within responsible business parameters, he hoped to temper anti-Progressive opposition in Montgomery. "If we [the proponents of a viable Board of Health] wish to stand against the storms of public criticism and natural reaction to all progressive movements," he warned, "we must lay our foundations well."[16] Welch knew that meaningful social reforms would require a fundamental shift in how the state government functioned. Progressivism, in essence, required governments to accept far greater responsibility—and, by implication, authority—over people's lives. Welch wanted a dramatic change to occur in how Alabamians perceived the role of government.

This attitudinal adjustment was well under way by 1918. The war—or rather the revelations about the wretchedness of Alabama that emerged during mobilization efforts—spurred the public shift in perspective.[17] "A gradual realization," wrote Loraine Bedsole Bush of the poor social conditions in Alabama, "resulted in a determination upon the part of many inquiring minds to discover exactly [Alabama's social] status."[18] Using America's positive wartime experiences as the prime example, many reformers argued that government was indeed capable of performing vital functions in the interest of the collective good. Despite the nearly immovable conservative forces in state government that had for almost two decades resoundingly rejected or ignored Progressive legislation they declared would limit personal liberty, and despite the fact that by war's end the Progressive movement had virtually disappeared at the national level, the impetus for socially progressive reforms at the state level in Alabama intensified dramatically by the end of 1918. All that remained before fundamental changes occurred was for the people to elect state leaders willing to accept the paradigm shift.

Alabama's wartime governor, however, hardly fit the bill as socially progressive. Charles Henderson, elected in 1914 as an avowed fiscal and social conservative, shunned virtually all calls for increased state spending for socially progressive programs. Born and raised in Pike County, Henderson became an exceedingly wealthy businessman and civic leader in Troy. After serving two terms on the Alabama Railroad Commission, he easily defeated his Republican rival for the governorship. Though agreeable to modest improvements in education and penal reform, Henderson steadfastly opposed meaningful initiatives to properly fund public education, eradicate child labor, improve public health, or end the convict lease system.[19] Yet, the startling rejection rates of Alabama conscripts and the obviously woeful health conditions that plagued Alabamians deeply concerned him.

Responding to such bleak statistics, Henderson contacted the Russell Sage Foundation of New York, which had conducted similar inquiries in other southern states, for a thorough investigation into Alabama's overall social conditions. In June 1918, the governor formally requested that Dr. Hastings Hart, the nationally known social worker who had authored the foundation's other southern reports, investigate conditions in Alabama as soon as possible. The governor later explained to the legislature that "Dr. Hart is an authority on social work and maintains a close connection with what is being done [with respect to social problems and programs] in every section of our country." Henderson said he requested Hart's services so the legislature "may have a more thorough understanding of the State's institutions, as to what is being done, and as to what has been accomplished in our social welfare work."[20]

During the following four months, Hart traveled throughout Alabama examining virtually every state-run institution. His itinerary included visits to universities and colleges, reformatories for males and females (both blacks and whites), institutions for the mentally and physically disabled, and prisons. Hart conducted dozens of on-site inspections and hundreds of interviews, collecting substantial data about overall social conditions. His *Social Problems of Alabama,* written during the state's 1918 gubernatorial campaign, was indeed an eye-opening document that shed light on just how abysmal social conditions in Alabama truly were.[21]

Smarting from deeply suffered insults to southern manliness, the people of Alabama—and, more important, some of the state Democratic Party leadership—began to demand fundamental changes within the political arena. Indicative of such reform impulses inspired by wartime experiences was the gubernatorial candidacy of Thomas Kilby, who initiated his run for the governor's seat in early 1918 and immediately began building a powerful support base. Though as fiscally conservative as Henderson, Kilby understood the dismal conditions that existed in many parts of the state, and it was perfectly clear that a Kilby administration would usher in Progressive reforms—particularly within the context of promoting social justice, public health, and child welfare. As historian Wayne Flynt has noted, Kilby's run for governor signified that "all of the stars in the reform firmament were aligned" in favor of government activism to combat social inequality and outmoded state-run institutions.[22]

Such a celestial alignment clearly indicates that the shift in perspective concerning the proper role of government evolved full bore during the 1918–1919 period. Loraine Bedsole Bush reported that there was "a decided social awakening on the part of all people" of Alabama.[23] During that summer's campaign for the Democratic nomination, Kilby ran on an agenda based almost entirely on Progressive reforms. By midsummer two-thirds of the state's newspapers had endorsed Kilby, and he was a distinct favorite over his conservative Democratic rival, William W. Brandon.

Kilby likewise gained the support of the state's medical community during the campaign—largely through the behind-the-scenes efforts of State Health Officer Welch. Kilby had pledged to support the public health reforms Welch would propose in his *Annual Report* for 1918. Welch worked enthusiastically. He asked one colleague, a "Dr. Greene," to endorse Kilby publicly because "I have secured from Mr. Kilby unequivocal assurances of his active aid in obtaining an appropriation of $150,000 for public health work in the State." Four days later, in a letter to "Dr. Walker," Welch asserted that not only had Kilby verbally agreed to the proposed $150,000 allocation should he be elected, but he also had signed a contract with Welch to signify his absolute support of meaningful public health reforms. Because of his ties to the state government, Welch asked both Drs. Greene and Walker not to reveal his lobbying on Kilby's behalf. "I am trusting to your wisdom," he explained to Dr. Walker, "to handle this delicate situation diplomatically. Under no circumstances let anyone know that I have communicated with you." He asked Dr. Greene to write Kilby with an endorsement on the basis of information gained from a "mutual friend" that public health would receive great support from a Kilby administration. "It would be very unfortunate," he continued, "for anyone to find out that I had made this request of you or that Mr. Kilby had made any promises to me." He cautioned Dr. Walker that "you, perhaps, will have to let [other doctors] know" of the contract between himself and Kilby, "but do it in such a way that they cannot prove that you said any such thing." "In other words," he explained, "it is a game of poker to be played with men for cards. I guess you know how to play poker."[24]

Kilby continued to build support for his campaign and developed an especially progressive platform. Besides his commitment to public health, Kilby promised honesty and efficiency in government, increased support for public education, revision of the state tax laws, abolition of the convict lease system, stricter child labor laws and regulations, and support for the Eighteenth Amendment to the U.S. Constitution. Reeling from the undeniably embarrassing conscription numbers and the universally bleak public health picture, the conservative Democrats, led by the Brandon campaign, stood little chance of defeating Kilby, who won election by nearly ten thousand votes.[25]

The weeks following Kilby's election were especially eventful. The fighting in Europe had finally drawn to a close, and news of the armistice sparked "wild demonstrations" across the state. Swarms of Montgomery and Birmingham residents thronged the streets, jubilant that the kaiser was defeated and that Alabama soldiers soon would be coming home. The *Birmingham Age-Herald* predicted with great satisfaction that the armistice "marked the beginning of a new era for humanity."[26] Patriotism and devotion to American values, optimism for a brighter future, and genuine satisfaction that Alabamians had so enthusiastically served the nation in its great time of trial characterized all these celebrations. It was not too long, however, before the euphoria of the armistice wore off and the realities of life in Alabama reemerged.

In December 1918, just one month after the armistice, Hastings Hart published his report on social conditions in Alabama, and his findings deflated much of the short-lived optimism that followed the armistice. In a methodic and impartial manner, Hart not only uncovered a wide range of seriously disturbing social problems but also suggested how the state could best remedy such appalling conditions. The government, counseled Hart, needed at once to allocate considerable new funds to a wide array of state-operated institutions and social programs. Though some progress had been made in terms of social justice, a fundamentally new approach to governance was needed that reflected a genuine commitment to education, child welfare, and public health. Echoing McCormick and Welch, Hart delivered a simple message: Alabamians would continue to live unhealthily in abject poverty and ignorance so long as the government ignored the many social problems that chronically plagued the state.[27]

"The war work" in Alabama, wrote Hart "is closely and necessarily involved with its social work." Immediate social reforms were needed "to furnish healthy soldiers and sailors; improve educational methods to furnish intelligent soldiers and capable workers." Furthermore, counseled Hart, the state should "provide adequate insane asylums; tuberculosis sanitariums and hospitals to care for infirm soldiers; reformatory prison methods to increase the supply of efficient workers which has been diminished by the war; general improvement of social work and social institutions to meet the new social conditions, moral, educational, industrial and political, which are being created by the war."[28]

Hart insisted that by making such reforms, Alabama could better contribute to the war effort. It was perfectly clear, however, that he had a far broader agenda for the state than merely adopting wartime reforms. He advised Alabamians to alter their social and civic conceptions to allow the government to care effectively for its indigent and infirmed citizens. He suggested that Alabamians concentrate as diligently on the social conditions of their own people as they had on the European war, noting that they, with great patriotism and devotion, had purchased $50 million in Liberty Bonds and paid $25 million in taxes for the training and provisioning of U.S. troops. "What will you do to train and feed and pay the doctors, nurses, teachers and caretakers who are fighting here in Alabama?" he asked. What should be done "to protect you from the evils of vice, crime, disease and pauperism?"[29]

Hart further asked whether Alabamians would be willing to better fund schools, reformatories, and hospitals for the "insane" and to deal with the "feeble-minded" and the epileptics who were "in urgent need of care." "They suffer sadly," he wrote. "Many become paupers or criminals; many die before their time for want of care; many, because of neglect, become parents of children afflicted like themselves." "In other words," Hart asked, "will you do for your own people, in Alabama, what you have done so freely and cheerfully for those in foreign countries?"[30]

Citing deficiencies in state spending in education, public health, sanitation, reformatories, institutions for the mentally and physically disabled, and prisons, Hart highlighted Alabama's shameful social conditions. He noted that public health conditions in the state were especially appalling; people suffered from scurvy, rickets, pellagra, hookworm, and a number of similar conditions easily remedied through nutritious food and proper health care. And yet, the State Board of Health was so poorly funded that its effectiveness in combating these and other diseases was all but nugatory. In what had to have been a most embarrassing revelation, *Social Problems in Alabama* showed that the state allocated $28,000 for the prevention of hog cholera, $25,000 for the eradication of cattle ticks, and $5,000 for the Live Stock Sanitary Board—for a total of $58,000—but the legislature appropriated only $25,000 to the Alabama State Board of Health. The Montgomery government evidently found it prudent to invest more than twice as much money for the health of hogs and cattle than it did for the health of its citizens. With the exception of Arkansas, Alabama was at the bottom of the list in terms of funding its Board of Health. Whereas Florida, Virginia, and Texas allocated on average $126 per 1,000 inhabitants to health and nutrition programs, Alabama spent a paltry $11 per 1,000 citizens. The result of such miserliness was a population whose overall health was well beneath regional and national standards. In sum, many Alabamians were living in conditions that by late-twentieth-century standards would rank them among the poorest of the third world countries. To obviate such terrible conditions, Hart recommended that the State Board of Health's annual appropriation be increased to $150,000.[31] He concluded that "whereas opinions may be held as to the necessity for economy, I can see no escape from the necessity for a large increase in the expenditures for the promotion and the preservation of the lives and health of the people."[32]

Hart also targeted the abysmal conditions that existed within the educational system. Here again Alabama ranked among the lowest southern states in terms of spending. The state's contribution of $2.04 per student was but one-third of the national average of $6.03. Likewise, teachers' salaries ranked well beneath the national average, the school year in Alabama was thirty-six days per year shorter than overall U.S. schools, and truancy in the state was at near-epidemic levels.[33] The Hart report clearly highlighted the problems inherent in poor educational funding, but, as with public health issues, Alabama had never invested in public education to any great extent. Fundamentally conservative values, a deep-seated and often malignant anti-intellectual strain, and the chronic lack of reliable tax revenues had all prevented Alabama lawmakers from adequately funding schools.[34]

Governor Henderson, who was then serving his lame-duck tenure while awaiting Thomas Kilby's inauguration in January 1919, was apparently less than pleased with Hart's findings. It has been written that Henderson well deserves the title "business governor" due to his unabashed faith in economy and efficiency and his firm conviction that socially progressive programs made little economic sense.[35] Reacting negatively to pressure for the enactment of a new Progressive agenda as prescribed within the Hart report, Henderson warned in a message to the legislature that "radical changes are taking place in the minds of many people, including some of our governmental officials as well, that mark departures from that system of government which we have been taught to idealize and under which we have prospered and grown so satisfactorily." It would not at all be wise "to depart, either in principles or in practice" from the conservative values of governance. Henderson then asked what type of government would be best for the people of Alabama. "Is it to be the democracy of our fathers adjusted to meet the demands of present day civilization? Will it be a democracy of order without the suppression of the individual?" Or, he asked, would it be a government "made up of the vagaries borrowed of those who have been supporting centralized autocracy?" Henderson's message was plain: it was no time for radical new concepts of government, experiments in social planning, or programs based on popular "vagaries" that might undermine laissez faire principles in government. In other words, socially progressive policies should continue to be considered anathema to sound government.[36]

In striking contrast to Henderson's farewell message, Kilby proposed a long list of reform initiatives in his inaugural speech on January 20, 1919: increased spending for education, public health, and child welfare; expanded services for the mentally ill; new prison facilities; and an end to the barbaric convict lease system. Kilby championed other initiatives, including the state's first workmen's compensation laws and a $25 million bond issue for new road construction.[37] The state government obviously needed substantially increased funds if the legislature enacted all the governor's reforms. But, as Hart had noted, the state assessed personal property at a paltry 25 percent of its true value instead of the 60 percent allowable by law. He suggested that if the state collected the full assessed amount of all property taxes, it could expand social programs considerably without incurring any additional debt.[38] Such tax reform was exactly what Governor Kilby accomplished during his tenure in office, and new tax revenues soon translated into the realization of fundamental reforms.

Kilby's agenda was one of business progressivism, but one nevertheless dedicated to the concept that government had a responsibility to the general welfare of the population.[39] The governor later thanked Hastings Hart and the Russell Sage Foundation for the investigation and for raising public consciousness as to the government's proper responsibilities. "Your report was well circulated in the state," the governor wrote, "and went far toward the creation of public sentiment which supported the legislature in the carrying out of progressive ideas."[40] Kilby noted that *Social Problems in Alabama* had "been of great service in awakening our people to the realization of conditions and the necessity for their improvement."[41]

Kilby also made good on the "contract" he signed with Dr. Welch to reform the Board of Health and redirect the state's attention toward public health issues. "There is nothing more worthy of your time and attention than the matter of conserving the health and lives of the people of the State," he explained to the legislature. The government "is not fully alive to our obligations to properly care for the mental and physical derelicts of the State. . . . We do not seem to fully realize what can be done for the prevention of disease and the preservation of human life, for we have failed to make proper use of the discoveries of medical science along those lines." The new governor instructed the legislature to create an official state Department of Public Health and to empower it—and properly fund it—so it could become the line of first defense against the spread of communicable diseases. "The proper administration of health laws is of first importance," he said, "because it involves the welfare and lives of the people."[42]

The state legislature took several months to enact Kilby's public health department proposal. Three groups opposed the plan: a few medical doctors who did not want Welch to have increased authority, "patent medicine people" who "waged a bitter and relentless war" from fear that the new department would undermine medicine sales, and most of the state's newspapers.[43] Nevertheless, the legislature finally acted in late September 1919, clear testimony that a majority of the legislators had accepted the paradigm shift in government's responsibilities. "We weathered the storm," Welch reported; the Board of Health's "most sanguine hopes have been realized." The legislature allocated $90,000 for the new department for 1919–20, $125,000 for 1920–21, and $150,000 for each year thereafter.[44]

Governor Kilby initiated other important Progressive reforms. He expanded services and increased funding to Bryce Hospital in Tuscaloosa, a state facility for treating the mentally disabled, and he obtained more money for Alabama's chronically underfunded industrial schools. Although his business progressivism prevented him from dismantling Alabama's shameful but profitable convict lease system, Kilby did improve prison conditions and build a new correctional facility that bears his name. The governor also more than doubled education expenditures. "Our entire citizenship is alive to the strategic importance of education as never before. . . . Today new conditions have arisen and new demands confront us," he said. Drawing a direct connection to the war and the thousands of failed intelligence exams, Kilby noted that the "World War has given education a most positive emphasis." Education would not only prepare citizens "to do their life work efficiently," it likewise would "inspire within [the people of Alabama] ideals that will make real and perpetual our recent victory."[45] By 1923 state funding for public education surpassed $8 million and represented the state's greatest commitment to public education to that date.[46]

Much to his credit and representative of his commitment to the welfare of Alabama's indigent children, Kilby created the Alabama Department of Child Welfare and appointed Loraine Bedsole (Bush) Tunstall as its director.[47] Tunstall, a nationally known social worker and a prominent member of the National Child Labor Committee, assumed responsibility for enforcing child labor laws, particularly in the textiles mills, and for developing standards of care and treatment in reformatories and other state institutions for children. Tunstall's expertise in child welfare complemented Kilby's social justice programs.

Governor Kilby's legislative successes, as noted by Hastings Hart in his subsequent report on social conditions in Alabama published in 1922, advanced Alabama "from the rear ranks to the front rank of states of the union in her social progress."[48] Though Hart substantially overstated the impact of Kilby's reforms, the state government's newfound faith in reform clearly signaled that the state had accepted social progressivism as an essential component of good government. And whereas the Progressive Era throughout most of the nation ended with the American entrance into World War I, the experiences of Alabamians during the war inspired not only a continuation of Progressive ideals but an expansion of them as well. Considering the state's long and undistinguished history of minimum government regulation, the paltry educational resources annually allocated by the legislature, the unfair and inefficient tax structure, and the virtually nonexistent governmental support of basic social services, any reforms that succeeded in the face of such fundamentally conservative values were substantial.

The Great War thus had a profound impact on Alabama. Though tempting to do so, it would be overstating the case to say that the changes resulting from the war were revolutionary. Even with the urban economic prosperity that was sustained throughout the 1920s and the steady growth in manufacturing and production, Alabama's population remained fundamentally agrarian, poorly educated, and impoverished.[49] The increased state allocations for education and social services, appreciable as these were, provided but a small percentage of the funds that would have been necessary to reverse decades of labor exploitation and governmental neglect of education, welfare, and health care. At the same time, cultural restraints such as ingrained traditionalism that by definition eschewed social changes, dogged individualism that undermined community-based improvement efforts, anti-intellectualism that held that book learning would do the average field hand little good, and a fatalistic outlook on life that often lowered people's expectations of themselves and of their community all played a role in stifling revolutionary—or even truly liberal—social reforms.

But then again, lasting social change is rarely revolutionary, and the reform impulses during the war era lent considerable impetus to an evolutionary process of modernization in Alabama. In terms of economic growth alone, the Great War altered the state considerably. Federally funded facilities in the state produced unprecedented economic growth and in so many respects provided visible evidence of the war's modernizing impact. Furthermore, interest in promoting business and economic growth at both the municipal and state levels reflected a revitalization of New South doctrines. At the same time laissez-faire ideologies were greatly weakened by the mounting conviction that government could be the agent of industrial and manufacturing growth and that it could combat social decay and inequities without necessarily destroying individual liberties.

National mobilization for the Great War also prompted greater acceptance of government's responsibility for the general well-being of the population. The realization that decades of neglect and blindness to social ills, the revelation that Alabama suffered from an unhealthy and largely ignorant population, and the awareness that Alabama's laboring class—particularly its underage members—should no longer be considered an easily exploited resource all prompted a reassessment of past policies and a newfound determination to remedy years of abuse and neglect. Consequently, Alabamians began to accept a direction more in keeping with modern concepts of governance. New programs for the promotion of public health and child welfare, laws to restrict child labor, greatly increased education budgets, more humane facilities for the indigent and infirm, and the eventual abandonment of the state's barbaric convict lease system were all products of these trends and of the era. Though Alabama would continue to lag far behind most U.S. states in terms of health and education, reforms initiated during the immediate postwar years fundamentally nationalized, liberalized, and modernized the state—a process largely attributable to the watershed that was World War I.

Captain Mortimer H. Jordan, a resident of Jefferson County who fought with the 167th Infantry Regiment in France, was amused that his British counterparts referred to all American troops as Yankees. "Think of it," he wrote. "Southern troops being called Yankees! And not minding it in the least, either. Surely times do change."[50] Captain Jordan's observations were more accurate than perhaps he would have preferred. But then again, perhaps he was one of the many Alabamians who welcomed the significant changes experienced during the war era. Either way, his statements well reflected the reality.

11
Memorializing World War I in Alabama

Robert J. Jakeman

On February 3, 1919, less than three months after the armistice that ended World War I, Alabama became the first state to enact legislation to create a statewide memorial to the service of its citizens in the Great War.[1] The law established the Alabama Memorial Commission (AMC), headed by the governor, and directed it to "adopt plans," raise funds to purchase a site, and construct "a suitable memorial to commemorate the part of Alabama and Alabamians in the world war."[2] The commissioners moved quickly, and by spring 1919 they had embarked on an ambitious campaign to raise $500,000 to erect a commemorative building directly south of the state capitol that would house two state agencies—the Department of Archives and History and the Department of Education.

Despite the state's early start, the project stalled until 1940, when the United States was on the brink of another world war. That year, the completed building was dedicated in two separate ceremonies, one on Flag Day and the other on Armistice Day. The ceremony on June 14, 1940, dedicated the second floor as the "Hall of Flags." Five months later, on November 11, the Society of American Archivists dedicated the portions of the building devoted to archival activities. In his keynote address, Archivist of the United States R. D. W. Connor remembered Thomas McAdory Owen, who founded the Alabama Department of Archives and History (ADAH) in 1901, the first government archival agency in the nation, and served as its director until his death on March 25, 1920. Connor described the War Memorial Building as "the capstone of Dr. Owen's work" and noted that it was "his inspiration in the initial stages of [the] project that [brought] it to a successful conclusion."[3]

Connor's remarks focused mainly on Owen's career and his central role in the creation of the ADAH, with only a brief reference to the Alabama Memorial Commission and Owen's role as its "executive officer." He deftly sidestepped any reference to the extraordinary delay between Owen's vision of a world war memorial building to house ADAH and its fulfillment more than twenty years later. He did not comment on the initial plans that called for the structure to serve as the home of both ADAH and the Alabama Department of Education. Moreover, he politely avoided pointing out that only an infusion of federal Works Progress Administration funds had brought the dormant project to life and ultimate completion.[4]

The two-decade delay notwithstanding, Alabama approached the brink of World War II having finally completed its World War Memorial. Thus the state fulfilled its obligations to erect a structure that would at once memorialize Alabamians who served in the Great War and provide a suitable home for ADAH. A *Montgomery Advertiser* editorial in April 1919 had predicted that Alabama's World War Memorial would take the form of "a building so stately, so dignified and so appropriate, that people from afar will come to wonder at the achievements of the people of Alabama in commemorating the valor of their soldiers." According to the *Advertiser*, it was only incidental that the memorial building would serve as the home of the state agency responsible for preserving the state's records and promoting knowledge of its history. Its primary purpose would be to "appeal to the ideal and inspire the spiritual" in Alabamians, to be "the focus of the State's patriotism."[5]

Despite these sentiments, it is doubtful that many Alabamians in the twenty-first century would identify the structure as a memorial commemorating their state's contributions and sacrifices in World War I. Instead, the building is widely known simply as "the state archives" or "the Archives and History building" and only incidentally—if at all—as the Alabama World War Memorial. An October 2007 search of the World Wide Web confirmed that the building is not generally recognized as a memorial to Alabamians who served in the Great War. Using the popular search engine Google, the query "Alabama World War Memorial" yields but ten hits. A similar query using the phrase "Alabama War Memorial" delivers 1,190 hits, but not for the building housing ADAH; instead, it returns results relating to the American Legion memorial by that name at the corner of Jackson and Monroe Streets in Montgomery, a memorial to all war veterans from the state.

Overlooking the ADAH building's commemorative role as a war memorial is nothing new, however. Perhaps the best evidence that the building quickly lost its memorial status—if indeed it ever truly had it—comes from a paper on the Alabama state capitol and environs presented by Algernon Blair. A prominent businessman and contractor known and respected by corporate and government leaders throughout the state, Blair read his paper at a 1943 meeting of "The Thirteen," an exclusive organization of thirteen prominent Montgomerians. He described the development of the capitol complex and gave a detailed account of the acquisition of the site for the building and its design and construction by Birmingham architects Warren, Knight and Davis.[6] At no point in his twenty-nine-page paper, however, did Blair refer to the structure as Alabama's World War Memorial. Instead, he simply called it "the Department of Archives and History Building." He presented his paper to a group that counted Thomas Owen as a charter member and, in 1943, included Peter Brannon, a longtime ADAH staff member. That a man as prominent and well connected as Blair would fail to refer to the structure as the state's World War Memorial suggests that from the outset the building was not widely recognized as the state's memorial to the Great War.[7]

The War Memorial Building's failure to attain memorial status was not an unexpected development, at least to some Alabamians. In the weeks and months after the legislation to create a memorial was approved, some citizens began to criticize the idea of erecting a building—rather than "a real monument or shaft"—to honor the fallen. One critic, Frank S. Moody of Tuscaloosa, asked pointedly, "Is there anything in a building that we can associate with the memory of our soldiers?"[8]

Nevertheless, the proponents of the plan to erect a memorial building proceeded under the able leadership of Owen, but ultimate fulfillment of their goals proved exceedingly difficult and slow. In addition to coping with complaints of critics such as Moody, they encountered fund-raising problems from the outset. A depressed agricultural economy and weariness from the constant appeals for contributions and sacrifice that they had endured during the war meant that many Alabamians were unable or unwilling to donate to the cause. Moreover, Owen's sudden death in 1920 at age fifty-three deprived the struggling movement of dynamic leadership at a crucial time, and it lost momentum. Although his successors continued the campaign, they raised scarcely a tenth of the $500,000 goal, and it all went toward the purchase of land for the building. They subsequently lobbied for state funding to construct the building, but the onset of the Great Depression ended any hope of securing state dollars for the project. Finally, the advent of federally funded public projects under Franklin Roosevelt's New Deal brought new hope and ultimate fulfillment.

The first formal proposal that Alabama's war memorial would take the form of a building came from the Alabama Council of Defense. The council's final report contained a section titled "Memorial for Soldiers," which proposed "a building of adequate proportions and enduring usefulness, and which will tend to keep alive the records and exploits of those sons of Alabama who made the supreme sacrifice."[9] Although the report did not specifically call for the creation of a memorial building housing ADAH, the language of the proposal left little doubt regarding its intent. Owen served on the council in his capacity as state war historian and almost certainly had a hand in shaping the proposal. His section of the report, outlining efforts to collect and preserve a documentary record of the participation of Alabamians in the war, however, made no reference to a memorial.[10]

The Council of Defense's recommendation for a building in lieu of—to use the words of Frank Moody—"a real monument or shaft" reflected a broader national trend of "living memorials" to the war dead. Proponents of living memorials maintained that traditional monuments would lose their significance to subsequent generations. Instead, they advocated creating a facility—a community building, a stadium, a park—that not only honored the memory of the fallen but also served the needs of the living. Harold S. Buttenheim, editor of *American City,* declared in a December 1918 article that "a memorial worthy of the recent conflict must be dynamic." A proper tribute, he advised, "must be a building commemorating the service of the living by giving service, rather than a statue or a shaft in which there could not pulse the life blood of a new day."[11]

One important manifestation of this idea was a national campaign for erecting memorial structures that could serve as centers for community life. By late 1918 or early 1919 a group of "one hundred representative men and women from all parts of the county" formed the National Committee on Memorial Buildings (NCMB) to "assist in the promotion and guidance of the nation-wide movement to erect community buildings as war memorials." General John J. Pershing endorsed the movement, writing NCMB chairman Paul D. Cravath in April 1919 that community buildings "as living tributes to those who served in the war . . . appeals very strongly to me." Other organizations were active as well. The War Camp Community Service—a charitable agency that provided morale and welfare services to troops during the war—established a Bureau of Memorial Buildings to serve as a clearinghouse for information on "planning, erecting and administering community houses, auditoriums, recreation centers and other 'living' memorials." Before the end of 1919, the NCMB became the Advisory Committee on Memorial Buildings to the War Camp Community Service.[12]

The degree to which this national movement influenced developments in Alabama is unclear, but there were undoubtedly some connections. For example, the Bureau of Memorial Buildings published a series of twelve bulletins in 1919 and 1920 titled *Community Buildings as War Memorials* with individual issues focusing on various aspects of creating memorial buildings. The tenth number in the series described the status of efforts to erect "large memorial buildings" in eighteen major cities across the nation. "The State of Alabama," the bulletin reported, "has decided that its memorial shall take the form of a beautiful and stately building erected at Montgomery."[13]

By early 1919, according to the NCMB, approximately four hundred cities and towns had definite plans for erecting a community house as a war memorial or were seriously considering the idea. But enthusiasm for "Liberty Buildings," as they were sometimes called, was not universal. In January 1919, the American Federation of Arts (AFA) issued a circular letter on war memorials that included recommendations on various types of memorials. Regarding memorial buildings, the AFA acknowledged that a structure "devoted to high purposes, educational or humanitarian," could serve as "an example and inspiration to present and future generations." The letter cautioned, however, that a structure that is "entirely utilitarian can not altogether satisfy the desire for a commemorative work of art." Judging from its recommendations for other types of memorials, the federation showed a clear preference for monumental memorials such as fountains, gateways, and tablets. "The most impressive monument," according to the federation, "appeals to the imagination alone." It noted that well-known commemorative structures such as the Arc de Triomphe and the Lincoln Memorial "are devoid of practical utility, but they minister to a much higher use." The same spirit could be imparted to projects of a smaller scale: "A little roadside shrine or cross, a village fountain or a memorial tablet, speaks the same message as the majestic arch or shaft or temple, and both messages will be pure and fine and perhaps equally far-reaching, if the form of that message is appealing and beautiful." If memorial planners should insist on a "utilitarian structure," the AFA cautioned that it must "impress the beholder by beauty of design, the permanent nature of the material used and the fitness of the setting."[14]

The tenth annual convention of the AFA, held in May 1919, exposed the diverging views of artists and city planners. The first day of the meeting focused on war memorials, and Charles Moore, chairman of the National Commission of Fine Arts, set the agenda for the day's discussions when he "distinguished between war memorials of *ideal significance* purely and those that are to be used as *structures for public purposes.*" Harold S. Buttenheim spoke in favor of memorial community buildings, but others "staunchly upheld" the concept of the "ideal memorial." For example, Elihu Root—who founded the AFA in 1909—argued that "art alone can carry on in times of peace that spirit of high idealism which called us into the war."[15]

The American debate over the appropriate nature of memorials—whether as ideal or utilitarian structures—did not have a counterpart in Europe, where the scope of the casualties was so vast and so far beyond any previous experience that it profoundly changed the way these nations coped with the memory of the war. As historian George L. Mosse has observed, "More than twice as many men died in action or of their wounds in the First World War as were killed in all major wars between 1790 and 1914." According to Mosse, this was battlefield slaughter of a "new dimension," which resulted in a "greater effort to mask and transcend death in war than had ever been made before."[16] Losses on such a scale resulted in an impulse in Europe to create national shrines, and the most profound expression of this impulse was the creation of memorials to "unknown soldiers," a recognition that modern war caused death on a scale so vast as to make identification of many of those killed impossible.[17]

The sense of loss and the desire to find some meaning in the widespread slaughter of the war that swept Europe did not have an exact counterpart in the United States. Whereas the Europeans had endured the war since 1914, the United States entered the conflict in April 1917 and did not commit troops in large numbers until the following fall. The scale of U.S. losses was miniscule compared with that of its European allies or the Central Powers.[18] Consequently, the "urge to find a higher meaning in the war experience [of World War I] and to offer some justification for the sacrifice and loss" that was so widespread in Europe, especially among veterans, was less intense in the United States.[19] Indeed, the United States had already coped with the new reality of modern war—mass death—fifty years earlier during the Civil War, and its casualty figures in that conflict were substantially higher than those it suffered in World War I.[20]

Although the United States did not exhibit the passionate drive to develop sacred war monuments to help the living find meaning in the wholesale slaughter of modern war, there was, nevertheless, a recognition that the nation's role in the war needed symbolic acknowledgment. The "community buildings as war memorials" movement in the United States did not, therefore, attract a following in Europe, where the tension between the sacredness of a memorial and the desire to commemorate the dead by serving the needs of the living was resolved in favor of the sacred. According to Mosse, the idea of creating memorial buildings to serve some practical purpose was "impossible to imagine in Germany" after World War I, "where a memorial in the shape of a library was considered unpatriotic."[21] In the United States, however, imagining memorial buildings that served a practical purpose was not considered unpatriotic, even though critics such as the American Federation of Art expressed a preference for "ideal" monuments over functional structures.

Although the idea of a liberty building had its critics, a cadre of state officials in Alabama had clearly embraced the concept and began to move decisively ahead with the idea. By February 18, 1919, scarcely two weeks after the state legislature approved the creation of a building, the governor organized the Alabama Memorial Commission, consisting of seventeen members, five ex-officio and twelve appointed by the governor. The ex-officio members, as defined by the enabling legislation, included Governor Thomas E. Kilby (who served as chairman); Speaker of the House of Representatives Henry P. Merritt; Senate President Pro Tempore T. J. Bedsole; Attorney General J. Q. Smith; and the director of the Department of Archives and History, Thomas M. Owen (who served as secretary). The appointed members were drawn from across the state, with the heaviest representation from Birmingham.[22]

Owen was the only ex-officio member who was not an elected official, a testament not only to his interest in the project's potential to create a facility for his agency but also to his gravitas as a respected and influential figure in state government. As noted earlier, he had directed ADAH since it was founded in 1901; he had also served on at least two other commissions authorized by the state legislature, and he had considerable experience getting things accomplished in state government.[23]

Born in 1866, Owen earned a law degree from the University of Alabama in 1887, began to build a practice, and entered local politics in Jefferson County. But by the early 1890s, he had developed a passion for Alabama history that would ultimately eclipse his budding legal and political career. In 1893 he married Marie Bankhead, daughter of John Hollis Bankhead, an experienced politico who would become a leading member of Alabama's congressional delegation in coming years. Marie's brothers would become influential leaders in Congress during the Roosevelt administration, and her niece Tallulah added glamour to the Bankhead name when she emerged as a successful and flamboyant stage and screen actress. Thus Owen had married into one of the most politically influential families in the state, a relationship that would provide him and ADAH with important connections and influence for years to come.

By 1898 Owen's passion for Alabama history had become all-consuming, and he devoted his personal and family connections to securing legislative approval for the creation of an "Alabama History Commission" charged with surveying the status of historical activities in Alabama and preparing a report of its findings for the governor.[24] Under Owen's aggressive and able leadership, the commission conducted a comprehensive survey of historical activities in other states and of historical records relating to Alabama. In 1900 the commission published an exhaustive 450-page report of its work and recommended the creation of an official agency to collect and manage the archives of the state, establish a state library and state museum, and, in general, ensure that the state's historical resources were identified, preserved, and managed on behalf of the citizens of Alabama.[25] By early 1901 the legislature had approved the creation of the Alabama Department of Archives and History and named Owen its director. Thus ADAH became the nation's first independent, state-funded agency responsible for the care and management of the records of government, and it was soon recognized nationally as a model for other states to emulate.[26]

With Owen at the helm, the fledging agency developed rapidly despite its limited budget and the makeshift space it occupied in the state capitol. His improvised quarters in the senate cloakroom gave Owen frequent contact with lawmakers when the legislature was in session, and he earned their respect and gratitude by placing the informational resources of his department at their disposal. He collected records, papers, books, and artifacts so successfully that he quickly filled to overflowing his allotted space.[27] In 1907 Owen had the opportunity to serve on another important commission—one that would provide ADAH with better facilities—when he was appointed to the Alabama Capitol Building Commission. Responsible for overseeing an expansion of the state capitol, the commission finished its work four years later, giving ADAH a portion of the new south wing that was added to the structure.[28]

ADAH's role expanded significantly in 1907 when it took responsibility for both public and school libraries in the state. That same year the agency also began to provide systematic and comprehensive reference services for the state legislature. By 1918 ADAH had become an integral part of state government, serving both cultural and administrative functions. The extent of Owen's success in building his agency into an important component of state government is apparent in the report prepared by Hastings H. Hart of the Russell Sage Foundation in 1918. Hart had found the services of ADAH so useful in his research that he declared it "one of the most important agencies in state government."[29]

Thus, by the onset of World War I, Owen had, on at least two occasions, successfully used the apparatus of special legislative commissions to good effect, first to create the department he envisioned and then to ensure that an expansion of the state capitol provided additional space for his operations. Such success meant that as a member of the Alabama Council of Defense, Owen was positioned to influence its recommendations regarding the state's plans for a war memorial. He served as the "State War Historian" for the Council of Defense, and in that capacity he devoted himself and his department to "a full and exhaustive collection of European war books, military and technical books, histories and historical sketches of all federal, military, welfare and commercial activities operating in the state, and the personal records of all officers and enlisted men in the military or naval service of the United States from Alabama."[30] The role Owen assumed for himself and his department regarding World War I was an extension of his previous work to ensure that the records and memory of Alabamians in the Civil War were preserved and honored, efforts that paid important dividends during the ADAH's early years. Owen no doubt considered his work to document and commemorate the service of Alabamians in World War I simply another opportunity to demonstrate ADAH's social and cultural value to the state. The final report of the Council of Defense contains no direct evidence that Owen played a role in crafting its recommendation to erect a memorial not "simply of artistic conception or imposing design, but a building of adequate proportions and enduring usefulness . . . which will tend to keep alive the records and exploits of those sons of Alabama who made the supreme sacrifice, and yet prove a benefaction to the veterans of the great world war."[31] Nevertheless, Owen's hand is apparent in the language and the subsequent establishment of the instrument to accomplish the council's recommendation—another special legislative commission, the Alabama Memorial Commission.

At the close of his term, the outgoing governor, Charles Henderson, embraced the idea of creating a commission to develop plans for the state's war memorial. On January 14, 1919, he addressed the legislature and reflected on the contributions of Alabama's soldiers and sailors to the war. In a reference to the state's venerated Civil War dead, Henderson told the legislators that the "records" the returning veterans "now bring and present to us [are] fresh laurels for the graves of our heroes." Such deeds of valor, he declared, "should ever be perpetuated in our minds and in the memories of those who come after us [by] the erection, in public places, of enduring monuments. The capitol grounds are the most suitable location for such a tribute." Consequently, he urged the legislature to "father the movement by the creation of a commission to receive subscriptions and to take such other action as may be necessary for the consummation of the plan."[32] A week later the newly inaugurated governor, Thomas E. Kilby, addressed the legislature and likewise urged the lawmakers to act. He declared that Alabama's "valiant sons . . . have written a burning page upon the annals of our State and nation and we should see to it that the record of their deeds be not lost or forgotten." He exhorted the legislature to "join with the other states and the nation in erecting memorials commensurate with the immeasurable sacrifices they made for Freedom, Justice and Right."[33]

Two weeks later, the legislature had approved the act creating the Alabama Memorial Commission. The act appropriated fifty thousand dollars toward the memorial with the proviso that the state's funding "shall not be available until the sum of two hundred thousand dollars has been raised by voluntary contribution throughout the State, and such sum shall not be actually expended from the State treasury until the expenditure first of the amounts voluntarily contributed." The act appropriated ten thousand dollars immediately to underwrite "organization, salaries, printing, advertising and other expenses" of the fund-raising campaign.[34]

When the AMC held its organizational meeting in Governor Kilby's office on February 18, it set a goal of raising "a minimum" of $500,000 "by popular subscription," an amount equivalent to almost $6 million in 2006. To raise this ambitious sum, the AMC placed four "campaign officers" in charge of the fund-raising effort: W. S. Stallings of Birmingham, state campaign director; State Treasurer R. L. Bradley, campaign treasurer; Spright Dowell of Montgomery, campaign director for schools; and Fred H. Gormley of Birmingham, newspaper publicity director. The commission decided to focus its fund-raising efforts on both the schools and the public at large. It designated May 9, 1919, as "Memorial Building Day in the schools," hoping to convince school administrators to hold patriotic programs that would encourage students to donate to the campaign. Anticipating a wave of patriotic fervor when Alabamians celebrated their first Independence Day holiday since war's end, they designated June 27–July 4, 1919, as the week to rally statewide public support and contributions. Literature distributed by the AMC advised that "all general inquiries should be addressed to the [Alabama Memorial Commission] Secretary and Historian," Thomas McAdory Owen, a clear indication of his central role in the effort.[35]

On April 3 the commission approved a resolution that specified the memorial would take the form of a building "of such design and architecture as will best illustrate and commemorate the record of Alabama and Alabamians in the world war." To ensure that it would be "statewide in both its purposes and uses," the commission stipulated that the building would be situated at a "site on or near the capitol grounds" in Montgomery. Regarding the building's purposes, the "Department of Archives and History shall have the custody . . . of . . . the memorial building and its historical contents" so that "records of the past, present and future" would be preserved for "posterity." Although ADAH would control the building and its historical materials, the structure would also provide offices for the State Department of Education.[36]

In the weeks between the AMC's organizational meeting and the April 3 resolution, however, the commission had held various public meetings to hear the views of the public regarding the form of the state's war memorial. The most significant opposition to erecting a memorial building to house ADAH and its collections came from those who advocated establishing a memorial hospital for veterans and their families, a group that numbered in the "tens of thousands" according to one newspaper report.[37] Supporters of the hospital proposal, led by physician W. B. Crumpton, argued that establishing a state veterans hospital as a memorial would not only honor the memory of those who died during the war but also serve the needs of a very important group of the living, the returning veterans. The members of the AMC gave the hospital supporters a full hearing, perhaps because their proposal included "a generous financial offer which would have given impetus to the memorial campaign at its inception." Nevertheless, the commission ultimately rejected the idea because of an attorney general's opinion that the AMC did not have the legal authority to build a hospital as a memorial. Hoping perhaps to avoid a divisive public squabble, Crumpton published an open letter that urged his allies to "lay hold, with liberal hand, and aid in the drive for the Archives and History Building."[38] Crumpton may have also hoped that exhibiting the spirit of a good loser would ultimately produce dividends for his cause. According to at least one report, the enabling legislation of the AMC would "undoubtedly be amended at the summer session of the Legislature, so that the commission can supplement its efforts, after providing for the memorial hall, to use its machinery for the erection of a State Hospital and turn over for such an institution the funds left after the memorial building is erected."[39] Despite these public expressions of goodwill and support, at least some of the hospital advocates were not willing to give up the fight. Two weeks after the AMC passed its resolution, the Jefferson County Medical Society continued to argue that a hospital was "the best form for a soldier memorial" and passed its own resolution supporting the idea. When Fred Gormley contacted Owen about the situation, Owen confidently advised that the commission should "continue to ignore the whole matter from what ever quarter the agitation may come."[40]

Criticism did indeed come from other quarters. The comments of Frank S. Moody published in the Livingston newspaper *Our Southern Home* in late April (discussed above) also alarmed Gormley. He sent Owen a clipping of the article in early May, along with the report that a recent editorial in the *Florence Times* had cited "an organized effort to secure from the Legislature a reversal of the decision of the Commission." Owen once again reassured Gormley, counseled restraint, and told him that he expected "that the agitation will be short-lived."[41]

Having stood firm on its decision regarding the nature and functional purposes of the memorial, the AMC moved quickly to establish its "machinery" for planning the memorial and launching the fund-raising campaign. The commissioners believed that it was crucial to take action while the memory of the war was fresh and the state's patriotic fervor was, presumably, still strong. They secured the services of an architectural firm, Warren, Knight and Davis of Birmingham, to develop a conceptual design for the building to use in the campaign materials.[42] They published various pieces of campaign literature, beginning on April 12 with "Circular No. 1," which provided information on the membership of the commission, plans for the campaign, and the full texts of the enabling legislation and the resolution adopted April 3.[43] The commissioners published at least three subsequent items specifically to support the campaign effort.[44]

Having designated May 9, 1919, as "Memorial Building Day" for state schools, the commission published a fifteen-page booklet containing recommendations for organizing and conducting a school program designed to solicit donations for the memorial from teachers and students. Hoping to separate the school campaign from the general campaign to come later in the summer, those who wrote the instructions cautioned that "contributions are to be made *solely by teachers and children*, the minimum average contribution should be five dollars per teacher, and fifty cents per pupil." Schools that found the May 9 date unsuitable were urged to select another date, "but under no conditions later than June 1," no doubt to avoid conflict with the general campaign efforts to come. For schools that closed before May 9, the AMC recommended that "the local teacher prepare special community exercises or make a personal canvass *among the children* in the interest of the memorial fund."[45]

In anticipation of the summer campaign, the AMC began to recruit chairmen for each county. Once a likely candidate agreed to serve, the governor made the official appointment. For example, on April 18 Governor Kilby signed a proclamation appointing C. E. Thomas to serve as campaign chairman of Autauga County.[46] Sometimes, however, the individuals approached expressed reservations about committing themselves to a statewide effort in the face of their community's interest in a local memorial. In late April, W. T. Neal of Escambia County wrote Governor Kilby that he needed to know more about the proposed state war memorial before he could accept the position of county chairman. He advised the governor that there was "strong sentiment here for erecting a memorial to the boys from this county, especially in view of the fact that Company G from Brewton had a larger number of men in the Rainbow division than any other Company." Several soldiers from Escambia County perished in France, he told Kilby, "and we think we should do something locally to commemorate their bravery and patriotism."[47] Efforts to recruit county chairmen continued into the summer; for example, in late June, only a few days before the campaign week was scheduled to begin, Owen was still seeking a chairman for Dallas County.[48]

Some county chairmen, however, took up the work of the campaign with great enthusiasm. In Bullock County, Henry J. Rosenstihl organized two public fund-raising rallies, one for whites and one for African Americans. Governor Kilby applauded his efforts to include blacks: "'Let

Everyone Give' should be one of your slogans. It is our desire that every man, woman, and child in Alabama should have some share in the memorial."[49] In July, W. H. Shaw reported that although Colbert County would raise its quota of $6,132 by July 4, he nevertheless "met with some opposition among men of prominence whose support I expected." Despite the problems, he told the governor, "this to me has been a pleasant task."[50]

The opposition Shaw encountered in Colbert County did not prevent the county from meeting its campaign quota, but in other places the situation was decidedly different. T. J. Bedsole, senate president pro tempore and an ex-officio member of the AMC, served as chairman for Clarke County in the southwestern part of the state. At the beginning of June he warned Owen of problems competing with churches; in the wake of the war they had launched their own campaigns, and some ministers were telling flocks to put donations to the church first "and let the others go."[51] By early July the situation in Clarke County had deteriorated. Bedsole reported to W. S. Stallings that although Grove Hill, the county seat, would meet its quota, other beats in Clarke County "will fall short." The county was well organized for the campaign, Bedsole explained, but the local economy was severely depressed: "Crops are the poorest that we have seen in years. . . . In some sections of this County, especially on the rivers, the farmers will hardly make anything. I do not think we can count on more than $3000.00 to $3500.00 for this County. . . . Conditions are awful. . . . We won't make 1/3 of a crop . . . under the very best conditions."[52]

A similar situation occurred in Franklin County in the northwest corner of the state. On June 7, J. Mason Douglass, an attorney in the county seat of Russellville, wrote Governor Kilby an impassioned six-page letter urging postponement of the campaign. Douglass told Kilby that he had served two years in the U.S. Army as "an officer in the Machine Guns" and spent nine months in France until wounds sent him home. Thus, he wrote, he "yield[ed] to no one in State pride or respect for the splendid accomplishments of Alabama soldiery." Nevertheless, he maintained that the current campaign is "ill timed and will be a burden on the people." He told Kilby that Franklin County had "gone over the top in every [wartime] campaign," including "five government drives, the Red Cross, War Work, Armenian Fund, Salvation Army Drives, [and] the Methodist Centennary *[sic]* Drive." "Now comes this drive," he continued, "one of the noblest in purpose and close to the heart of our people in its sanctity of feeling, but coming at a most *inopportune time* and calculated amongst those who are in touch with the facts and the people to preclude the possibility of future drives by burdening the spirit and over taxing the financial capacity of the people." The financial situation in the county, Douglass explained, was dire. Mines were closed, and farmers were in danger of financial ruin because of incessant heavy rains, which "washed away" crops in the "bottom lands" and prevented planting and tilling in other areas. For state government to persist in its memorial building campaign threatened to erode public confidence at a time when "support of all the people will be required for bond issues, road construction, and other forward improvements." Moreover, Douglass continued, the people of Franklin County had reservations about the AMC's plan for the memorial. According to Douglass, they "do not understand, nor, under the [present] circumstances . . . can they be sufficiently instructed what this memorial is to be." They knew, of course, "that it is to be a building," but such a memorial "does not reach their hearts and imagination." He summed up the problem succinctly for the governor by reflecting on the purposes of memorials:

> *There are two values in memorials;* they may be combined or they may be separate. The one is sentimental, the other, practical. In the eyes of the average man the present memorial form does not assume either. It is too much of an administrative building to serve . . . a sentimental value, too remote from everybody save a few to serve a practical value. I wish that [all] buildings of the state regardless of their purpose might be held in the respect with which the Athenians were wont to regard their buildings. But this is not Athens, and our people, rural and remote from Montgomery, unaccustomed to deal in matters of strong attachments to objects of sentiment, fail to understand the matter.

Douglass concluded by urging the governor, on behalf of his fallen comrades, to postpone the campaign until the fall: "If the dead could speak, they would not rush the people . . . into a premature plan at a premature time." And speaking as "one of the living . . . who has been there," the veteran told Kilby that "there is no such pressing need for immediate construction as to justify this undue burden upon the people." "It is easy to make eulogistic speeches," he admonished the governor, "it is easy to make glorious statements. *But wait for better times, for the full return of prosperity, for the return of all our soldiers, and then go forth in sleepless vigilance to secure an unprecedented support from all the people.*"[53]

No reply to Douglass appears in the records at ADAH relating to the memorial building, but Owen's response to Charles E. McCord, a correspondent from Autauga County who expressed similar reservations, suggests how he would have dealt with the complaints from Franklin County.[54] Owen reminded McCord that "throughout the entire country the people are aroused to the setting up of appropriate memorials, not only to commemorate the service of the men who made the supreme sacrifice . . . but also to [honor] the great body of home activities, which made success at the home front possible." Regarding the AMC's decision to commemorate war service by erecting a building rather than a monument, Owen cited the example of the biblical Jacob, who in early life "set up a stone as a memorial to his great experiences with the Jehovah." But as the Jewish nation matured, Owen told McCord, they subsequently "set up at Jerusalem a temple, not in the seats of the twelve tribes, but in the heart of their land, in order that all the people might have some one central place to which they could rally in their religious and political and social life." He then referred to more recent examples, such as Westminster Abbey, "where for hundreds of years all England has turned as to a point of inspiration," and Battle Abbey, "in which thousands of relics of war are assembled." Like these sites in England, the proposed war memorial building in Alabama, Owen predicted, would stand for generations as "an honor to the men of this generation who shared in the great battles for world liberty."[55]

Despite Owen's confident rhetoric and his admonitions to persevere in the face of criticism, the campaign faltered. The AMC once again tried to rally support and contributions from schoolteachers and students by publishing materials for Armistice Day programs in the fall.[56] But the economic situation, weariness over war-related fund drives, and skepticism over the idea of a memorial building occupied by a state agency were substantial obstacles to success. Although the AMC continued sporadic efforts to raise money, by 1924 only $55,000 had been raised, scarcely 10 percent of the half-million-dollar goal. Most of that amount was spent on purchasing lots on the block south of the state capitol, the site currently occupied by the state archives building.[57] But perhaps the most damaging blow to the effort was the illness and death of Thomas Owen, the architect of the proposal and its guiding light. The loss of his leadership and steady hand crippled the struggling campaign. During the summer of 1919 Owen realized that the war memorial campaign was faltering, so he began to call on members of the ADAH board of trustees to assist in their respective counties. In mid-June he wrote W. H. Blake and asked that Blake do what he could to ensure that Colbert County raised "double its quota" for the memorial building. Owen explained that he previously had kept the activities of ADAH and the AMC separate, but now that the "form and design of the memorial have been settled," he needed the help of the ADAH trustees. He told Blake that he was incredibly busy because much of the AMC "work of organization is falling on my shoulders" at a time that the legislature was in session and making demands on his time as well. "However, the future has so much . . . promise because of the memorial," he told Blake, "and the outlook for our work is so fine, that I am willing to sacrifice everything for it."[58] Nine months later Owen dropped dead of a heart attack. His passing was headline news in state newspapers, and the *Montgomery Advertiser* told its readers that "he literally worked himself to death" promoting history and the mission of ADAH.[59] An editorial in the *Advertiser* that appeared the day after his death was titled "The Builder"; it declared that Owen "loomed larger in the estimation of the people of Alabama than any other public official in charge of a department of the State's government."[60]

A week after Owen died, the ADAH board of trustees selected his wife, Marie, to succeed him as director. Marie Bankhead Owen had suffered two losses in March. At the beginning of the month her father, Senator John Bankhead, had died, and by the end of the month she was a widow. Despite her losses—or perhaps because of them—Marie took up the work of her husband with great enthusiasm. Her first priority was completing a project that had long occupied her husband's interest, his *History of Alabama and Dictionary of Alabama Biography,* a lengthy, four-volume reference set that remains an essential resource for students of Alabama history. Shortly after her husband's death, Marie told the publisher that she would deliver a completed manuscript in sixty days, but completing the project took more than a year. Equally important in Marie's mind was fulfilling her husband's dream of erecting a separate building for ADAH.[61]

Marie struggled to keep the memorial building campaign alive while she was grieving over her losses, adjusting to her new responsibilities as the director of a state agency, and completing work on her husband's *History of Alabama* manuscript. In late 1921 she took steps to revive the campaign. She sent a form letter to all county chairmen, updating them on the project. Funds raised in the campaign of 1919–20, she reported, were used to purchase "a part of the land on which the Alabama Memorial Building will be erected." But the project needed more money to "buy a whole block." She admitted that because of the death of her husband "this movement was halted for a while," but she promised to resume the effort despite the challenges of "the financial depression through which we have been passing."[62]

By 1924, however, Marie had abandoned any hope that the AMC's campaign might ultimately produce funds to construct a building or even purchase the site for the structure. Responding to an inquiry from T. H. Roberson of Franklin County, she advised that the campaign had produced funds only sufficient to purchase half of the block south of the capitol, the site planned for the memorial building, and expressed hope that ultimately the state would purchase the remaining lots. "The Memorial Building itself," she observed, "will have to be erected by Legislative appropriation as the Counties failed to raise their quotas. The present Legislature is friendly to an appropriation for the Memorial Building . . . and the Governor has promised to include a Memorial Building appropriation in the list of things he will mention when he calls an extra session of the Legislature." She reassured Roberson that "the building will absolutely be erected at no distant date as it is the memorial due to Alabama and Alabamians, both [to] our soldier and civilian forces who made such heroic sacrifices during that period of our history."[63]

Unfortunately, Marie's confidence in the governor and legislature was misplaced, for no appropriation came out of the summer 1924 session. Hope once again loomed large in 1927 when a bill was introduced to appropriate funds for a memorial building that would also provide offices for state American Legion officers. Owen prepared a statement "To the People of Alabama" titled "State Historian Advises People of Need for Fire Proof Building. Urges Support of Ashcroft Bill." Despite an aggressive lobbying and publicity effort, the initiative faltered and produced no results.[64]

Any hope that the state would fund construction of the building perished with the onset of the Great Depression, which cast state government into a severe fiscal crisis. Nevertheless, ADAH's need for space to house its collections continued to grow. The extent of the need became apparent in 1932 when the Brookings Institution published a five-volume report on Alabama's state and local governments.[65] The report was commissioned by Governor Benjamin M. Miller shortly after he took office in 1931. Its findings showed clearly the inadequacies of ADAH's facilities, with staff working in two buildings and collections stored in four other buildings that lacked proper fire protection and storage equipment. Despite the many valuable collections in ADAH's custody, current accommodations for the agency did not provide reference space for researchers.[66] The year 1935 brought a new governor to Montgomery, Bibb Graves, who won with the support of a coalition of liberals, labor, and New Dealers. Once in office Graves tapped into New Deal funding and launched a major building program for the capitol complex. By the 1930s Marie Owen's brothers, John and William Bankhead, held influential positions in Congress and were key allies of President Roosevelt. Consequently, she was ideally positioned to obtain funding for the ADAH facility that she and her husband had long sought, though this time not from private donations or from the state but from the federal government.[67]

Thus, despite the failed campaign, despite the long delay, and despite the legislature's failure to appropriate funds, Mrs. Owen persevered and brought to closure the project her husband had started scarcely a year before his sudden death. At one level, she clearly succeeded: Alabama had a World War Memorial Building and ADAH had a magnificent facility. Certainly that was the assessment R. D. W. Connor, Archivist of the United States, conveyed in his dedicatory remarks on Armistice Day 1940 (see above), and his sentiments were entirely appropriate for that celebratory occasion. But if the *Montgomery Advertiser* editorial that appeared in April 1919 accurately articulated the fundamental objective of the project—to construct a memorial that would "appeal to the ideal and inspire the spiritual" in Alabamians and be the focal point "of the State's patriotism"—its success must be judged as marginal at best.[68] The goal of erecting a memorial through the generous donations of Alabamians who were flushed with patriotism and bursting with pride in the performance of their troops proved illusive. Fund-drive fatigue, crop failures, and a depressed economy all conspired against the plan to fund the project with private donations. Had Thomas Owen survived and maintained the ability to proceed with his characteristic drive and vision, perhaps he could have overcome such obstacles. Perhaps not.

Regardless of the mechanism, regardless of the source of funds, and regardless of the delay, Alabama ultimately obtained a magnificent building with the words "Alabama World War Memorial" engraved in large bold letters, words that remain there for all to see and contemplate if they only will. The fundamental purpose of this and all war memorials persists—to help the living find meaning in the death and destruction of war, but the success of a memorial is as much a responsibility of its intended audience as its design and execution. Perhaps the creation of a memorial to a "war to end all wars" in 1940, at a time when another global conflagration was erupting, made it impossible for Alabama's War Memorial Building to help its immediate audience find meaning in an earlier war. And ensuing generations of Alabamians have endured the Korean War, the Vietnam War, two wars in the Persian Gulf, a war in Afghanistan, a cold war, and a war on terrorism that appears to be ongoing. Finding meaning in such a parade of conflicts presents challenges unimagined in 1919, and yet the obligations of the living to ascribe meaning to those who sacrificed their lives in combat persist. In his poem "The Young Dead Soldiers," Archibald MacLeish gives eloquent and poignant voice to that solemn responsibility: "Our deaths are not ours; they are yours; they will mean what you make them."[69]

Notes

Chapter 1

1. "An Address to a Joint Session of Congress, 2 April 1917, 8.30 pm," in *The Papers of Woodrow Wilson,* vol. 41, *January 24–April 6, 1917,* ed. Arthur Link (Princeton, NJ, 1983), 521.

2. Colin Davis, *Power at Odds: The 1922 National Railroad Shopmen's Strike* (Urbana, IL, 1997), 10–11.

3. Ibid., 36–39; William J. Cunningham, "The Railroads under Government Operation. I. The Period to the Close of 1918," *Quarterly Journal of Economics* 35, no. 2 (February 1921): 290–93, 332; K. Austin Kerr, "Decision for Federal Control: Wilson, McAdoo, and the Railroads, 1917," *Journal of American History* 54, no. 3 (December 1967): 550–60; Walter D. Hines, *War History of American Railroads,* Economic and Social History of the World War, American Series (New Haven, CT, 1928), 7–9, 12–23, 40.

4. *Birmingham News,* May 18, 1917.

5. David M. Kennedy, *Over Here: The First World War and American Society* (New York, 1980), 93–143; Page Smith, *America Enters the World* (New York, 1985), 567–80; Ronald Schafer, *America in the Great War: The Rise of the War Welfare State* (New York, 1991), 31–46; Arthur S. Link and William B. Catton, *American Epoch: A History of the United States since the 1890s,* 3rd ed. (New York, 1967), 1:202–9; Marc Allen Eisner, *From Warfare State to Welfare State: World War I, Compensatory State-Building, and the Limits of the Modern Order* (University Park, PA, 2000), 56–76.

6. See, for example, Albert Burton Moore, *History of Alabama* (University, AL, 1934), 753–63; William Warren Rogers, Robert David Ward, Leah Rawls Atkins, and Wayne Flynt, *Alabama: The History of a Deep South State* (Tuscaloosa, AL, 1994), 402–8; Harvey H. Jackson III, *Inside Alabama: A Personal History of My State* (Tuscaloosa, AL, 2004), 159–61; Wayne Flynt, *Alabama in the Twentieth Century* (Tuscaloosa, AL, 2004), 381–83.

7. Stewart E. Tolnay and E. M. Beck, *A Festival of Violence: An Analysis of Southern Lynchings, 1882–1930* (Urbana, IL, 1995), 3, 17–27, 57, 273.

8. Anne Permaloff and Carl Grafton, *Political Power in Alabama: The More Things Change . . .* (Athens, GA, 1995), 1.

9. Allen Johnson Going, *Bourbon Democracy in Alabama, 1874–1890* (Tuscaloosa, AL, 1992), 9–26, 33; Michael R. Hyman, *The Anti-Redeemers: Hill-Country Political Dissenters in the Lower South from Redemption to Populism* (Baton Rouge, 1985), 176–86; William Warren Rogers, *The One-Gallused Rebellion: Agrarianism in Alabama, 1865–1896* (Baton Rouge, 1970), 31–55; Rogers et al., *Alabama,* 259–76, 343–54.

10. Going, *Bourbon Democracy in Alabama,* 147–69; Robert G. Sherer, *Black Education in Alabama, 1865–1901* (Tuscaloosa, AL, 1997), 1–16.

11. Going, *Bourbon Democracy in Alabama,* 154, 157–58; U.S. Bureau of the Census, "Table 9: School Attendance," *Thirteenth Census of the United States Taken in the Year 1910: Abstract of the Census: Statistics of Population, Agriculture, Manufactures, and Mining for the United States, the States, and Principal Cities, with Supplement for Alabama Containing Statistics for the State, Counties, Cities, and Other Divisions* (Washington DC, 1913), 592 (hereafter all references to census reports will be cited by the title *U.S. Census* followed by the decennial number); Winston County [AL] Genealogical Society, "1910 Census Data," available at http://wcgs.ala.nu/cendata1910.htm (accessed November 11, 2003).

12. Rouchen Horton, "A Brief Study of Illiteracy in the United States," *Peabody Journal of Education* 1, no. 2 (September 1923): 111.

13. Price comparison made from S. Morgan Freedman, "The Inflation Calculator," available at http://www.westegg.com/inflation (accessed December 21, 2006).

14. Moore, *History of Alabama,* 690; Jonathan M. Weiner, *Social Origins of the New South* (Baton Rouge, 1978), 5, 9–12, 33, 66–73; Jack Temple Kirby, *Rural Lost Worlds: The American South, 1920–1960* (Baton Rouge, 1987), 26–29; U.S. Bureau of the Census, "Series K 298–306. Hay, Cotton, and Cottonseed Acreage, Production, and Price: 1790–1957," in *Statistical History of the United States from Colonial Times to the Present* (Stamford, CT, 1965), 301–2.

15. Moore, *History of Alabama,* 688–90. See also "Table 4: Value of All Crops and Principal Classes Thereof, and Acreage and Production of Principal Crops, by Counties: 1909," *U.S. Census 1910,* vol. 4, *Agriculture, 1909 and 1910, Report by States—Alabama* (Washington, DC, 1913), 46–52; and "County Table 4: Value of All Crops, and Acreage and Production of Principal Crops: 1919," *U.S. Census 1920,* vol. 6, pt. 2, *Agriculture, Reports by States—Alabama* (Washington, DC, 1922), 502–7.

16. Moore, *History of Alabama,* 696n, 698n; Brooks Blevins, *Cattle in the Cotton Fields: A History of Cattle Raising in Alabama* (Tuscaloosa, AL, 1998), 43–75.

17. Moore, *History of Alabama,* 681–82; Norwood A. Kerr, *A History of the Alabama Agricultural Experiment Station, 1883–1983* (Auburn, AL, 1985), 3–41.

18. Moore, *History of Alabama,* 683.

19. *U.S. Census 1910*, vol. 9, *Manufacturers, 1909, Reports by States—Alabama* (Washington, DC, 1913), 27.

20. Moore, *History of Alabama*, 682, 686–87, 691.

21. Ibid., 685–86, 692–93.

22. Winston County [AL] Genealogical Society, "1910 Census Data."

23. Rogers et al., *Alabama*, 270–74, 377.

24. "Table 1: Comparative Summary for 1909, 1904, and 1899: The State—All Industries Combined and Selected Industries," *U.S. Census 1910*, vol. 9, *Manufactures, 1909* (Washington, DC, 1913), 29; Marie Bankhead Owen, *Alabama: A Social and Economic History of the State* (Montgomery, 1938), iv.

25. Wayne Flynt, *Mine, Mill, and Microchip: A Chronicle of Alabama Enterprise* (Northridge, CA, 1987), 140; Robert Eugene Perry, "Middle-Class Townsmen and Northern Capital: The Rise of the Alabama Cotton Textile Industry, 1865–1900" (PhD diss., Vanderbilt University, 1986); Moore, *History of Alabama*, 712–13; "Table 1: Comparative Summary for 1909, 1904, and 1899," *U.S. Census 1910, Manufacturers*, 29.

26. Moore, *History of Alabama*, 705; for gross value of products, compare Statistics of Manufactures, "Table 1: Comparative Summary for 1909, 1900, and 1899" with "Mining in Alabama: Table 1," in *U.S. Census 1910: Abstract of the Census: Statistics of Population, Agriculture, Manufactures, and Mining for the United States*, 671, 680.

27. Deirdre Coakley, *Portrait of a City: An Informal History of Gadsden, Alabama, 1846–1966* (Gadsden, AL, 1996), 10–11, 31–32, 55–56; Harvey H. Jackson III, *Rivers of History: Life on the Coosa, Tallapoosa, Cahaba, and Alabama* (Tuscaloosa, AL, 1995), 146–47, 155; Grace Hooten Gates, *The Model City of the New South: Anniston, Alabama, 1872–1900* (Huntsville, AL, 1978); "Table 2: Population of Incorporated Places, 1910, 1900, 1890," *U.S. Census 1910, Abstract with Supplement for Alabama* (Washington, DC), 586.

28. Marjorie Longnecker White, *The Birmingham District: An Industrial History and Guide* (Birmingham, AL, 1981), 106–13; Leah Rawls Atkins, *The Valley and the Hills: An Illustrated History of Birmingham and Jefferson County* (Woodland Hills, CA, 1981), 69–70, 102–3; Edward Shannon Lamonte, *Politics and Welfare in Birmingham, 1871–1975* (Tuscaloosa, AL, 1995), ix; W. David Lewis, *Sloss Furnace and the Rise of the Birmingham District: An Industrial Epic* (Tuscaloosa, AL, 1994), 61–102, 176; Ethyl Armes, *The Story of Coal and Iron in Alabama* (Birmingham, AL, 1910; reprint, New York, 1973), 238–308, 330–46.

29. Henry M. McKiven, Jr., *Iron and Steel: Class, Race, and Community in Birmingham, Alabama, 1875–1920* (Chapel Hill, NC, 1995), 7, 41, 43–46, 115.

30. Ibid., 89–111.

31. Daniel Letwin, *The Challenge of Interracial Unionism: Alabama Coal Miners, 1878–1921* (Chapel Hill, NC, 1998), 89–99, 142–52; Flynt, *Mine, Mill, and Microchip*, 117–18; Lewis, *Sloss Furnaces*, 312; Brian M. Kelly, "Having It Their Way: Alabama Coal Operators and the Search for Docile Labor, 1908–1921," in *It Is Union and Liberty:*

Alabama Coal Miners and the UMW, ed. Edwin L. Brown and Colin J. Davis (Tuscaloosa, AL, 1999), 38–40; Daniel Letwin, "The Early Years: Alabama Miners Organize, 1878–1908," in *It Is Union and Liberty,* 17–37.

32. Letwin, *Interracial Unionism,* 150, 152; Letwin, "Early Years," 33; Lewis, *Sloss Furnaces,* 312.

33. Kelly, "Having It Their Way," 39–40; Letwin, *Interracial Unionism,* 162–63; Flynt, *Mine, Mill, and Microchip,* 122–28.

34. Robert David Ward and William Warren Rogers, *Alabama's Response to the Penitentiary Movement, 1829–1865* (Gainesville, FL, 2003), 82, 104, 110; Mary Ellen Curtin, "Legacies of Struggle: Black Prisoners in the Making of Postbellum Alabama, 1865–1895" (PhD diss., Duke University, 1992), 116–20.

35. Curtin, "Legacies of Struggle," 128–44; Rogers et al., *Alabama,* 313–14, 422–23; Lewis, *Sloss Furnaces,* 312; Robert David Ward and William Warren Rogers, *Convicts, Coal, and the Banner Mine Tragedy* (Tuscaloosa, AL, 1987), 26–50, 77–93. See also Matthew J. Mancini, *One Dies, Get Another: Convict Leasing in the American South, 1866–1928* (Columbia, SC, 1996), and Mary Ellen Curtin, *Black Prisoners and Their World, Alabama, 1865–1900* (Charlottesville, VA, 2000).

36. Ellis W. Hawley, *The Great War and the Search for a Modern Order: A History of the American People and Their Institutions, 1917–1933,* 2nd ed. (New York, 1992), 1–16; Michael McGerr, *A Fierce Discontent: The Rise and Fall of the Progressive Movement in America, 1870–1920* (New York, 2003), 40–74.

37. Dewey W. Grantham, *Southern Progressivism: The Reconciliation of Progress and Tradition* (Knoxville, 1983), xv–xvi.

38. James F. Doster, *Railroads in Alabama Politics,* University of Alabama Studies No. 12 (University, AL, 1957), 9–14, 32–38, 85–86.

39. Ibid., 163–220; Sheldon Hackney, *Populism to Progressivism in Alabama* (Princeton, NJ, 1969), 12–19, 128–30, 251–78, 288–98; Rogers et al., *Alabama,* 321–22, 348–49, 357–61.

40. Hackney, *Populism to Progressivism,* 300–302; *Code of Alabama,* 1897, sections 1372–79, cf. ibid., 1907, sections 1255–56, Alabama Department of Archives and History, Montgomery.

41. Hackney, *Populism to Progressivism,* 175–78, 230, 235–36, 254.

42. Mary Martha Thomas, *The New Woman in Alabama: Social Reform and Suffrage, 1890–1920* (Tuscaloosa, AL, 1992), 2, 4; Rogers et al., *Alabama,* 379.

43. Rogers et al., *Alabama,* 383–86; Thomas, *New Woman,* 5–9, 43.

44. Thomas, *New Woman,* 70–72.

45. Ibid., 74–77.

46. Ibid., 82–83.

47. Ibid., 54, 57–58.

48. Hasting H. Hart, *Social Problems in Alabama* (Montgomery, 1918); Thomas, *New Woman,* 60; Rogers et al., *Alabama,* 413–14.

49. Thomas, *New Woman,* 49–51.

50. Ibid., 118–203; Aileen Kraditor, *The Ideals of the Woman Suffrage Movement, 1890–1920* (New York, 1981), 195–96; Rogers et al., *Alabama,* 379–82.

51. Eisner, *From Warfare State to Welfare State,* 2, 45–47.

Chapter 2

1. Simpson [Eastern Department Headquarters] to Commanding Officer, State Mobilization Camp, Telegram, April 6, 1917; Bulletin No. 31, Eastern Department Headquarters, April 3, 1917, Adjutant General's Office, Administrative Files, 1881–1953, Alabama Department of Archives and History, Montgomery (hereafter cited as AGO, ADAH); *Illustrated Review, Fourth Alabama Infantry, United States Army, Montgomery, Alabama, 1917* (Montgomery, n.d.).

2. Chief, Militia Bureau to the Adjutant General, Alabama, Memorandum, May 18, 1917; "A Proclamation by the President of the United States of America," July 3, 1917; General Orders No. 10, the Adjutant General's Office, July 28, 1917; the Adjutant General to Commanding Officer, Alabama National Guard, Memorandum, July 31, 1917, all in AGO, ADAH.

3. Department Adjutant, Southeastern Department Headquarters to Commanding Officer, Alabama Field Hospital No. 1, Memorandum, June 19, 1917; Captain Oscar W. Underwood, Jr., First Alabama Cavalry to Adjutant, First Alabama Brigade, Memorandum [June 1917], all in AGO, ADAH.

4. First Alabama Infantry Headquarters, Memorandum, May 22, 1917, AGO, ADAH.

5. Commanding Officer, First Alabama Infantry to Commanding General, Southeastern Department, Memorandum, June 12, 1917, and 2d Indorsement, June 19, 1917; Commanding Officer, Second Alabama Infantry to Commanding General, Southeastern Department Headquarters, Memorandum, July 26, 1917; Fourth Alabama Infantry Headquarters, Memorandum, May 15, 1917, all in AGO, ADAH.

6. Captain Isham Kimbell, Medical Corps, Examining Officer, Memorandum, June 15, 18, 1917; Commanding Officer, Second Alabama Infantry to Commanding General, Southeastern Department Headquarters, Memorandum, July 26, 1917, all in AGO, ADAH.

7. Ibid.

8. Bulletin No. 25, Eastern Department Headquarters, March 29, 1917, AGO, ADAH. Although several diaries and personal accounts are available for the overseas experiences of Alabama Guardsmen, the author located none for the period of guard duty in the state.

9. Commanding Officer, First Alabama District to Commanding General, First Alabama Brigade, Memorandum, May 10, 1917; Adjutant, Eastern Department Headquarters to Commanding General, Alabama Brigade, Memorandum, April 10, 23, 28, 1917; Commanding Officer, State Mobilization Camp to Commanding Officer, Second Alabama Infantry, Memorandums, April 10, 12, 1917, all in AGO, ADAH.

10. Adjutant, Eastern Department Headquarters to Commanding General, Alabama Brigade, Memorandum, April 10, 1917, all in AGO, ADAH.

11. Commanding Officer, First Alabama District to Commanding Officer, First Alabama Brigade, Memorandum, April 21, 1917; Commanding Officer, Second Alabama Infantry Detachment to Commanding General, Eastern Department, Memorandum, April 8, 1917; T. M. Stevens to General Robert E. Steiner, April 3, 1917; Richard Sylvester to the Adjutant General, State of Alabama, February 24, 1917; J. C. F. Clark to General R. E. Steiner, April 4, 1917; Adjutant General to Camp Commander, Memorandum, April 6, 1917, all in AGO, ADAH. The Memphis Terminal Corporation was in Tennessee, but a detachment of Alabama Guardsmen was on duty in the area.

12. Commanding Officer, State Mobilization Camp to Mayor, City of Clanton, Memorandum, April 28, 1917. Copies were also sent to Chilton County Sheriff and to the Alabama Power Company. Thomas W. Martin to Brigadier General Robert E. Steiner, May 26, 1917, all in AGO, ADAH.

13. J. B. Patterson to Major T. C. Locke, April 17, 1917, AGO, ADAH; State Mobilization Camp Headquarters, Memorandum, April 18, 1917, AGO, ADAH; [Robert E. Steiner] to C. H. Markham, April 18, 1917, AGO, ADAH; Commanding Officer, State Mobilization Camp to Captain Ravee Norris, Memorandum, April 19, 1917, Records of the Adjutant General's Office, 1917– [AGO], RG 407, National Archives and Records Administration, Washington, DC (hereafter cited as AGO, RG 407, NARA); Commanding Officer, State Mobilization Camp to President, Rock Island Railroad, Memorandum, May 9, 1917, AGO, ADAH; Adjutant, State Mobilization Camp to D. W. Lang, L and N Railroad Company, Memorandum, June 13, 1917, AGO, ADAH; Commander, First Alabama Brigade to Commanding General, Southeastern Department, Memorandum, May 22, 1917, AGO, ADAH.

14. Department Adjutant, Eastern Department to Commanding Officer, Second Alabama Infantry, Memorandum, April 3, 1917, AGO, ADAH.

15. Adjutant, State Mobilization Camp to Passenger Agent, Western of Alabama Railway, Memorandum, May 13, 1917; Commanding Officer, Company M, First Alabama Infantry to Commanding Officer, First Alabama Infantry, Memorandum, May 23, 1917, all in AGO, ADAH.

16. Brigadier General Robert Steiner to Commanding General, Southeastern Department, Telegram, May 15, 1917, AGO, ADAH.

17. First Alabama Infantry Headquarters, Memorandum, April 13, 1917; Commanding Officer, Company C, First Alabama Infantry to Commanding Officer, First Alabama Infantry, Memorandum, May 23, 1917, and 1st Indorsement, June 4, 1917; Return of the First Regiment of Alabama Infantry, April 1917; State Mobilization Camp, Memorandum, April 19, 1917; Adjutant, Eastern Department Headquarters to Commanding General, Alabama Brigade, Memorandum, April 21, 1917; Commanding Officer, First Alabama Infantry to Commanding Officer, Bay Minette Detachment, Memorandum, April 13, 1917, and 1st Indorsement, April 14, 1917; Captain Howard S. J.

Walker to Commanding Officer, First Alabama Infantry, Memorandum, May 23, 1917, all in AGO, ADAH.

18. Post Return of First Alabama Infantry, May 1917; Special Orders No. 137, First Alabama Infantry Headquarters, June 27, 1917, all in AGO, ADAH.

19. Commanding Officer, First Alabama Infantry to Commanding General, Southeastern Department, Memorandum, May 19, 1917, AGO, ADAH.

20. Post Return of First Alabama Infantry, May 1917, AGO, ADAH.

21. Adjutant, First Alabama Infantry to Commanding Officer, Company B, First Alabama Infantry, Memorandum, May 11, 1917, and 1st Indorsement, May 24, 1917, AGO, ADAH.

22. First Infantry Headquarters, Memorandum, April 8, 1917; R. C. Reiman to Captain Leon Schwarz, July 4, 1917, all in AGO, ADAH.

23. Commanding Officer, State Mobilization Camp to Commanding Officer, First Alabama Infantry, Memorandum, June 12, 1917; *Montgomery Advertiser* [June 12, 1917], clipping, all in AGO, ADAH.

24. Commanding Officer, First Alabama Infantry to Commanding Officer, Bay Minette Detachment, Memorandum, April 13, 1917, AGO, ADAH.

25. C. E. Vernell to M. Gavin, June 23, 1917; J. B. Turner to Colonel F. M. Maddox, June 25, 1917, all in AGO, ADAH.

26. First Alabama Infantry Headquarters, Memorandum, May 12, 1917, AGO, ADAH.

27. Narcissa L. Shawhan to Commanding Officer, First Alabama Regiment, June 11, 1917; Supply Company Headquarters, Memorandum, May 29, 1917, all in AGO, ADAH.

28. Narcissa L. Shawhan to Commanding Officer, First Alabama Regiment, June 11, 1917; Supply Company Headquarters, Memorandum, May 29, 1917, all in AGO, ADAH.

29. Colonel J. M. Arrasmith, Infantry, Special Instructor to Commanding General, Eastern Department, Memorandum, April 23, 1917, AGO, ADAH.

30. Commanding Officer, Third Battalion, Second Alabama Infantry to Commanding General, First Alabama Brigade, Memorandum, August 14, 1917; Second Alabama Infantry Headquarters, General Orders No. 3, April 21, 1917, all in AGO, ADAH.

31. Ibid.; "Orders for Sentinels on Frisco and Harahan Bridges, Memphis, Tenn." [1917]; [Robert] Steiner to Major Carl H. Seals, Telegram, April 22, 1917; Commanding Officer, Second Alabama Infantry Detachment to Commanding General, State Mobilization Camp, Memorandum, April 22, 1917; Commanding Officer, Second Alabama Infantry Detachment to Commanding Officer, State Mobilization Camp, 1st Indorsement, April 26, 1917, all in AGO, ADAH.

32. Commanding Officer, Second Alabama Infantry Detachment to Commanding General, State Mobilization Camp, Memoranda, April 23, 26, 1917, AGO, ADAH.

33. Commanding Officer, Second Alabama Infantry Detachment to Commanding General, State Mobilization Camp, Memorandum, June 4, 1917, AGO, ADAH.

34. First Alabama District Headquarters, Second Alabama Infantry, General Orders No. 8, April 28, 1917, AGO, ADAH.

35. Commanding Officer, Company M, Fourth Alabama Infantry to Commanding Officer, Fourth Alabama Infantry, Memorandum, April 8, 1917; Commanding Officer, Company M, Fourth Alabama Infantry to Commanding Officer, Second Alabama Infantry, Memorandum, April 12, 1917, all in AGO, RG 407, NARA.

36. Commanding Officer, Company M, Fourth Alabama Infantry to Lieutenant James W. Driver, Memorandum, April 18, 1917, AGO, RG 407, NARA; Commanding Officer, Company M, Fourth Alabama Infantry to Commanding Officer, First Alabama Brigade, Memorandum, April 19, 1917, AGO, ADAH.

37. Captain Graves to Commanding General Steiner, Telegram, April 18, 1917; Statement regarding accident by John C. Austin, n.d., all in AGO, ADAH.

38. Report of Board . . . on Death of Private Avner Jones, First Squadron, First Alabama Cavalry Headquarters, June 16, 1917, AGO, ADAH.

39. Commanding Officer, First Squadron, First Alabama Cavalry to Commanding Officer, State Mobilization Camp, Memorandum, April 23, 1917, AGO, ADAH.

40. Commanding Officer, State Mobilization Camp to Commanding General, Southeastern Department, Memorandum, April 28, 1917; Commanding Officer, First Squadron, First Alabama Cavalry to Commanding General, State Mobilization Camp, Memorandum, April 24, 1917, with attached statements of Private Fred Campbell and Private Marion Roberts, all in AGO, ADAH.

41. Commanding Officer, State Mobilization Camp to Major B. F. McMorris, Memorandum, April 25, 1917; Commanding Officer, First Squadron, First Alabama Cavalry to Commanding General, State Mobilization Camp, Memorandum, April 24, 1917, all in AGO, ADAH.

42. Although the inclination is to draw some conclusion about these shootings having racial overtones, the evidence simply does not support such a conclusion.

43. *Illustrated Review, Fourth Alabama Infantry;* Commanding Officer, Company M, Fourth Alabama Infantry to Commanding Officer, Fourth Alabama Infantry, Memorandum, June 11, 1917, AGO, RG 407, NARA; Robert E. Steiner to Major General Leonard Wood, July 9, 1917; Field Return of the First Alabama Infantry, July 26, 1917; Commanding Officer, First Alabama Infantry to Commanding General, First Alabama Brigade, Memoranda, July 2, 5, 8, 15, 1917; [F. M.] Maddox to Commanding Officer, State Mobilization Camp, Telegrams, July 9, 12, 19, 1917, all in AGO, ADAH.

44. William H. Amerine, *Alabama's Own in France* (New York, 1919), 50; *Illustrated Review, Fourth Alabama Infantry.*

45. Laura M. Elmore to R. E. Steiner, April 12, 1917; Mobilization Camp Headquarters, Memoranda, April 2, 17, 1917; E. J. Devinney to R. E. Steiner, April 14, 1917, all in AGO, ADAH.

46. Robert E. Steiner to Montgomery Light and Traction Company, June 16,

July 8, 1917; R. E. Steiner to Board of Revenue of Montgomery County, July 8, 1917; W. F. Black to Robert E. Steiner, July 14, 1917; Commanding Officer, First Alabama Brigade to Captain William A. Carlton, Memorandum, July 4, 1917; Aide-de-Camp, Acting Adjutant to Crampton Lumber Company, July 30, 1917, all in AGO, ADAH.

47. Commanding Officer, State Mobilization Camp to Regimental Commanders, Memorandum, May 18, 1917; [State Mobilization Camp, Quartermaster Corps], Memorandum, June 11, 1917; Assistant Surgeon, First Alabama Infantry to Commanding Officer, First Alabama Infantry, Memorandum, June 22, 1917; Brigadier General R. E. Steiner to Commanding Officer, Southeastern Department, 5th Indorsement, June 27, 1917, all in AGO, ADAH.

48. State Mobilization Camp Headquarters, Memorandum, May 6, 1917; State Mobilization Camp, Memorandum No. 140, September 11, 1917, all in AGO, ADAH. Many of Steiner's orders reflected the orders that Steiner received from his superiors, especially those regarding health and sanitation.

49. State Mobilization Camp Headquarters, Memorandum, April 4, 1917; Eastern Department Headquarters, Bulletin No. 51, April 17, 1917; State Mobilization Camp, Memorandum, April 27, 1917; State Mobilization Camp Headquarters, Memorandum, July 3, 1917, all in AGO, ADAH.

50. Southeastern Department Headquarters, Bulletin No. 51, June 20, 1917; First Alabama Infantry Headquarters, Memorandum, July 31, 1917, all in AGO, ADAH.

51. State Mobilization Camp Headquarters, Memorandum No. 90, August 26, 1917; State Mobilization Camp Headquarters, Memorandum, May 25, 1917, all in AGO, ADAH.

52. State Mobilization Camp Headquarters, Memorandum, July 3, 1917; Commanding Officer, First Alabama Brigade to Richard Tollis, Montgomery Light and Traction Company, Memorandum, June 27, 1917, all in AGO, ADAH.

53. State Mobilization Camp Headquarters, Memorandum, April 25, 1917; First Alabama Infantry Headquarters, Memorandum, April 27, 1917, all in AGO, ADAH.

54. First Alabama Infantry Headquarters, Memorandum, April 27, 1917; Commanding Officer, First Alabama Cavalry to Second Lieutenant E. D. Thames, First Alabama Cavalry, Memorandum, July 8, 1917, all in AGO, ADAH.

55. "Report of Inspection," May 14, 15, 1917; Lieutenant Colonel William J. Vaiden, First Alabama Cavalry to Commanding Officer, First Alabama Cavalry, Memorandum, June 26, 1917, all in AGO, ADAH. Much of the credit for improved sanitation conditions was due to the efforts of William Gorgas, surgeon general of the army. See John M. Gibson, *Physician to the World: The Life of General William C. Gorgas* (Tuscaloosa, AL; reprint, 1989), 232–35.

56. Commanding Officer, Mobilization Camp to Commanding Officer, First Alabama Cavalry, Memorandum, July 8, 1917; Commanding Officer, Mobilization Camp to Commanding Officer, Fourth Alabama Infantry, Memorandum, July 8, 1917; First Alabama Cavalry Headquarters to Commanding General, First Alabama Brigade, 1st Indorsement, July 9, 1917; Commanding Officer, Fourth Alabama Infantry to Com-

manding Officer, First Alabama Brigade, 1st Indorsement, July 9, 1917, all in AGO, ADAH.

57. H. H. Forcheimer, Alabama Medical Corps to Commanding Officer, First Alabama Infantry, Memorandum, August 2, 1917; Acting Sanitary Inspector to Camp Commander, State Mobilization Camp, Memorandum, August 7, 1917; Captain W. A. Padgett, Medical Corps to Commanding Officer, First Alabama Infantry, Memorandum, June 26, 1917; First Alabama Infantry Headquarters, Memorandum, April 20, 1917, all in AGO, ADAH.

58. State Mobilization Camp Headquarters, Memoranda, April 10, June 8, 1917; Captain W. A. Padgett to Commanding Officer, Company H, First Alabama Infantry, Memorandum, August 1, 1917, all in AGO, ADAH. See also Howard L. Holley, *The History of Medicine in Alabama* (Birmingham, AL, 1982), 285–86; and Shirley G. Schoonover, "Alabama Public Health Campaign," *Alabama Review* 28 (July 1975): 231–32.

59. Southeastern Department Headquarters, Circular (unnumbered), July 18, 1917; State Mobilization Camp Headquarters, Memorandum, April 14, 1917; Southeastern Department Headquarters, Memorandum, May 23, 1917; Commanding Officer, Field Hospital No. 1 to Commanding General, First Alabama Brigade, Memorandum, May 16, 1917; Commanding Officer, State Mobilization Camp to Commanding Officers, First, Second, and Fourth Alabama Infantry, First Alabama Cavalry, Memorandum, May 22, 1917; Assistant Surgeon, First Alabama Infantry to Commanding Officer, First Alabama Infantry, Memorandum, June 24, 1917, all in AGO, ADAH.

60. Camp Surgeon to Commanding Officer, First Alabama Brigade, Memorandum, September 8, 1917, AGO, ADAH.

61. Field Hospital No. 1, State Mobilization Camp, Memorandum, May 28, 1917, AGO, ADAH.

62. State Mobilization Camp Headquarters, Memorandum, July 3, 1917, AGO, ADAH.

63. Commanding Officer, State Mobilization Camp to Regimental, Separate Unit, and Detachment Commanding Officers, Memorandum, May 29, 1917; State Mobilization Camp Headquarters, Memorandum, July 3, 1917; Surgeon, First Alabama Infantry to Commanding Officer, First Alabama Infantry, Memorandum, June 12, 1917; Memorandum No. 102, State Mobilization Camp Headquarters, August 30, 1917, all in AGO, ADAH; Allan M. Brandt, *No Magic Bullet: A Social History of Venereal Disease in the United States since 1880* (New York, 1985), 74, 76.

64. General Orders No. 1, State Mobilization Camp Headquarters, March 30, 1917; Second Alabama Infantry Headquarters, Memorandum, July 16, 1917; "Scheme of Instructions," Fourth Alabama Infantry Headquarters, July 15, 1917; "Drill Schedule for First Alabama Cavalry," July 16, 1917; "Schedule of Instructions for First Alabama Brigade for Period of Six Weeks Beginning August 6th, 1917," all in AGO, ADAH. See also G. S. Turner and J. J. Fulmer, *Battle Fire Training* (Fort Leavenworth, KS, n.d.).

65. Commanding Officer, Ambulance Company No. 1 to Commanding Gen-

eral, State Mobilization Camp, Memorandum, April 30, 1917; Captain Thomas W. Palmer, Jr., First Alabama Cavalry to Commanding Officer, First Alabama Cavalry, Memorandum, June 17, 1917; Commanding Officer, Alabama Medical Corps to Commanding General, First Alabama Brigade, Memorandum, July 5, 1917; Commanding Officer, Field Hospital No. 1 to Commanding General, First Alabama Brigade, Memorandum, July 9, 1917; Return of Field Hospital No. 1, July 1917; Commanding Officer, Alabama Field Hospital to Commanding General, First Alabama Brigade, Memorandum [July 6 or 7, 1917], all in AGO, ADAH.

66. *Historical Annual, National Guard of the State of Alabama, 1938* (Baton Rouge, 1938), 16; General Orders No. 8, Thirty-First Division Headquarters, September 18, 1917, AGO, ADAH; Special Orders No. 4, Thirty-First Division Headquarters, September 10, 1917, AGO, ADAH.

67. WAP(?) to "Charlie," August 25, 1917; First Lieutenant Richard T. Rives, Company A, Signal Corps to Commanding General, First Alabama Brigade, Memorandum, September 9, 1917, all in AGO, ADAH.

68. Adjutant General of the Army to Commanding General, Southeastern Department, Memorandum and Appendix A, August 1, 1917, AGO, ADAH. The remaining states represented in the division were New Hampshire, Massachusetts, Indiana, Michigan, Rhode Island, Maryland, California, South Carolina, Missouri, Connecticut, Tennessee, Oklahoma, New Jersey, Nebraska, Oregon, Colorado, Maine, North Carolina, Kansas, Texas, Wisconsin, Georgia, and Pennsylvania.

69. Adjutant, Southeastern Department Headquarters to Commanding General, First Alabama Brigade, Memorandum, August 13, 1917; Commanding Officer, 167th Infantry to Commanding Officer, First Alabama Brigade, Memorandum, August 17, 1917, all in AGO, ADAH.

70. Medical Examiners to the Commanding General, First Alabama Brigade, Memorandum, August 14, 1917, AGO, ADAH.

71. Brigadier General Steiner, First Alabama Brigade to Commanding General, Southeastern Department, Telegram, August 27, 1917, AGO, ADAH.

72. Private E. C. Ming to Commanding Officer, Company G, 167th Infantry, Memorandum, August 24, 1917; Commanding Officer, Company G, 167th Infantry to Commanding Officer, 167th Infantry, 1st Indorsement, August 25, 1917 (quote); Commanding Officer, 167th Infantry to Commanding Officer, First Alabama Brigade, 2d Indorsement, n.d., all in AGO, ADAH.

73. John H. Gardiner, interview by Ivan H. Wallace, Jr., tape recording, Orlando, Florida, December 7, 1991, tape recording in possession of author.

74. [Harry L. Carter], "Little Events and Experiences of the World War, Lohndorf, Germany, January 1919," Typescript, 1, AGO, ADAH.

75. [Southeastern Department Headquarters] to Commanding General, First Alabama Brigade, Telegram, August 15, 1917, AGO, ADAH; [Carter], "Little Events," 1; Gardiner, interview.

76. Commander-in-Chief, American Expeditionary Forces to Commanding Gen-

eral, Forty-Second Division, Memorandum, March 26, 1919; "Battle Participation of the Forty-Second Division," n.d.; Commanding General, Forty-Second Division to Commanding General, Third Army, Memorandum, February 6, 1919; Commanding General, Forty-Second Division to Commanding General, First Army Corps, Memorandum, December 21, 1918; "Summary of History of Forty-Second Division," n.d.; "Brief History of the Forty-Second Division," n.d., all in Records of the American Expeditionary Forces (World War I), RG 120, National Archives and Records Administration (hereafter cited as AEF, RG 120, NARA); *Order of Battle of the United States Land Forces in the World War,* 3 vols. (Washington, DC, reprint, 1988), 2:272–85; Leonard P. Ayres, *The War with Germany: A Statistical Summary,* 2nd ed. (Washington, DC, 1919), 101–18.

77. Commander-in-Chief, American Expeditionary Forces to Commanding General, Forty-Second Division, Memorandum, March 26, 1919; "Battle Participation of the Forty-Second Division," n.d.; Commanding General, Forty-Second Division to Commanding General, Third Army, Memorandum, February 6, 1919; Commanding General, Forty-Second Division to Commanding General, First Army Corps, Memorandum, December 21, 1918; "Summary of History of Forty-Second Division," n.d.; "Brief History of the Forty-Second Division," n.d., all in AEF, RG 120, NARA; *Order of Battle,* 2:272–85; Ayres, *War with Germany,* 101–18; General Order No. 21-C, Forty-Second Division Headquarters, April 1919, quoted in Amerine, *Alabama's Own in France,* 296–98; Amerine, *Alabama's Own in France,* 4, 10, 136–54. For a fuller examination of the 167th's service, see Ruth Smith Truss, "The Alabama National Guard's 167th Infantry Regiment in World War I," *Alabama Review* 56 (January 2003): 3–34.

78. Amerine, *Alabama's Own in France,* 325–39.

79. Ibid., 252–67.

Chapter 3

1. William H. Amerine, *Alabama's Own in France* (New York, 1919), 37, 40, 47; Ruth Smith Truss, "The Alabama National Guard from 1900 to 1920" (PhD diss., University of Alabama, 1992), 207, 246–64, 294; *Montgomery Advertiser,* July 3, 1917; Michael V. R. Thomason, ed., *Mobile: The New History of Alabama's First City* (Tuscaloosa, 2001), 112.

2. Truss, "Alabama National Guard," 308–32; *Montgomery Advertiser,* July 1, 1917.

3. *Montgomery Advertiser,* July 3, 6–8, 1917.

4. Ibid., July 3, 6, 9–10, 27, 1917; Diagram of Camp Sheridan accompanying "Special Report, A Return to Camp Sheridan, Montgomery, Alabama," November 11, 1963, "Alabama in World War I," Folder 25, Public Information Subject Files—County Files, Montgomery County, SG6911, Alabama Department of Archives and History, Montgomery (hereafter cited as ADAH); Ralph D. Cole and W. C. Howells, *The Thirty-Seventh Division in the World War, 1917–1918* (Columbus, OH, 1926), 187.

5. *Montgomery Advertiser,* July 1, 3, 6, 1917, and July 14, 1940; Cole and Howells, *Thirty-Seventh Division,* 178–81, 187.

6. *Montgomery Advertiser,* July 1, 1917; Cole and Howells, *Thirty-Seventh Division,* 184, 187.

7. *Montgomery Advertiser,* July 6, 1917.

8. Ibid., July 8–10, September 20, October 2, 1917.

9. Ibid., July 27, August 31, 1917, May 30, 1918.

10. Ibid., August 31, September 1, 1917; May 30, 1918. On the construction of Camp Sheridan, see also Cole and Howells, *Thirty-Seventh Division,* 187–204.

11. *Montgomery Advertiser,* July 3, 6, 9, 27, October 22, 1917.

12. Ibid., April 28, 1918.

13. Wesley Phillips Newton, *Montgomery in the Good War: Portrait of a Southern City, 1939–1946* (Tuscaloosa, AL, 2000), 66; *Montgomery Advertiser,* June 2, 1918; Beth Taylor Muskat and Mary Ann Neeley, *The Way It Was: Photographs of Montgomery and Her Central Alabama Neighbors* (Montgomery, 1985), 130; Cole and Howells, *Thirty-Seventh Division,* 234–49.

14. *Montgomery Advertiser,* June 4, 1918.

15. Ibid., July 7–8, 10, 25–26, 1917; Truss, "Alabama National Guard," 333–45.

16. *Montgomery Advertiser,* August 31, September 1, October 1–3, 1917; William Warren Rogers, Robert David Ward, Leah Rawls Atkins, and Wayne Flynt, *Alabama: The History of a Deep South State* (Tuscaloosa, AL, 1994), 394; Cole and Howells, *Thirty-Seventh Division,* 207, 223.

17. *Montgomery Advertiser,* October 3, 1917.

18. Ibid., September 18, 1917; Typescript, "Remount Depot, Montgomery," Folder 510, Public Information Subject Files—County Files, Montgomery County, SG6911, ADAH.

19. Cole and Howells, *Thirty-Seventh Division,* 224, 319–33, 369–70; *Montgomery Advertiser,* August 31, October 3, 27, November 27, December 24, 1917; April 30, August 28, 1918.

20. Mary Beth Reed, Charles E. Cantley, and J. W. Joseph, *Fort McClellan, A Popular History* (Stone Mountain, GA, 1993), 69–73, 78; *Montgomery Advertiser,* June 26, 1918; *Anniston Star,* July 2–3, 6, 8–10, 15–16, 18, 22, August 14–16, 20, 22–23, 1917; John A. Cutchins and George Scott Stewart, Jr., *History of the Twenty-Ninth Division "Blue and Gray," 1917–1918* (Philadelphia, 1921), 1–5.

21. Reed, Cantley, and Joseph, *Fort McClellan,* 73–76; *Anniston Star,* August 26, 28, 1917; Cutchins and Stewart, *Twenty-Ninth Division,* 4–5.

22. Reed, Cantley, and Joseph, *Fort McClellan,* 76; *Anniston Star,* August 16, 1917.

23. *Anniston Star,* July 22, August 21, October 5, 1917; Reed, Cantley, and Joseph, *Fort McClellan,* 80–81.

24. Reed, Cantley, and Joseph, *Fort McClellan,* 77; *Anniston Star,* July 13, 15, 17, 19–20, 22, 24, August 13–15, 17, 19–24, 26–29, September 16, 27, October 4, 21, 1917; July 21, 1918; Cutchins and Stewart, *Twenty-Ninth Division,* 5, 8–10, 22, 27, 29, 47–54.

25. *Anniston Star,* August 13–15, September 30, October 1–2, 4–5, 21, 24, 26, December 20, 1917, July 21, 1918; *Montgomery Advertiser,* June 30, July 5, 1918; Reed, Cantley, and Joseph, *Fort McClellan,* 71, 78.

26. *Anniston Star,* September 26, October 2, 1917; Cutchins and Stewart, *Twenty-Ninth Division,* 11–15.

27. Samuel Eliot Morrison, *The Oxford History of the American People* (New York, 1965), 866; Allan R. Millet and Peter Maslowski, *For the Common Defense: A Military History of the United States of America* (New York, 1983), 332.

28. Reed, Cantley, and Joseph, *Fort McClellan,* 79; *Anniston Star,* October 5, 1917, July 21, 1918; *Montgomery Advertiser,* December 6, 1917, June 4, 1918. See also Frank E. Roberts, *The American Foreign Legion: Black Soldiers of the 93rd in World War I* (Annapolis, MD, 2004).

29. *Anniston Star,* October 17, 19, 1917; *Montgomery Advertiser,* October 24, 1917.

30. *Montgomery Advertiser,* November 29, 1917.

31. Ibid., July 7, August 28, 1918; Maurer Maurer, ed., *The U.S. Air Service in World War I* (Washington, DC, 1978), 1:92–115; James Lea Cate, "The Air Service in World War I," *Plans and Early Operations, January 1939 to August 1942,* vol. 1 of *The Army Air Forces in World War II,* ed. Wesley Frank Craven and James Lea Cate, 8–12 (Chicago, 1948); John B. Scott, Jr., *Memories of the Mount: The Story of Mt. Meigs, Alabama* (Montgomery, 1993), 140.

32. Jerome A. Ennels and Wesley Newton, *The Wisdom of Eagles: A History of Maxwell Air Force Base,* 2nd ed. (Montgomery, 2002), 18–20; *Montgomery Advertiser,* June 24, July 5, 11, 1918.

33. *Montgomery Advertiser,* July 16, 19, 23, 28, August 28, 1918; Ennels and Newton, *Wisdom of Eagles,* 19.

34. *Mobile Register,* April 21, June 5, 1918; Scott, *Memories of the Mount,* 141–42; *Montgomery Advertiser,* June 1, 6, 10, 16, 20, August 28, 1918.

35. Cole and Howells, *Thirty-Seventh Division,* 234–35, 376–77, 394–404; Cutchins and Stewart, *Twenty-Ninth Division,* 44–45, 55–56; *Anniston Star,* June 10, 24, 1918; *Montgomery Advertiser,* August 10, 1931, July 24, 1954.

36. *Montgomery Advertiser,* June 7, 9, 1918.

37. Ibid., June 11, 1918.

38. Ibid., June 13, 1918.

39. Ibid., July 20, 1918; *Anniston Star,* August 22, 1917.

40. *Montgomery Advertiser,* June 14, 18, 20, 23–24, July 11, 14, 1918.

41. Andrew Turnbull, *Scott Fitzgerald: A Biography* (New York, 1971), 80–90; Matthew J. Bruccoli, Scottie Fitzgerald Smith, and Joan P. Kerr, eds., *The Romantic Egoists* (Columbia, SC, 2003), 46–47. Fitzgerald's novel was published as *This Side of Paradise.*

42. *Anniston Star,* August 8, 13, 15, 22, 1918.

43. Jeanne Battle Owen Hagedorn, *A Certain Slant of Light: A Family History, 1850–1950* (n.p., n.d.), 56–57.

44. Ruth Truss, "The Alabama National Guard's 167th Infantry Regiment in World War I," *Alabama Review* 56 (January 2003): 23–24; Wesley Phillips Newton, "The Death of a Montgomery Soldier in the Great War," *Montgomery County Historical Society Herald* 9 (October 2001): 5–6; *Montgomery Advertiser*, July 29, 1928; *Anniston Star*, September 23, 26, 1918.

45. J. Wayne Flynt, *Alabama in the Twentieth Century* (Tuscaloosa, AL, 2004), 382; Rogers et al., *Alabama*, 406; *Anniston Star*, September 24, October 18, 1918; *Montgomery Advertiser*, September 17, October 1, 4, 10, 1918.

46. *Montgomery Advertiser*, October 15, 1918. Frank M. Andrews rose to the rank of lieutenant general after the war and became a leading advocate for an independent United States Air Force.

47. Ibid., November 12, 1918; *Anniston Star*, November 12, 1918; Turnbull, *Scott Fitzgerald*, 91–92; Reed, Cantley, and Joseph, *Fort McClellan*, 79.

48. *Montgomery Advertiser*, May 27, 30, June 9–10, 18–19, 21–23, 26, 1918.

49. William H. Zinsser to Thomas M. Owen, January 16, 1919, "Camp Sheridan," Folder 510, Public Information Subject Files—County Files, Montgomery County, SG6911, ADAH; *Montgomery Advertiser*, June 16, 22, 1918, May 10, 1919, November 28, 1920.

50. Ennels and Newton, *Wisdom of Eagles*, 21, 26–27.

51. *Anniston Star*, June 24, July 10–11, 16, 21, 24, August 9, 23, September 17, 18, 25, 1918.

52. Reed, Cantley, and Kerr, *Fort McClellan*, 81–83; David McPherson of Fort McClellan, telephone interview with the author, January 18, 2005.

Chapter 4

1. William Warren Rogers, Robert David Ward, Leah Rawls Atkins, and Wayne Flynt, *Alabama: The History of a Deep South State* (Tuscaloosa, AL, 1994), 371.

2. Charles Octavius Boothe, *Cyclopedia of the Colored Baptists of Alabama* (Birmingham, AL, 1895), 37.

3. August Meier and Elliott Rudwick, "The Boycott Movement against Jim Crow Street Cars in the South, 1900–1906," in *Along the Color Line: Explorations in the Black Experience*, ed. August Meier and Elliott Rudwick (Urbana, IL, 1976), 286; *Mobile Register*, May 17, 1905.

4. Alabama Colored Baptist State Convention, *Journal of the Forty-seventh Annual Session of the Alabama Colored Baptist State Convention Held with the Mt. Zion Baptist Church, Anniston, Alabama, November 18–21, 1914* (Nashville, TN, 1915), 60, available in the Special Collections Department, Samford University Library, Birmingham, AL (hereafter cited as Samford University).

5. Minutes of the New Hope Baptist Association, 1914, 10, Special Collections Department, Samford University.

6. Minutes of the Mt. Pilgrim Association, 1915, 20, Special Collections Department, Samford University.

7. Sandy E. Martin, *Black Baptists and African Missions: The Origin of a Movement, 1880–1915* (Macon, GA, 1989), 199.

8. Wayne Flynt, *Alabama Baptists: Southern Baptists in the Heart of Dixie* (Tuscaloosa, AL, 1998), 298.

9. Alabama Colored Baptist State Convention, *Journal of the Forty-eighth Annual Session of the Alabama Colored Baptist State Convention Held with the First African Baptist Church, Eufaula, November 24–28, 1915* (Selma, AL, 1915), 10, Samford University.

10. Alabama Colored Baptist State Convention, *Jubilee Volume of the Fiftieth Annual Session of the Alabama Colored Baptist State Convention Held with the 6th Avenue Baptist Church, Birmingham, Alabama, November 22–26, 1917* (Selma, AL, 1917), Samford University.

11. Gayraud S. Wilmore, *Black Religion and Black Radicalism* (Garden City, NY, 1972), 166; Rufus Perry, *The Cushite or the Descendants of Ham as Found in the Sacred Scriptures and in the Writings of Ancient Historians and Poets from Noah to the Christian Era* (Springfield, MA, 1893), 52–53; Albert J. Raboteau, *Canaan Land: A Religious History of African Americans* (Oxford, 1999), 51–56.

12. Alabama Colored Baptist State Convention, *Jubilee Volume of the Fiftieth Annual Session,* 38–39.

13. Ibid., 94.

14. W. E. B. DuBois, "Close Ranks," *Crisis,* July 16, 1917, 111.

15. Houston B. Roberson, "Fighting the Good Fight: A History of Dexter Avenue Baptist Church, 1865–1977" (PhD diss., University of North Carolina, 1997), 127–28; *Emancipator,* October 13, November 17, 1917.

16. *Birmingham Reporter,* April 13, 1918.

17. Ibid., March 9, June 22, 1918.

18. E. L. Barrett and J. H. Moorman, *Leaders of the Colored Race in Alabama* (Mobile, AL, 1928), 28.

19. William Breen, "Black Women and the Great War," *Journal of Southern History* 44 (August 1978): 432–36.

20. Ibid., 421 passim.

21. Mary Martha Thomas, *The New Woman in Alabama* (Tuscaloosa, AL, 1992), 69–91.

22. Miscellaneous speeches of J. H. Eason, located in the author's private collection.

23. Minutes of the Alabama Colored Baptist State Convention, 1918, Archives, Selma University, Selma, AL.

24. *Birmingham Reporter,* March 16, 1918.

25. Rogers, *Alabama,* 432. The best book on the Klan in Alabama is Glenn Feldman, *Politics, Society, and the Klan in Alabama, 1915–1949* (Tuscaloosa, AL, 1999).

26. Carl V. Harris, *Political Power in Birmingham, 1871–1921* (Knoxville, 1977), 34–35.

27. McArthur Jackson, "A Historical Study of the Founding and Development of

Tuskegee Institute" (PhD diss., University of North Carolina at Greensboro, 1983), 46–51.

28. Minutes of the Alabama Colored Baptist State Convention, 1919.

29. Minutes of the Alabama Colored Baptist State Convention, 1921, 40–41.

30. Ibid., 48–58.

31. John W. Goodgame, *A Collection of Sermons and Addresses by Rev. John W. Goodgame, Pastor of the Sixth Avenue Baptist Church, Birmingham, Alabama* (Birmingham, AL, n.d.), 18–22.

32. *Birmingham Reporter*, July 10, 1919.

33. Roberson, "Fighting the Good Fight," 129–30; *Emancipator*, June 21, 1919.

Chapter 5

1. For an overview of the Jim Crow era in Alabama and the South, see C. Vann Woodward, *The Strange Career of Jim Crow* (New York, 1957); Leon F. Litwack, *Trouble in Mind: Black Southerners in the Age of Jim Crow* (New York, 1998); Leon F. Litwack, "Jim Crow Blues," *Organization of American Historians Magazine of History* 18, no. 2 (January 2004): 7–11; Howard N. Rabinowitz, *Race Relations in the Urban South, 1865–1890* (New York, 1978); William Cohen, *At Freedom's Edge: Black Mobility and the White Southern Quest for Racial Control, 1861–1915* (Baton Rouge, 1991).

2. Louis R. Harlan, *Booker T. Washington: The Wizard of Tuskegee, 1901–1915* (New York, 1983), 408, 431–34; Nancy J. Weiss, "The Negro and the New Freedom: Fighting Wilsonian Segregation," *Political Science Quarterly* 84 (March 1969): 61–79; Kathleen Wolgemuth, "Woodrow Wilson and Federal Segregation," *Journal of Negro History* 44 (April 1959): 158–73; Mark Ellis, *Race, War, and Surveillance: African Americans and the United States Government during World War I* (Bloomington, IN, 2001), xiv–xv; Charles Flint Kellogg, *NAACP: A History of the National Association for the Advancement of Colored People, Vol. 1: 1909–1920* (Baltimore, 1973), 161–71.

3. Allen Woodrow Jones, "Alabama," in *The Black Press in the South, 1865–1979*, ed. Henry Lewis Suggs (New York, 1983), 41; Florette Henri, *Black Migration: Movement North, 1900–1920* (Garden City, NY, 1976), 269–70; Theodore Kornweibel, Jr., "Apathy and Dissent: Black America's Negative Responses to World War I," *South Atlantic Quarterly* 80, no. 3 (Summer 1981): 322–23.

4. Louis R. Harlan, *Booker T. Washington: The Making of a Black Leader, 1856–1901* (New York, 1972), 160–61, 218–19; August Meier, *Negro Thought in America, 1880–1915: Racial Ideologies in the Age of Booker T. Washington* (Ann Arbor, MI, 1969), 103–6.

5. Ellis, *Race, War, and Surveillance*, 6–7, 22.

6. *Montgomery Advertiser*, n.d., ca. April 21, 1917, quoted in Ellis, *Race, War, and Surveillance*, 9.

7. "Keep Cool: Avoid the Sensationalist," *Birmingham Ledger*, April 7, 1917.

8. Quoted in Ellis, *Race, War, and Surveillance*, 14.

9. *Birmingham Weekly Voice*, n.d., quoted in *Birmingham Ledger*, April 7, 1917.

10. *Birmingham Weekly Voice,* April 14, 1917.

11. Quoted in Ellis, *Race, War, and Surveillance,* 18.

12. N. E. Cashin and J. A. Wilson to Gov. Charles Henderson, April 19, 1917 (with enclosed petition "By the Colored Citizens of Morgan County"); Henderson to Wilson, April 23, 1917, Alabama Governor (1915–1919: Henderson), Administrative Files (hereafter cited as Henderson Files), SG225XX, Alabama Department of Archives and History (ADAH), Montgomery.

13. Dr. Thomas C. Savage to Gov. Charles M. Henderson, February 7, 1917; Dr. T. C. Reid to Henderson, April 10, 1917; Robert Mayer to Henderson, April 10, 1917; Demopolis Citizens' Petition to the Governor, n.d., ca. February–April 1917, all in Henderson Files, ADAH.

14. John C. Webb to Henderson, April 10, 1917, Henderson Files, ADAH.

15. Dr. T. C. Reid to Henderson, April 10, 1917, Henderson Files, ADAH.

16. Henderson to John C. Webb, April 12, 1917; Henderson to Robert Mayer, April 12, 1917; Henderson to Dr. T. C. Reid, April 13, 1917, Henderson Files, ADAH.

17. W. F. Garth to Henderson, April 8, 1917, Henderson Files, ADAH.

18. Henderson to Garth, April 14, 1917, Henderson Files, ADAH.

19. Albert Burton Moore, *History of Alabama* (Tuscaloosa, AL, 1951), 758; William Warren Rogers, Robert David Ward, Leah Rawls Atkins, and Wayne Flynt, *Alabama: The History of a Deep South State* (Tuscaloosa, AL, 1994), 405; Thomas Fleming, *The Illusion of Victory: America in World War I* (New York, 2003), 106, 118, 250.

20. Ellis, *Race, War, and Surveillance,* 23.

21. "Keep Cool: Avoid the Sensationalist," *Birmingham Ledger,* April 7, 1917.

22. Monroe Nathan Work, ed., *Negro Yearbook: Annual Encyclopedia of the Negro, 1917–18* (Tuskegee, AL, 1919), 8–12, 117; T. Lynn Smith, "The Redistribution of the Negro Population of the United States, 1910–1960," *Journal of Negro History* 51, no. 3 (July 1966): 158; Mayor Harry Pillans to Editor, *Cincinnati Post,* May 12, 1917; Pillans to Mayors of Philadelphia, Pittsburgh, Detroit, Chicago, St. Louis, and Homestead, January 24, 1917, Mobile City Commission Records, Mobile Municipal Archives, Mobile, AL; Henri, *Black Migration,* 52.

23. George Edmund Haynes, "Conditions among Negroes in the Cities," *Annals of the American Academy of Political and Social Science* 49 (September 1913): 110.

24. "Jim Is Coming Home," *Mobile Register,* April 15, 1917.

25. *Birmingham Ledger,* April 6, 1917.

26. "North Does Not Relish Its Negro Problem," ibid., May 31, 1917.

27. Henri, *Black Migration,* 53, 352.

28. Quoted in Emmett J. Scott, "Additional Letters of Negro Migrants of 1916–1918," *Journal of Negro History* 4 (October 1919): 444.

29. Quoted in Emmett J. Scott, "Letters of Negro Migrants, 1916–18," *Journal of Negro History* 4 (July 1919): 332.

30. Quoted in ibid., 329.

31. Quoted in Scott, "Additional Letters of Negro Migrants," 451–52.

32. Jones, "Alabama," 41.

33. *Birmingham Weekly Voice,* July 14, 1917.

34. Ibid., June 16, 1917. See also "The School Question," ibid., June 23, 1917.

35. Ellis, *Race, War, and Surveillance,* 21–22.

36. Smith, "Redistribution of the Negro Population," 161; Henri, *Black Migration,* 69.

37. N. E. Cashin and J. A. Wilson to Gov. Charles Henderson, April 19, 1917 (with enclosed petition "By the Colored Citizens of Morgan County"), Henderson Files, ADAH; C. H. Hudson, principal, Brundidge Public and Industrial School, to editor, *Montgomery Journal,* April 22, 1917; Kornweibel, "Apathy and Dissent," 322.

38. *Mobile Register,* April 8, 1917.

39. Ellis, *Race, War, and Surveillance,* 14; "Moton Urges Negro to Work for Country," *Montgomery Journal,* April 22, 1917.

40. Walter S. Buchanan to Gov. Charles Henderson, March 29, 1917, Henderson Files, ADAH.

41. Henderson to Buchanan, March 29, 1917, ibid.

42. *Montgomery Journal,* April 22, 26, 1917.

43. Rogers et al., *Alabama,* 402.

44. *Birmingham Weekly Voice,* May 12, 1917.

45. *Mobile Register,* April 8, 15, 1917.

46. "Negroes Loyalty Meeting," *Mobile Register,* April 17, 1917.

47. "Resolutions Adopted by Negro Miners at a Mass Meeting Held June 27, 1917, at Sipsey, Ala.," Henderson Files, ADAH.

48. Rogers et al., *Alabama,* 418–21.

49. Fleming, *Illusion of Victory,* 87; Ellis, *Race, War, and Surveillance,* 11.

50. "Giving Our Soldiers a Square Deal," *Montgomery Emancipator,* October 6, 1917.

51. *Montgomery Advertiser,* n.d., quoted in ibid.

52. Henri, *Black Migration,* 272–73, 289–91; John Hope Franklin, *From Slavery to Freedom: A History of Negro Americans* (New York, 1969), 455, 458–59; *Camp Dodger,* October 19, November 2, 1917; *Montgomery Emancipator,* February 16, 1918.

53. Byron Farwell, *Over There: The United States in the Great War, 1917–1918* (New York, 1999), 50–51; Fleming, *Illusion of Victory,* 95–96.

54. E. T. Attwell to Gov. Charles Henderson, May 8, 1917, Henderson Files, ADAH; Franklin, *From Slavery to Freedom,* 471; Attwell to Herbert Hoover, December 21, 1921, January 10, 1924, June 20, November 6, 1928; Attwell to Edgar Rickard, November 13, 1928; Misc. Correspondence, 1929–31, all in Secretary's File and Subject File, Herbert Hoover Presidential Library, West Branch, IA.

55. Attwell to Henderson, May 8, 1917, Henderson Files, ADAH.

56. Attwell to Henderson, May 3, 8, 1917, ibid. The quote "a little missionary work" is from the May 8 letter.

57. Henderson to Attwell, May 8, 1917, ibid.

58. *Birmingham Weekly Voice,* May 26, 1917.

59. Theodore Rosengarten, *All God's Dangers: The Life of Nate Shaw* (New York, 1975), 169; Kornweibel, "Apathy and Dissent," 323.

60. Quoted in Ellis, *Race, War, and Surveillance,* 47.

61. Jeanette Keith, "The Politics of Southern Draft Resistance, 1917–1918: Class, Race and Conscription in the Rural South," *Journal of American History* 87 (March 2001): 1335–61; Ronald Schaffer, "The Home Front," *Organization of American Historians Magazine of History* 17, no. 1 (October 2002): 23; Ellis, *Race, War, and Surveillance,* 16; Theodore Kornweibel, Jr., *"Investigate Everything": Federal Efforts to Compel Black Loyalty during World War I* (Bloomington, IN, 2004), passim.

62. *Alabama Adjutant General's Quadrennial Report, 1922* (Montgomery, 1922), 111–13.

63. *Birmingham Weekly Voice,* June 9, 1917.

64. Work, *Negro Year Book, 1917–18,* 88.

65. *Tuskegee News,* June 14, 1917.

66. Ellis, *Race, War, and Surveillance,* 16.

67. Henri, *Black Migration,* 264–65; Kellogg, *NAACP,* 221.

68. Quoted in Franklin, *From Slavery to Freedom,* 460.

69. Ibid., 457.

70. Harlan, *Making of a Black Leader,* 260–61; Ellis, *Race, War, and Surveillance,* 54–56, 230–31; "Eminent Negro Speaker Here," *Camp Dodger,* May 10, 1918.

71. Franklin, *From Slavery to Freedom,* 461; Ellis, *Race, War, and Surveillance,* 86.

72. *Birmingham News,* October 27, 1917, quoted in Work, *Negro Year Book, 1917–18,* 83; "Selma Ablaze with Patriotism," *Montgomery Emancipator,* April 20, 1918.

73. *Birmingham Weekly Voice,* June 9, 1917; Glenn Feldman, "Lynching in Alabama, 1889–1921," *Alabama Review* 48, no. 2 (April 1995): 134–39.

74. Thomas M. Owen, *History of Alabama and Dictionary of Alabama Biography* (Chicago, 1921), 4:1255; Meier, *Negro Thought in America,* 182–84; Kellogg, *NAACP,* 76–77.

75. Allen W. Jones, "Thomas M. Campbell: Black Agricultural Leader of the New South," *Agricultural History* 53, no. 1 (January 1979): 48; Work, *Negro Year Book, 1917–18,* 96–97; Franklin, *From Slavery to Freedom,* 468–69; "Negro Soldiers Real Fighters, Says Dr. Moton," *Camp Dodger,* August 16, 1918.

76. Work, *Negro Year Book, 1917–18,* 74–75.

77. Ellis, *Race, War, and Surveillance,* 158–59.

78. *Montgomery Emancipator,* July 26, 1919, quoted in Jones, "Alabama," 42.

79. Ellis, *Race, War, and Surveillance,* 207–8; John Patrick Finnegan, *Military Intelligence* (Washington, DC, 1998), 29.

80. Quoted in Ellis, *Race, War, and Surveillance,* 204.

81. R. R. Moton, *Finding A Way Out* (New York, 1920), 263.

82. Quoted in Ellis, *Race, War, and Surveillance,* 209; see also Franklin, *From Slavery to Freedom,* 469–70; Kellogg, *NAACP,* 274–75.

83. *Alabama Adjutant General's Quadrennial Report, 1922,* 154–68.

84. Ellis, *Race, War, and Surveillance*; Kornweibel, *"Investigate Everything."*

85. Feldman, "Lynching in Alabama," 136–41.

86. Blaine A. Brownell, *The Urban Ethos in the South, 1920–1930* (Baton Rouge, 1975), 48–49, 52, 58, 136–38, 142–46.

87. Robert R. Rea, *History at Auburn: The First One Hundred Years of the Auburn University History Department* (Auburn, AL, 1991), 19–21, 24–32.

88. Moore, *History of Alabama*, 759. Moore's book was revised in 1934 and again in 1951.

89. Rogers et al., *Alabama*, 408; Wayne Flynt, *Alabama in the Twentieth Century* (Tuscaloosa, AL, 2004), 318–35, 376–83.

Chapter 6

1. *Florence Times*, April 20, 1917.

2. Robert J. Norrell, *Reaping the Whirlwind: The Civil Rights Movement in Tuskegee* (New York, 1985); John Egerton, *Speak Now against the Day: The Generation before the Civil Rights Movement in the South* (Chapel Hill, NC, 1995); Neil R. McMillen, *Dark Journey: Black Mississippians in the Age of Jim Crow* (Urbana, IL, 1990).

3. Norrell, *Reaping the Whirlwind;* McMillen, *Dark Journey;* Samuel C. Hyde, Jr., ed., *Sunbelt Revolution: The Historical Progression of the Civil Rights Struggle in the Gulf South, 1866–2000* (Gainesville, FL, 2003).

4. "Muscle Shoals: A Plan for the Use of the United States Properties on the Tennessee River by Private Industry of the Manufacture of Fertilizers and Other Useful Products," Muscle Shoals Commission (1931), Tennessee Valley Technical Library, Muscle Shoals, AL; Telegram, John H. Bankhead, Sr., and Oscar Underwood to John W. Worthington, October 1, 1917, John H. Bankhead, Sr., Papers, LPR 49, Alabama Department of Archives and History, Montgomery, AL (hereafter cited as Bankhead Papers, ADAH); John Bankhead to John W. Worthington, February 25, 1918, Bankhead Papers, ADAH; Nashville Section of the Engineering Association of the South, *America's Gibraltar: Muscle Shoals, A Brief for the Establishment of Our Nitrate Plant at Muscle Shoals on the Tennessee River* (n.p., 1916), Special Collections, Collier Library, University of North Alabama, Florence, AL (hereafter cited as Collier Library).

5. U.S. Bureau of the Census, "Table 1, Farms and Farm Property by Counties, United States," *Thirteenth Census of the United States Taken in the Year 1910*, vol. 6, *Agricultural Reports by State, with Statistics for Counties* (Washington, DC, 1913), 33, 36; "Table 2, Number, Acreage, and Value of Farms Classified by Tenure, Color and Nativity of Farmers, and Mortgage Debt," ibid., 41; Pete Daniel, *Breaking the Land: The Transformation of the Cotton, Tobacco, and Rice Cultures since 1880* (Urbana, IL, 1985), 7–9; *Florence Herald*, October 18, 1917.

6. *Florence Herald*, October 18, 1917; U.S. Bureau of the Census, "Table 1, Composition and Characteristics of the Population for the State and for Counties," *Thirteenth Census of the United States Taken in the Year 1910*, vol. 2, *Population Reports by States*

with Statistics for Counties, Cities, and Other Civil Divisions (Washington, DC, 1913), 48, 55; "Table 4, Composition and Characteristics of the Population for the State and for Counties for Places of 2,500 to 10,000," ibid., 62; "Table 2, Number, Acreage, and Value of Farms Classified by Tenure, Color and Nativity of Farmers, and Mortgage Debt," *Thirteenth Census of the United States,* vol. 6, *Agricultural Reports*, 41, 43; *Florence Times,* May 18, 1917; *Florence Herald,* December 16, 1900.

7. McMillen, *Dark Journey,* 7–8.

8. Ibid.; Alabama Constitution (1901), art. 8, sec. 178 and 186; Jimmie Frank Gross, "Alabama Politics and the Negro, 1874–1901" (PhD diss., University of Georgia, 1969), 274–75.

9. *Florence Times,* April 20, 1917, April 5, 1901; *Florence Herald,* July 24, 1903; "Along the Color Line," *Crisis: A Record of the Darker Races* 3, no. 1 (November 1911): 12.

10. Elizabeth Womack McDonald, *History of the Florence City Schools, 1820–1967,* Alabama Collection, Collier Library; Alabama Constitution (1901), art. 14, sec. 256; *Florence Times,* April 12, 1901.

11. McDonald, *History of the Florence City Schools,* 30; *Florence Times,* October 20, 1899, April 12, 1901, February 8, 1918; *Florence Herald,* June 26, 1903; *Florence Democrat,* February 2, 1900.

12. *Clifton Mirror,* March 3, 1905; *Florence Evening Bulletin,* February 22, 1901; *Florence Times,* September 1, 1903.

13. Ronald Schaffer, *America in the Great War: The Rise of the War Welfare Sate* (New York, 1991), 75–90; John Hammond Moore, "Charleston in World War I: Seeds of Change," *South Carolina Historical Magazine* 1 (1985): 46, 49; McMillen, *Dark Journey,* 302, 303–6.

14. U.S. Congress, House, Select Committee on Expenditures in the War Department, *War Expenditures: Hearings before the Select Committee on Expenditures in the War Department,* 66th Cong., 1st and 2nd sess. (Washington, DC, 1921), 3:30–31; *Florence Times,* November 16, 1917, March 29, June 7, 1918; *Florence Herald,* December 13, 1917, "U.S. Nitrate Plant Number 2: Muscle Shoals, Alabama, Souvenir of Inspection Team by Officials and Citizens of the Tri-Cities" (1919), Florence Vertical File, Archives and Special Collections, Collier Library.

15. "U.S. Nitrate Plant Number 2"; *Florence Times,* March 1, 1918.

16. Manuscript Census Returns, *Fourteenth Census of the United States Taken in the Year 1920,* Lauderdale County, Alabama, Population Schedules, Wilson Dam Precinct, National Archives Microfilm Series T-625A, Reel 27, Washington, DC.

17. Ibid.

18. "The Horizon," *Crisis,* 15, no. 1 (November 1917): 37; "The Horizon," *Crisis* 16, no. 6 (October 1918): 293; *War Expenditures: Hearings,* 32–33; *Florence Times,* March 1, 1918.

19. *Sheffield Standard,* January 12, 1917; *Florence Times,* December 21, 1917.

20. *Florence Herald,* March 2, May 2, 1918, *Florence Times,* April 12, 1918.

21. *Florence Times,* January 25, March 1, 1918; *Florence Herald,* March 21, 1918.

22. *Florence Times,* January 25, March 1, 1918; *Florence Herald,* March 21, 1918.

23. *Florence Herald,* March 21, 1918; *Florence Times,* February 8, 1918.

24. Daniel Schaffer, "War Mobilization in Muscle Shoals, Alabama, 1917–1918," *Alabama Review* 39 (January 1986): 133–34, 141–42; *Florence Times,* November 1, 1918; *War Expenditures: Hearings,* 41.

25. Minutes of the Florence Board of Commissioners, May 21, 1918, City Clerk's Office, Florence Municipal Building, Florence, Alabama; *Florence Times,* November 1, 1918; *Florence Herald,* October 31, 1918.

26. *Florence Herald,* March 14, 21, 1918; *Florence Times,* May 3, 1918; Fred C. Butler, Memoranda of Unsatisfactory Community Conditions in Existence at Ordnance Projects, to Chairman, Committee on Conditions of Living (n.d.), Records of the War Labor Policies Board, RG 1, National Archives and Records Administration (hereinafter cited as WLPB, RG 1, NARA).

27. Henry M. McKiven, Jr., *Iron and Steel: Class, Race, and Community in Birmingham, Alabama, 1875–1920* (Chapel Hill, NC, 1995), 4.

28. L. A. Gabriel to A. L. Lewis, July 21, 1918, WLPB, RG1, NARA; Charles Flint Kellogg, *NAACP: A History of the National Association for the Advancement of Colored People* (Baltimore, 1967), 1:269.

29. *War Expenditures: Hearings,* 42–43.

30. Sally E. Hadden, *Slave Patrols: Law and Violence in Virginia and the Carolinas* (Cambridge, MA, 2001), 167–220; Jon K. Damico, "The Rush to the Colors: North Louisiana Responds to the Great War, 1917," *Southern Studies* 6, no. 2 (Summer 1995): 25–43; *Florence Times,* February 22, 1918; Minutes of the Florence Board of Commissioners, July 9, 1918.

31. McMillen, *Dark Journey,* 305; *Florence Herald,* January 24, 1918; *Florence Times,* March 15, 1918; Minutes of the Florence Board of Commissioners, May 21, 1918.

32. Reports concerning the dismissal of the black bricklayers fail to explain why the NAACP was unsuccessful in attempting to reinstate the workers; Kellogg, *NAACP,* 268–69; "Story of the Branches," *Crisis* 17, no. 6 (April 1919): 281.

33. Jessie Thomas Moore, Jr., *A Search for Equality: The National Urban League, 1910–1961* (University Park, PA, 1981), 47–50.

34. Kellogg, *NAACP,* 266–70; George E. Haynes, *The Negro at Work during the World War and during Reconstruction,* Second Study on Negro Labor (Washington, DC, 1920), Records of the U.S. Department of Labor, RG 174, National Archives and Records Administration (hereafter cited as DoL, RG 174, NARA); Memorandum from George Haynes to William B. Wilson, Secretary of Department of Labor, July 22, 1918, WLPB, RG 1, NARA.

35. Memorandum from George Haynes to William B. Wilson, Secretary of Department of Labor, July 22, 1918, WLPB, RG 1, NARA; Haynes, *Negro at Work.*

36. Louis Post to Walter S. Buchanan, August 3, 1918, WLPB, RG 1, NARA; Memorandum from George Haynes to James Ford, October 31, 1918, WLPB, RG 1, NARA; Haynes, *Negro at Work.*

37. Haynes, *Negro at Work;* Report from George Haynes to William B. Wilson, Secretary of Department of Labor, March 20, 1919, WLPB, RG 1, NARA.

38. *War Expenditures: Hearings,* 8–50 passim.

39. Schaffer, "War Mobilization in Muscle Shoals" 143–45; *Florence Times,* November 15, 1918.

40. Schaffer, "War Mobilization in Muscle Shoals," 146; Vincent Saunders, "The Horizon," *Crisis* 17, no. 2 (December 1918): 90; Saunders, "The Horizon," *Crisis* 17, no. 3 (January 1919): 144; "Lynching Record for the Year," *Crisis* 17, no. 4 (February 1919): 181.

41. "Brief Summary of Anti-Lynching Work," *Crisis* 17, no. 4 (February 1919): 183; Saunders, "The Horizon," *Crisis* 18, no. 1 (May 1919): 37.

42. Report from George Haynes to William B. Wilson, Secretary of Department of Labor, June 18, 1919, WLPB, RG 1, NARA; quoted from Report from George Haynes to William B. Wilson, Secretary of Department of Labor, August 27, 1919, WLPB, RG 1, NARA; Henry P. Guzda, "Labor Department's First Program to Assist Black Workers," *Public Historian* 4, no. 4 (Fall 1982): 43–44.

Chapter 7

1. Melton McLaurin and Michael Thomason, *Mobile: The Life and Times of a Great Southern City* (Woodland Hills, CA, 1981), 95–96.

2. *Mobile Register,* August 6, 8, 1914 (hereafter cited as *Register*).

3. Ibid.; Walter Mills, *The Road to War: America 1914–1917* (New York, 1935), 37–38.

4. George B. Tindall, *The Emergence of the New South, 1913–1945* (Baton Rouge, 1967), 33–37; Kathleen Burk, *Britain, America and the Sinews of War, 1914–1918* (Boston, 1985), 52–56, 58–59.

5. Ralph E. Poore, "Alabama's Enterprising Newspaper, *The Mobile Press Register* and Its Forebears, 1913–1991" (unpublished manuscript, 1992), Mobile Public Library.

6. *Register,* August 6, 9, 10, 1914.

7. Ibid., December 23, 25, 1914.

8. Ibid., May 12, 1915.

9. Harry Pillans to Z. M. P. Inge, May 26, 1915, RG 6: Records of the Board of Commissioners of the City of Mobile, 1911–1985, Series 84: Warves, 1911–1984, Box 3, Mobile Municipal Archives, Mobile, AL (hereafter cited as RG 6, Series 84, Mobile Municipal Archives); Harry Pillans, "An Enlargement of a River Port by Reclamation in the Bay at Its Outlet," *World Ports* 10 (July 1922): 62–67; *Register,* April 1, July 10, August 10, 1917.

10. Pillans, "Enlargement of a River Port," 62–64; Tollef Tollefsen, "Interesting Times: The State Harbor Commission, 1915–23" (unpublished typescript, 2004), 7–8, 19–20, University of South Alabama Archives, Mobile, AL (hereafter cited as USA Archives).

11. F. G. Bromberg to George Wills, January 18, 1916, Frederick G. Bromberg Papers, Southern Historical Collection, University of North Carolina, Chapel Hill; David E. Alsobrook, "Alabama's Port City: Mobile during the Progressive Era, 1896–1917" (PhD diss., Auburn University, 1983), 231–32; Byron Farwell, *Over There: The United States in the Great War* (New York, 1999), 272–73; Meirion Harries and Susie Harries, *The Last Days of Innocence: America at War, 1917–1918* (New York, 1997), 28.

12. *Register,* 78th Annual Trade Edition, September 1, 1918.

13. First National Bank of Mobile, *Highlights of 75 Years in Mobile, 1865–1940* (Mobile, 1940), 78–79; *Report of the Board of Commissioners of the City of Mobile, September 30, 1916* (Mobile, 1916), 3, 7, 15; *Report of the Board of Commissioners of the City of Mobile, September 30, 1917* (Mobile, 1917), 3.

14. *Register,* March 22, 1917.

15. Tennant McWilliams, *Hannis Taylor: The New Southerner as an American* (Tuscaloosa, AL, 1978), 38, 69–70, 75–77; Tennant McWilliams, *The New South Faces the World: Foreign Affairs and the Southern Sense of Self, 1877–1950* (Baton Rouge, 1988), 47–67; Michael Thomason, ed., *Mobile: The New History of Alabama's First City* (Tuscaloosa, AL, 2001), 146–47.

16. Gordon Harvey, "Without Conscious Hypocrisy: Woodrow Wilson's Mobile Address of 1913," *Gulf Coast Historical Review* 10, no. 2 (Spring 1995): 25–46.

17. *Register,* March 2, 1917.

18. Ibid., April 3, 6, 1917.

19. Ibid., April 17, 1917.

20. Ibid., April 6, 1917.

21. Ibid., March 2, 14, 1917; C. R. M. F. Crutwell, *The History of the Great War, 1914–1918,* 2nd ed. (Oxford, 1961), 380–88; Allen Churchill, *Over Here! An Informal Recreation of the Home Front in World War I* (New York, 1968), 53.

22. Tollefsen, "Interesting Times," 9–10, 22–23; Pillans, "Enlargement of a River Port," 62–64; Pillans's correspondence on the Arlington project with various people, 1918–1922, in RG 6, Series 84, Mobile Municipal Archives; *Register,* May 30, June 6, August 24, September 17, 26, 1915, July 10, 1917.

23. Tollefsen, "Interesting Times," 28–33; *Report of the Board of Commissioner, September 30, 1917,* 3–5.

24. *Register,* June 6, July 25, August 1, September 19, 1917; James A. B. Scherer, *The Nation at War* (New York, 1918), 181–82; Harries and Harries, *Last Days of Innocence,* 150–51, 198.

25. Churchill, *Over Here,* 60.

26. *Register,* November 16, 24, 1918. Hurley was quoted as saying, "We may expect no reduction (in shipbuilding) for years to come" while visiting in Mobile late in the month.

27. Ibid., July 3, 77th Annual Trade Edition, September 1, 1917; *Fore and Aft,* August 2, 1919. The minesweeper *Swan* was launched the same day but not finished until January 27, 1919.

28. *Fore and Aft,* October 26, 1918; *Register,* 77th Annual Trade Edition, September 1, 1917.

29. Frank Boykin to Edward Boykin, August 10, 1964, Frank Boykin Letters, Vertical File, USA Archives; Edward Boykin, *Everything's Made for Love* (Mobile, 1973); Kenneth Stubbs, *Race to the Front: The Material Foundations of Coalition Strategy in the Great War* (Westport, CT, 2002), 187; Pillans to Maurice Hirsh, September 25, 1918, RG 6, Series 84, Box 3, Mobile Municipal Archives.

30. *Register,* August 5, 6, September 1, November 25, 1917.

31. Ibid., November 25, December 4, 1917.

32. Ibid., May 12, September 1, 1917.

33. Ibid., March 9, August 2, 28, September 11, 1918.

34. Ibid., August 4, September 1, 22, 1918.

35. Ibid., January 13, July 27, 1917, August 8, September 9, October 6, November 1, 10, 1918.

36. Ibid., June 28, August 14, 26, 1918.

37. Ibid., May 25, 1918.

38. Ibid., June 30, 1918; Boykin, *Everything's Made for Love,* 48–49; Frank Boykin to Edward Boykin, August 10, 1964, Frank Boykin Letters, Vertical File, USA Archives.

39. *Fore and Aft,* August 2, 1919; *Register,* August 31, 1919, 79th Annual Trade Edition; September 1, 1920, 80th Annual Trade Edition, August 28, 1921.

40. *Register,* September 26, November 3, 1918.

41. For an example of the city's support, see Pat Lyons's "Proclamation, August 8, 1918," RG 6: Records of the Board of Commissioners of the City of Mobile, 1911–1984, Series 79: U.S. Government, 1917–1984, Box 11, Mobile Municipal Archives (hereafter cited as RG 6, Series 79, Mobile Municipal Archives). The *Register*'s support for all such drives was unwavering and enthusiastic. *Register,* May 22, 1917, April 4, 14, May 17, 1918.

42. *Register,* April 6, 13, 1918.

43. Pat Lyons to Patrick J. O'Shaughnessy, April 16, 1918, RG 6, Series 79, Mobile Municipal Archives. For the McAdoo quote, see *Register,* April 14, 1919.

44. *Register,* May 18, 19, 28, 1918.

45. Ibid., September 3, 1918.

46. Ibid.

47. Ibid., September 8, 14, 15, 1918.

48. Churchill, *Over Here,* 182.

49. *Register,* July 5, 1918; *Fore and Aft,* August 2, 1919.

50. *Register,* July 2, 4, 5, 1918.

51. Ibid., April 8, 1917, July 6, 1918; Churchill, *Over Here,* 165–67.

52. Manuscript copy on GRS stationary of typescript letter, April 24, 1918, Correspondence File, Box 4, and Meeting Minutes, April 30, 1918, Box 113, both in German Relief Society Papers, USA Archives.

53. Alsobrook, "Alabama's Port City," 23, 232–34.

54. *Register,* July 27, 28, 1918.

55. Ibid., August 2, 9, 12, 22, 24, 1918.

56. Ibid., November 11, 1917.

57. Ibid., June 2, 5, 7, 1918.

58. Ibid., June 6, 1918.

59. Ibid., June 16, 17, 18, 1918.

60. Ibid.

61. Copy from NAACP Collection, Library of Congress, of "Application for Charter of Mobile, Alabama Branch of The National Association of Colored People, April 2, 1919," Microfilm Reel 3, Box 3, John L. LeFlore Papers, 1926–1976, USA Archives. The national NAACP approved the application early in May. Forty-nine people are listed as charter members.

62. *Register,* July 21, 1918.

63. Ibid., July 21, 28, 1918; William J. Breen, *Uncle Sam at Home: Civilian Mobilization, Wartime, Federalism, and the Council of National Defense, 1917–1919* (Westport, CT, 1984), 97–98.

64. *Register,* October 27, 1917, May 30, June 1, 1918; Alsobrook, "Alabama's Port City," 399–445. By mid-August the *Register* was calling the troops "doughboys."

65. David Alsobrook, "Soiled Doves and the Mobile City Commission: Regulation of Prostitution in the Port City during the Progressive Era, 1895–1920," paper given at the Alabama Historical Association meeting in Mobile, April 19, 2002, USA Archives.

66. *Register,* June 12, 14, 24, August 29, December 9, 12, 1917, February 10, March 10, April 4, 1918.

67. *Report of the Board of Commissioners of the City of Mobile for the Year Ending September 30, 1918* (Mobile, 1918), 5; *Register,* February 3, March 9, 23, 1918.

68. *Register,* October 7, December 9, 1917, January 6, 1918. Mobile was briefly considered as a site for a naval base. Jennifer D. Keene, *The United States and the First World War* (Harlow, UK, 2000), 40.

69. *Register,* June 16, September 1, 1918, 78th Annual Trade Edition.

70. *Quadrennial Report of the Alabama Adjutant General, 1922* (Montgomery, 1922), 110–13, Alabama Department of Archives and History, Montgomery (hereafter cited as ADAH).

71. *Register,* April 17, July 22, 1918.

72. Ibid., April 6, 1919.

73. Ibid., April 15, 26, June 18, 1918.

74. Churchill, *Over Here,* 105–6, 145, 217.

75. *Register,* September 16, 17, October 6, 7, 11, 13, 1918.

76. Ibid., September 22, October 5, 6, 13, 27, November 3, 10, 11, 1918.

77. Ibid., November 11, 13, 1918.

78. Ibid., September 26, October 26, November 3, 1918.

79. Ibid., November 5, 1918.

80. Ibid., October 2, 8, 12, 13, 18, 19, November 5, 1918.

81. *Annual Report of the State Board of Health of Alabama, 1918* (Montgomery, 1918), 52; *Annual Report of the State Board of Health of Alabama for Two Years, January 1, 1919 to December 31, 1920* (Montgomery, 1920), 58, 60, ADAH. For a comprehensive analysis of the worldwide pandemic, see John Barry, *The Great Influenza: The Epic Story of the Deadliest Plague in History* (New York, 2004).

82. *Register,* October 19–20, 1918.

83. Ibid., November 8, 1918; Churchill, *Over Here,* 203–4.

84. *Register,* November 2, 1918.

85. *Fore and Aft,* November 6, 1918.

86. *Register,* November 15, 16, 1918.

87. Ibid., November 24, 1918.

88. Ibid., September 1, 1921, 81st Annual Trade Edition.

89. Ibid., September 9, 11, 1921.

90. A. N. Marquis, ed., *Who's Who in America* (Chicago, 1924), 13:25.

91. [Michael McEvoy], "History of the Waterman Steamship Corporation," typescript [1959], 16–17, Waterman Steamship File, Vertical Files, USA Archives.

92. At its Chickasaw shipyard, U.S. Steel built fourteen large steel vessels; Mobile Shipbuilding built eighteen of wood or steel; Ley built two concrete ships; Henderson built four of wood; Murnan built two of wood; ADDSCO built six of various types.

93. *Alabama Official and Statistical Register, 1913* (Montgomery, 1913), 211, 213; *Alabama Official and Statistical Register, 1947* (Montgomery, 1947), 365, 394.

94. Alsobrook, "Alabama's Port City," 28–29.

95. *Register,* September 1, 1922, 82nd Annual Trade Edition.

96. Ibid. The issue continued to be hotly debated after the war. Pillans to H. K. Milner, July 18, 1921, RG 6, Series 84, Box 3, Mobile Municipal Archives.

97. Thomason, *Mobile,* 181–84.

98. Edward Ullman, "Mobile: Industrial Seaport and Trade Center" (PhD diss., University of Chicago, 1943), 23.

99. *Register,* September 1, 1919, 79th Annual Trade Edition.

100. Ibid., 81st Annual Trade Edition, 82nd Annual Trade Edition.

101. Tollefsen, "Interesting Times," 23–24, 30.

102. The league was organized on May 30, 1917, and remained active through World War II and beyond. Catherine B. Battson, *A History of the Mother's Army and Navy League* (Mobile, n.d. [ca. 1951]), 19, Local History and Genealogy, Mobile Public Library; *Register,* November 22, 1918.

Chapter 8

1. Council of National Defense, *First Annual Report of the Council of National Defense for the Fiscal Year Ended June 30, 1917* (Washington, DC, 1917), 6.

2. Ibid., 10.

3. Council of National Defense, *Report on Organization and Activities of State Councils of Defense: Bulletin No. 38* (Washington, DC, 1917), 1–2.

4. Alabama State Council of Defense, *Report of the Alabama Council of Defense: Covering Its Activities from May 17, 1917 to December 31, 1918* (Montgomery, 1919), 5–6.

5. Ibid.

6. Ibid.

7. Ibid., 7–9.

8. William J. Breen, *Uncle Sam at Home: Civilian Mobilization, Wartime Federalism, and the Council of National Defense, 1917–1919* (Westport, CT, 1984), 5–14.

9. Alabama State Council of Defense, *Proceedings of the Alabama State Council of Defense, June 1, 1917* (Montgomery, n.d.), 1–29.

10. Ibid.

11. Alabama State Council of Defense, *Report,* 40–41.

12. Ibid., 41.

13. *Montgomery Advertiser,* April 19, 1917.

14. Ibid.

15. Ibid.

16. *Cullman (AL) Democrat,* December 20, 1917; *Montgomery Advertiser,* December 10, 21, 29, 1917.

17. Albert B. Moore, *A History of Alabama and Her People* (Chicago, 1927), 3:716.

18. Home Defense Guards File, Alabama Governor (1915–1919: Henderson), Administrative Files (hereafter cited as Henderson Files, ADAH), SG22539, Alabama Department of Archives and History, Montgomery, AL.

19. *Montgomery Advertiser,* June 2, 1917.

20. Governor Charles Henderson to unnamed correspondent, April 1917, Henderson Files, ADAH.

21. Frank S. Moody to Governor Henderson, April 18, 1917, ibid.

22. H. L. McElderry to Governor Henderson, April 17, 1917, ibid.

23. McClane Tilton, Jr., to Governor Henderson, April 17, 1917, ibid.

24. G. H. Malone to Governor Henderson, April 18, 1917, ibid.

25. W. T. Andrews to Governor Henderson, May 28, 1917, ibid.

26. B. F. Elmore to Governor Henderson, May 18, 1917, ibid.

27. R. H. Richardson to Governor Henderson, May 28, 1917, ibid.

28. John Moffat to D. Adams, Jr., March 1, 1918, ibid.

29. L. M. Hooper to Governor Henderson, February 23, 1918, ibid.

30. Ibid., February 22, 1918.

31. See County Councils of Defense Folders, 1917–1918, ibid.

32. C. A. Stiefelmeyer to Governor Henderson, February 18, 1918, ibid.

33. Council of National Defense, *Information Circular No. 25* (Washington, DC, January 12, 1918); ibid., *Information Circular 29* (Washington, DC, April 27, 1918); ibid.,

Information Circular 44 (Washington, DC, May 25, 1918); ibid., *Information Circular 45* (Washington, DC, June 1, 1918); ibid., *Information Circular 54* (Washington, DC, August 3, 1918).

34. Ibid., *Information Circular No. 49* (Washington, DC, June 29, 1918).

35. Alabama Council of Defense, *Report,* 94.

36. Tom Smith to Governor Henderson, June 29, 1917, Henderson Files, ADAH.

37. U.S. Congress, House, *Liberty Bond Authorization Act,* 65th Congress, 3rd Session, H.R. 2762, ibid.

38. Council of Defense, Folder 2, ibid.

39. *Alexander City (AL) Outlook,* June 6, 1917.

40. *Opelika (AL) Daily News,* June 15, 1917.

41. *Montgomery Advertiser,* December 14, 1917.

42. *Dadeville (AL) Spot Cash,* May 3, 1918.

43. *Cullman Democrat,* April 18, 1918.

44. Alabama Council of Defense, *Report,* 94.

45. Harold Laswell, *Propaganda Techniques in World War I* (Cambridge, MA, 1971), 18.

46. Stephen Vaughn, *Holding Fast the Inner Lines: Democracy, Nationalism, and the Committee on Public Information* (Chapel Hill, NC, 1980), 16–17.

47. Ibid., 17.

48. Ibid., 18.

49. George Creel, *The Creel Report* (New York, 1972), 12.

50. Ibid., 66.

51. *Alabama Defense Record,* May 16, 1918–November 1, 1918; Alabama State Council of Defense, *Proceedings,* 4.

52. Alabama State Council of Defense, *Report,* 34.

53. George Creel, *Rebel at Large* (New York, 1947), 162.

54. George M. Cruikshank, ed., *The History of Four Minute Men of Alabama* (Birmingham, AL, 1921), 16.

55. Creel, *Creel Report,* 24.

56. Alabama Council of Defense, *Report,* 91.

57. Ibid., 91–93.

58. Cruikshank, *History of the Four Minute Men,* 25; Alabama State Council of Defense, *Report,* 91.

59. Alabama State Council of Defense, *Report,* 92.

60. Ibid., 93.

61. Ibid., 15.

62. *General Laws (and Joint Resolutions) of the Legislature of Alabama Passed at the Session of 1915* (Montgomery, 1915), 80–81.

63. Alabama State Department of Education, *Report of Special Drive against Illiteracy among Men of Draft Age, 1918* (Montgomery, 1918), 5.

64. Ibid., 6.

65. Ibid., 14–15.

66. Alabama State Council of Defense, *Report,* 95.

67. *Montgomery Advertiser,* May 2, 1917.

68. Ibid., September 16, 1917.

69. Ibid., December 18, 1917.

70. Ibid., September 16, December 2, 1917.

71. *Dadeville Spot Cash,* August 17, 1917.

72. Joseph L. Lanier, *First Seventy-Five Years of West Point Manufacturing Co., 1880–1955* (Princeton, NJ, 1955), 1–33.

73. *Defenders of Democracy* [ca. 1919], Folder 6, Lanett Cornerstone Collection, Cobb Memorial Archives, Shawmut, AL.

Chapter 9

1. Archer Jones, *The Art of War in the Western World* (Oxford, 1987), 46–47, 643.

2. Ibid., 435–36, 459–63.

3. Robert Cowley, "The Unreal City," *MHQ: The Quarterly Journal of Military History* 6, no. 2 (1994): 13–18.

4. Tom G. Hall, "Wilson and the Food Crisis: Agricultural Price Control during World War I," *Agricultural History* 47 (January 1973): 25.

5. Arthur S. Link, *Woodrow Wilson and the Progressive Era, 1910–1917* (New York, 1954), 188.

6. Mary Martha Thomas, *The New Woman in Alabama: Social Reform and Suffrage, 1890–1920* (Tuscaloosa, AL, 1992), 1.

7. *Birmingham News,* April 19, 1895, quoted in "History of Third District, Alabama Federation of Women's Clubs, 1915–1923, with Background History, 1895–1915," 9, typed manuscript from the Schlesinger Library, Radcliffe Institute, Harvard University.

8. Barnett Wood, unpublished memoir on the history of the Tintagil Club, October 1987, 1–2; Tintagil Club Program, 1901–1902, 1910–1911, 1916–1917; "Constitution of the Tintagil Club," Article 2 (all Tintagil Club papers in possession of club historian Mrs. Edith Crook, Montgomery, AL); Thomas, *New Woman in Alabama,* 43.

9. *Magazine Club Yearbook, 1913–1914; Ionian Club Yearbook, 1902–1903; Twentieth Century Club Yearbook, 1915–1916;* and *Sesame Club Yearbook, 1917–1918,* all in the Alabama Associations Collection, 1850–1984, LPR 136, Alabama Department of Archives and History, Montgomery (hereafter cited as ADAH).

10. Untitled spreadsheet of council presidents and *1954 Café Society Program* from archives of Montgomery Section of National Council of Jewish Women, Montgomery, AL.

11. *Mother's Circle Yearbook, 1916–1917,* Alabama Associations Collection, 1850–1984, LPR 136, ADAH.

12. Albert Burton Moore, *History of Alabama* (University, AL, 1934), 686–87;

Elizabeth Lynne Anderson, "Improving Rural Life in Alabama: The Home Demonstration Program, 1911–1972" (master's thesis, Auburn University, 1984), 31–33; *Montgomery Advertiser,* April 15, May 6, 1917.

13. Mary Feminear, "Report of Mary Feminear, State Chairman of Home Economics and Food Conservation. Food Administration Department [for Alabama]," January 25, 1918, [Box 5], File 58—Home Economics, Correspondence of R. M. Hobbie, State and Local Records—Alabama, Records of the U.S. Food Administration, RG 4, National Archives and Records Administration Southeast Region, Atlanta, GA (hereafter NARA—SE); *Birmingham News,* April 22, May 20, June 21, 1917; *Birmingham Age Herald,* May 15, 1917; R. L. Polk Company, *City Directory, Birmingham, Alabama, 1917,* 395; *City Directory, Birmingham, Alabama, 1919,* 350; *City Directory, Birmingham, Alabama, 1920–21,* 489; monetary equivalence calculated from Lawrence H. Officer and Samuel H. Williamson, "Purchasing Power of Money in the United States from 1774 to 2006," http://measuringworth.com/calculators/ppowerus (accessed October 10, 2007).

14. *Prattville (AL) Progress,* January 4, 11, March 1, 8, April 12, 26, August 2, 30, 1917; *Montgomery Advertiser,* May 27, 1917.

15. *Montgomery Advertiser,* May 13, 1917.

16. Ibid., May 6, 1917.

17. Royal Home Canner Company, Inc., *The Royal Road to Independence: Catalog K* (n.p., [1916]).

18. *Montgomery Advertiser,* May 6, 1917; *Prattville Progress,* October 11, 1917, May 30, 1918.

19. *Montgomery Advertiser,* May 6, 1917.

20. Ibid.; Thomas Owen, *History of Alabama and Dictionary of Alabama Biography,* 4 vols. (Chicago, 1921), 3:635, 700–701, 935; Nelson Pruyn Hoff, *Alabama Blue Book and Social Register, 1929* (Birmingham, 1929), 333, 335, 349; Surname File, Green, M–Greenwalt, M844743, Reel 236, Frames 865–948; Surname File, Jones, J. V.–Jones, N. L., M850602, Reel 308, Frames 549, 552; Surname File, Quealy–Ragland, M861552, Reel 465, Frames 438–551, 672–73, all at ADAH.

21. *Montgomery Advertiser,* May 13, 1917.

22. Ibid., May 6, 13, 1917.

23. Ibid., May 10, 13, 16, 18, 20, 1917.

24. Ibid., May 24, 1917.

25. *Montgomery Times,* June 5, 1917.

26. *Montgomery Advertiser,* May 27–28, June 3, 1917.

27. *Montgomery Advertiser,* June 3, 10, July 2, 1917; Feminear, "Report of Mary Feminear."

28. *Montgomery Advertiser,* June 3, 9–10, 22, 1917; *Montgomery Times,* June 15, 19, 28, July 7, 1917.

29. *Montgomery Times,* June 28, July 7, 1917; *Montgomery Advertiser,* August 26, 1917.

30. *Montgomery Advertiser,* April 28, May 12, 26, 1918.

31. On Quisenberry, see Surname File, Quealy–Ragland, M861552, Reel 465, Frames 778–96, ADAH; on Nunn, see political announcements on editorial page of *Prattville Progress,* March 14, 1918; *Montgomery Times,* May 15, 1918.

32. *Montgomery Advertiser,* May 26, 1918.

33. *Montgomery Times,* May 15, 1918; *Montgomery Advertiser,* May 26, 1918.

34. Feminear, "Report of Mary Feminear"; *Montgomery Advertiser,* July 14, 1918.

35. *Montgomery Times,* July 17, 1918; *Montgomery Advertiser,* July 28, August 4, 1918.

36. Advertisement for Piggly Wiggly at 123 Commerce Street, *Montgomery Times,* May 24, 1918; *Montgomery Advertiser,* September 22, 1918; James M. Mayo, *The American Grocery Store: The Business Evolution of an Architectural Space* (Westport, CT, 1993), 89–92; "The Piggly Wiggly System," pamphlet available in Special Collections Department, Memphis Public Library, Memphis, TN; Nancy F. Koehn, "Henry Heinz and Brand Creation in the Late Nineteenth Century," *Business History Review* 73 (Autumn 1999): 363–64.

37. *Montgomery Advertiser,* June 4, 1918.

38. Ibid., August 18, 1918.

39. Ibid., July 14, 1918; Kendall Taylor, *Sometimes Madness Is Wisdom: Zelda and Scott Fitzgerald, A Marriage* (New York, 2001), 54–61; James R. Mellow, *Invented Lives: F. Scott and Zelda Fitzgerald* (Boston, 1984), 51–61; Nancy Milford, *Zelda: A Biography* (New York, 1970), 32–36.

40. Minutes, Regular Meeting, April 2, 1923, from archives of Montgomery Section of National Council of Jewish Women, Montgomery, AL.

41. Adele Kahn Weil Scrapbook, 1901–1938, SPR207, ADAH.

Chapter 10

1. Mary Martha Thomas, *The New Woman in Alabama: Social Reforms and Suffrage, 1890–1920* (Tuscaloosa, AL, 1992); Shirley Garrett Schoonover, "Alabama's Quest for Social Justice during the Progressive Era" (master's thesis, Auburn University, 1970).

2. Allen W. Jones, "Political Reforms of the Progressive Era," in *From Civil War to Civil Rights: Alabama 1860–1960,* comp. Sarah Woolfolk Wiggins (Tuscaloosa, AL, 1987), 203–20; William Warren Rogers, Robert David Ward, Leah Rawls Atkins, and Wayne Flynt, *Alabama: The History of a Deep South State* (Tuscaloosa, AL, 1994), 355–75.

3. Rogers et al., *Alabama,* 414; Shirley Schoonover, "Alabama Public Health Campaign, 1900–1919," *Alabama Review,* 28, no. 3 (July 1975): 232.

4. Charles Henderson, "Final Message to Legislature, 14 January 1919," 11–12, in Alabama Governor (1915–1919: Henderson), Administrative Files (hereafter cited as Henderson Files, ADAH), SG22537, Alabama Department of Archives and History, Montgomery; see also J. H. McCormick, "Public Health," in *Child Welfare in Alabama: An Inquiry by the National Child Labor Committee under the Auspices and with the Co-*

operation of the University of Alabama, National Child Labor Committee (New York, 1918), 11.

5. Schoonover, "Alabama Public Health Campaign," 232.

6. McCormick, "Public Health," 11.

7. See, for example, Rod Andrew's "Soldiers, Christians, and Patriots: The Lost Cause and Southern Military Schools, 1865–1915," *Journal of Southern History* 64, no. 4 (November 1998): 677–710.

8. Ruth Smith Truss, "The Alabama National Guard's 167th Infantry Regiment in World War I," *Alabama Review,* 56, no. 1 (January 2003): 7; Schoonover, "Alabama Public Health Campaign," 232.

9. Schoonover, "Alabama Public Health Campaign," 232; McCormick, "Public Health," 12; Wayne Flynt, *Alabama in the Twentieth Century* (Tuscaloosa, AL, 2004), 196; Rogers et al., *Alabama,* 366; Schoonover, "Alabama's Quest for Social Justice," 104–10.

10. Loraine Bedsole Bush, "A Decade of Progress in Alabama," *Journal of Social Forces* 2, no. 4 (May 1924): 540.

11. McCormick, "Public Health," 11.

12. Ibid., 12.

13. Schoonover, "Alabama Public Health Campaign," 231.

14. Samuel W. Welch, "Annual Report of the State Board of Health of Alabama, January 1st to December 31st 1918" (Montgomery, 1919) in Henderson Files, ADAH.

15. Ibid., 9.

16. Ibid., 8–9.

17. Flynt, *Alabama in the Twentieth Century,* 196.

18. Bush, "Decade of Progress in Alabama," 540.

19. Lee N. Allen, "Charles Henderson, 1915–1919," in *Alabama Governors: A Political History of the State,* ed. Samuel L. Webb and Margaret E. Armbrester (Tuscaloosa, AL, 2001), 162–65.

20. Charles Henderson, "To the Senate and House of Representatives," January 14, 1919, 8–9, in Henderson Files, SG22541, ADAH.

21. Hastings Hart, *Social Problems in Alabama: A Study of the Social Institutions and Agencies of the State of Alabama as Related to Its War Activities* (New York, 1918).

22. Flynt, *Alabama in the Twentieth Century,* 195.

23. Bush, "Decade of Progress in Alabama," 542.

24. Welch to Dr. Greene, July 20, 1918, and Welch to Dr. Walker, July 24, 1918, in Henderson Files, SG22537, ADAH.

25. Michael Breedlove, "Thomas E. Kilby, 1919–1923," in *Alabama Governors,* 167; Rogers et al., *Alabama,* 416.

26. Rogers et al., *Alabama,* 407–8.

27. Hart, *Social Problems in Alabama.*

28. Ibid, 9. Hart wrote his report before the armistice. He made a clear connection between social reforms and the need for Alabama to provide strong and healthy soldiers.

29. Ibid., 10

30. Ibid., 11.

31. Hart's recommendation that the Board of Health's budget be increased to $150,000 suggests likely collusion between Thomas Kilby, Samuel Welch, and Hart sometime during early July 1918.

32. Hart, *Social Problems in Alabama,* 34.

33. Ibid., 15–16.

34. Ibid., 16; Flynt, *Alabama in the Twentieth Century,* 220–31.

35. Allen, "Charles Henderson, 1915–1919," 162.

36. Henderson, "To the Senate and House of Representatives."

37. Breedlove, "Thomas E. Kilby," 167–69.

38. Hart, *Social Problems in Alabama,* 35.

39. Emily Owen, *Thomas Kilby in Local and State Government* (Anniston, AL: Birmingham Publishing Co., 1948), 43–67.

40. Thomas Kilby to Dr. H. H. Hart, December 6, 1919. Alabama Governor (1919–1923: Kilby), Administrative Files, (hereafter cited as Kilby Files, ADAH), SG006999, Alabama Department of Archives and History, Montgomery.

41. Ibid., June 27, 1919.

42. Thomas Kilby, *Inaugural Address, January 20, 1919* (Montgomery, 1919), 12.

43. Samuel W. Welch, *Annual Report of the State Board of Health of Alabama for the Two Years January 1st 1919 to December 31st 1920* (Montgomery, 1922), 7.

44. Ibid., 7–8.

45. Kilby, *Inaugural Address,* 14; see also "Inauguration, 1919," Kilby Files, SG006999, ADAH.

46. Breedlove, "Thomas E. Kilby," 168. Even with Kilby more than doubling the state education budget, as late as 1927 Alabama still ranked forty-fifth of forty-eight states in literacy rates. Flynt, *Alabama in the Twentieth Century,* 223.

47. Alabama Women's Hall of Fame, "Loraine Bedsole Tunstall (1879–1953)," http://www.awhf.org/tunstall.html (accessed April 12, 2006).

48. Hastings H. Hart, *Social Progress of Alabama: A Second Study of the Social Institutions and Agencies of the State of Alabama, Made at the Request of Governor Thomas E. Kilby* (Montgomery, 1922), 12.

49. Flynt, *Alabama in the Twentieth Century,* 184–87.

50. Leah Rawls Atkins, *The Valley and the Hills, An Illustrated History of Birmingham and Jefferson County* (Tarzana, CA, 1981), 103.

Chapter 11

1. Alabama Memorial Commission, *Campaign Handbook: Suggestive Speech and Publicity Material for Use of Speakers, Directors and Others, in the Campaign for Funds for the Alabama Memorial* (Montgomery, 1919), 9.

2. "An Act to Create the Alabama Memorial Commission," *General Laws (and*

Joint Resolutions) of the Legislature of Alabama Passed at the Session of 1919 (Montgomery, 1919), 18–19.

3. "State Archives Dedicated by Society of American Archivists," *Alabama Historical Quarterly* 2 (Fall 1940): 278–79.

4. Ibid.

5. *Montgomery Advertiser,* April 4, 1919.

6. John M. Schnorrenberg, *Remembered Past, Discovered Future: The Alabama Architecture of Warren, Knight and Davis, 1906–1961; Catalogue of Exhibitions at Birmingham Museum of Art, Birmingham Public Library, University of Alabama at Birmingham Visual Arts Gallery* (Birmingham, AL, 1999), 112–14.

7. *Algernon Blair (1873–1952): Churchman, Builder, Great Citizen: Tributes by His Friends at Montgomery, Alabama, October 13, 1953* (Montgomery, 1953); Algernon Blair, *Alabama State Capitol and Grounds: Paper Read before the Thirteen, May 13, 1943* (Birmingham, AL, 1943).

8. *Our Southern Home* (Livingston, AL), April 30, 1919.

9. *Report of the Alabama Council of Defense, Covering Its Activities from May 17, 1917, to December 31, 1918* (Montgomery, 1919), 36–37.

10. "Report of the State War Historian," in ibid., 65–71.

11. "Liberty Buildings as Victory Monuments: Suggestions to Communities Planning Memorials to Heroes of the Great War," *American City* 19 (December 1918): 471.

12. Bureau of Memorial Buildings, War Camp Community Service, *Community Buildings as War Memorials: What Sort of Memorial?* Bulletin No. 1 (New York, 1919).

13. Bureau of Memorial Buildings, War Camp Community Service, *Community Buildings as War Memorials: Architecture of Large Memorial Buildings,* Bulletin No. 10 (New York, 1919), 18.

14. The American Federation of Art's circular letter was reprinted in *National Municipal Review* 8 (March 1919): 135–38.

15. "Tenth Annual Convention of the American Federation of Arts," *American Magazine of Art* 10 (July 1919): 326–30, and at http://www.oldandsold.com/articles14/new-york-96.html (quotation from online source, emphasis added). On the history of the AFA, see the organization's Web site at http://www.afaweb.org/.

16. George L. Mosse, *Fallen Soldiers: Reshaping the Memory of the World Wars* (New York, 1990), 3–4.

17. Ibid., 94–98.

18. U.S battle deaths amounted to approximately 50,000, whereas France lost 1.3 million in battle, Britain 0.9 million, Russia 1.7 million, Italy 0.5 million, Germany 1.8 million, and Austria-Hungary 0.9 million. R. Ernest Dupuy and Trevor N. Dupuy, *The Encyclopedia of Military History from 3500 B.C. to the Present,* 2nd ed. (New York, 1986), 990.

19. Mosse, *Fallen Soldiers,* 6.

20. Total military deaths in the Civil War numbered approximately 623,000 (362,000 Union, 261,000 Confederate). Allan R. Millett and Peter Maslowski, *For*

the Common Defense: A Military History of the United States of America (New York, 1984), 229.

21. Mosse, *Fallen Soldiers*, 100.

22. The legislation called for twelve appointed members, but the composition of this group varied somewhat, judging from the published literature of the AMC. The following ten appointed members appear consistently in the literature: Borden Burr, Birmingham; W. R. Chapman, Dothan; Albert C. Davis, Montgomery; N. D. Denson, Opelika; James B. Ellis, Selma; C. A. O'Neal, Andalusia; A. G. Patterson, Albany; L. Pizitz, Birmingham; Joseph O. Thompson, Birmingham; and Richard Wilkinson, Montgomery. The names of two additional members appear inconsistently in the literature: Henry J. Willingham, Florence, and Richard V. Taylor, Mobile.

23. Published sources on Owen's life and career include Robert Reynolds Simpson, "Origin of State Departments of Archives and History in the South" (PhD diss., University of Mississippi, 1971); Robert R. Simpson, "The Origins of the Alabama Department of Archives and History," *Alabama Review* 34 (Summer 1972): 155–70; James F. Doster, "Thomas McAdory Owen, Sr." in *Keepers of the Past,* ed. Clifford L. Lord (Chapel Hill, NC, 1965), 97–108; Mary A. Finch, "Thomas McAdory Owen: Preserver of Alabama History" (master's thesis, Auburn University, 1991); Milo B. Howard, Jr., "Thomas McAdory Owen: Alabama's Greatest Bibliographer," *Alabama Review* 28 (January 1975): 3–15; R. D. W. Connor, "Dedication of the Archival Section of the Alabama World War Memorial Building," *American Archivist* 4 (April 1941): 77–83; Alden Monroe, "Thomas Owen and the Founding of the Alabama Department of Archives and History," *Provenance* 11 (2003): 22–35; Wendell H. Stephenson, "Some Pioneer Alabama Historians III: Thomas McAdory Owen, Sr.," *Alabama Review* 2 (January 1949): 45–62.

24. Richard J. Cox, "Alabama's Archival Heritage, 1850–1985," *Alabama Review* 40 (October 1987): 289.

25. Thomas McAdory Owen, ed., *Report of the Alabama History Commission to the Governor of Alabama, December 1, 1900* (Montgomery, 1901).

26. Monroe, "Thomas Owen," 26–31.

27. Ibid., 32.

28. Alabama Historical Records Advisory Board, *Assessing Alabama's Archives: A Plan for the Preservation of the State's Historical Records; The Full Report* (Montgomery, 1985), 36–37.

29. Hastings H. Hart, *Social Problems in Alabama: A Study of the Social Institutions and Agencies of the State of Alabama as Related to Its War Activities* (New York, 1918), 21.

30. Ibid.

31. *Report of the Alabama Council of Defense,* 36–37.

32. Alabama Memorial Commission, *Campaign Handbook,* 21–22.

33. Ibid., 25.

34. Ibid., 14.

35. Ibid., 3. Monetary equivalence calculated from Lawrence H. Officer and Samuel

H. Williamson, "Purchasing Power of Money in the United States from 1774 to 2006," http://measuringworth.com/calculators/ppowerus (accessed October 10, 2007).

36. "Design of the Alabama Memorial: Resolution Adopted by the Alabama Memorial Commission, April 3, 1919," Alabama Memorial Commission, *Campaign Handbook,* 15–16.

37. *Montgomery Journal,* April 15, 1919; reprinted in Alabama Memorial Commission, *Campaign Handbook,* 17–18.

38. Alabama Memorial Commission, *Campaign Handbook,* 15.

39. Ibid.

40. Thomas McAdory Owen to Fred H. Gormley, April 21, 1919, Records of the Alabama Department of Archives and History, Administrative Files (hereafter cited as ADAH Administrative Files), SG16339, Alabama Department of Archives and History, Montgomery.

41. Owen to Gormley, May 6, 1919, in ibid.

42. Schnorrenberg, *Remembered Past, Discovered Future,* 112. The architects' perspective rendering appeared as the frontispiece of the commission's *Campaign Handbook.* It also appeared as a postcard and in various newspaper articles.

43. *Alabama Memorial Commission: Memorial to Commemorate the Part of Alabama and Alabamians in the World War; Act Creating Commission; Resolution Adopting Form of Material* (n.p., April 12, 1919).

44. In addition to the *Campaign Handbook,* cited in full above, the AMC published two booklets for the school campaign: *Suggestive Program for Use in the Schools of the State: Memorial Building Day, May 9, 1919* (Montgomery, 1919) and *Suggestive Program for Use in the Schools of the State: Armistice Day, November 11, 1919* (Montgomery, 1919).

45. Alabama Memorial Commission, *Suggestive Program for Use in the Schools . . . May 9, 1919,* 4. The intended audience for this publication, as well as for the one produced for Armistice Day, was apparently any state school in Alabama, black or white, if the absence of any reference to race in the material is any indication.

46. Autauga County Folder, ADAH Administrative Files, SG16338, ADAH.

47. W. T. Neal to Kilby, April 25, 1919, Escambia County folder, in ibid.

48. Owen to W. W. Harper, June 24, 1919, County Chairmen Folder, in ibid.

49. Kilby to Rosenthil, June 23, 1919, Bullock County Folder, in ibid.

50. Shaw to Kilby, July 1, 1919, Colbert County Folder, in ibid.

51. Bedsole to Owen, June 2, 1919, Clarke County Folder, in ibid.

52. Bedsole to Stallings, July 2, 1919, Clarke County Folder, in ibid.

53. J. Mason Douglass to Thomas E. Kilby, June 7, 1919, Franklin County Folder, in ibid. Emphasis in quotations in original.

54. C. E. McCord to Owen, June 18, 1919, Autauga County Folder, in ibid.

55. Owen to Charles E. McCord, June 24, 1919, Autauga County Folder, in ibid.

56. Alabama Memorial Commission, *Suggestive Program for Use in the Schools . . . November 11, 1919.*

57. Marie Bankhead Owen to T. H. Roberson, April 23, 1924, Franklin County Folder, ADAH Administrative Files, SG16338, ADAH.

58. Owen to W. H. Blake, June 18, 1919, Colbert County Folder, in ibid.

59. *Montgomery Advertiser,* March 26, 1920.

60. Ibid., March 27, 1920.

61. Robert J. Jakeman, "Marie Bankhead Owen and the Alabama Department of Archives and History, 1920–1955," *Provenance* 21 (2003): 36–65.

62. Marie Bankhead Owen to "Friend," November 8, 1921, County Chairmen Folder, ADAH Administrative Files, SG16338, ADAH.

63. Marie Bankhead Owen to T. H. Roberson, April 23, 1924, Franklin County Folder, in ibid.

64. See American Legion Folder, in ibid.

65. Brookings Institution, *Report on a Survey of the State and County Governments of Alabama,* 5 vols. (Montgomery, 1932). For references to ADAH, state records, and legislative reference, see 1:59–60, 63, 73, 85, 87, 117, 104, 125–31, 135, 137, 203, 251–56, 320–21, 392–98, and 403–4.

66. Jakeman, "Marie Bankhead Owen," 49–50.

67. Ibid., 52–53.

68. *Montgomery Advertiser,* April 4, 1919.

69. The full text of the poem, written for a memorial service for Library of Congress staff members who had died in World War II, is available at http://www.loc.gov/teachers/lyrical/poems/dead_soldiers.html.

Contributors

David Alsobrook (PhD, Auburn University, 1983), director of the Museum of Mobile, retired from the National Archives and Records Administration in 2007 after thirty years of service. His NARA assignments included supervisory archivist at the Carter Presidential Library and director at the George H. W. Bush Presidential Library and the Clinton Presidential Library. He has published essays and book reviews in various scholarly and popular journals, primarily relating to race relations, politics, and society in Alabama and the South.

Wilson Fallin, Jr. (PhD, University of Alabama, 1994) is professor of history at the University of Montevallo. He is a member of the board of directors of the Birmingham Civil Rights Institute and for ten years was historian of the National Baptist Convention. In addition to several articles and book chapters, he has written three books: *The African American Church in Birmingham, Alabama, 1815–1963: A Shelter in the Storm* (1997); *The History of Birmingham-Easonian Baptist Bible College: One Hundred Years of Black Religious Education, 1904–2004* (2004); and *Uplifting the People: Three Centuries of Black Baptists in Alabama* (2007).

Robert J. "Jeff" Jakeman (PhD, Auburn University, 1988) was on active duty with the U.S. Air Force from 1972 to 1980 and was reactivated for the Gulf War. Before retiring from the reserves as a colonel in 1997, he was a historical officer at the Maxwell Air Force Base Historical Research Agency and the reserve counterpart to the commandant of Squadron Officer School. In 1992 he joined the faculty of the Auburn History Department, served as editor of *The Alabama Review* (1995–2008), and is the manager of the online *Encyclopedia of Alabama*. He has written *The Divided Skies: Establishing Segregated Flight Training at Tuskegee, Alabama, 1934–1942* (1992) as well as articles on archival topics and military aviation.

Dowe Littleton (MA, Auburn University, 1991) currently serves as the reading clerk for the State of Alabama Senate, a position he has held since 1993. He began his state career in the Government Records Division of the Alabama Department of Archives and History in 1984. His essay in this collection grew from his master's thesis, *The Alabama State Council of Defense, 1917–1919*.

Wesley Phillips Newton (PhD, University of Alabama, 1964), emeritus professor, taught at Auburn University between 1964 and 1987. In World War II he served in the United States Army as an infantry rifleman, was wounded at the Battle of the Bulge, and became a prisoner of war. He has published articles in scholarly journals and has written a number of books, including *Montgomery in the Good War: Portrait of a Southern City, 1939–1946* (University of Alabama Press, 2000); *To Command the Sky: The Battle for Air Superiority over Germany, 1942–1944* (coauthored with Stephen McFarland, published by the Smithsonian Institution Press/University of Alabama Press, 1991 and 2005); and *The Wisdom Of Eagles: A History Of Maxwell Air Force Base* (coauthor with Jerome A. Ennels, published by River City Press, second edition, 2002).

Martin T. Olliff (PhD, Auburn University, 1998) has been the director of the Archives of Wiregrass History and Culture and an associate professor of history at Troy University—Dothan Campus since 2002. Between 1996 and 2002, he was the assistant archivist at Auburn University. He has published a number of articles on chefs and on Alabama history.

Victoria E. Ott (PhD, University of Tennessee, 2003) serves as an assistant professor of history at Birmingham-Southern College. She has published a number of articles on the Civil War home front, and her *Confederate Daughters: Coming of Age during the Civil War* was published by Southern Illinois University Press in March 2008. Her contribution to this collection was originally published in the *Southern Historian* (Spring 2001).

Robert Saunders, Jr. (PhD, Auburn University, 1994) is an associate professor of history and the chair of the Department of History and Political Science at Troy University—Dothan Campus, where he has taught since 1997. His book *John Archibald Campbell: Southern Moderate, 1811–1889* was published by the University of Alabama Press in 1997.

Michael V. R. Thomason (PhD, Duke University, 1968) is a professor emeritus of history at the University of South Alabama, having taught there from 1970 until 2006. He founded the University of South Alabama Archives in 1978 and served as its director until his retirement. During his career he published several well-known and respected books on the history of Alabama and Mobile and was the editor of the *Gulf South Historical Review* from its first issue in 1985 through its last in 2006.

Ruth Smith Truss (PhD, University of Alabama, 1992) has taught at the University of Montevallo since 1993, where she is currently an associate professor of history. She has published a number of articles and reviews on military history, particularly the history of the Alabama National Guard.

Index

167th Infantry Regiment, 19, 37, 38, 47, 62, 94, 135, 200; combat in France, 39–40
365th Infantry Regiment, 74
366th Infantry Regiment, 98
372nd Infantry Regiment, 54
528th Service Battalion, 97–98
804th Pioneer Negro Infantry Regiment, 98
Acker, W. F., 53
Adams, Oscar W., 73, 164
African Americans, 6–7, 15–16, 20–21, 33, 51, 81–84, 101, 106, 130, 137–138, 213–214; activism, 77–79, 102–104, 115–117; civil rights, 95–98, 102, 120; conscription, 91–93; discrimination against, 4–5, 43, 114–116, 123; disfranchisement of, 13, 66, 67, 68, 77, 104–105, 140; equality sought as reward for service, 67, 81, 96, 98; historiography, 98–100; and Liberty Loan drives, 132, 160; loyalty, 69–72, 73–75, 77, 80, 81, 87–90, 93, 101, 132, 133–134; lynching, 4, 68, 76, 79, 95, 96, 118–120; and religion, 66–80; as soldiers, 54–55, 62, 94, 136; war work, 49, 164, 167, 172; as workers, 48, 89–90, 108–110, 128–129
African Methodist Episcopal Church, 106
Agricultural Extension Service, 158
Agriculture, Alabama, 5–8, 103
Air Force, U.S., 64–65
Air Nitrates Company, 107–108, 112, 114, 118
Air University, 64
Alabama A&M College, 7, 88, 117
Alabama Baptist Missionary Convention, 67
Alabama Board of Health, 188–189, 195
Alabama Capitol Building Commission, 208
Alabama Cast Iron Pipe Company (ACIPCO), 12
Alabama Child Labor Committee, 185
Alabama Children's Home Society, 181
Alabama College for Women, 175
Alabama Colored Baptist State Convention, 67–68, 73–74, 76
Alabama Council of Defense, 21, 84, 96, 117, 152–168, 183, 204, 209; committees of, 154–156; county organization, 156–157; reorganization in 1918, 158–159, 167–168; speakers bureau, 164
Alabama Defense Record, 162–163, 165
Alabama Department of Archives and History (ADAH), 23, 201–204, 207–209, 211, 216–219
Alabama Department of Child Welfare, 198
Alabama Department of Education, 201–202, 211
Alabama Department of Labor, 158
Alabama Department of Public Health, 190, 197

Alabama Dry Dock and Shipbuilding Company (ADDSCO), 127–129, 133, 138–139
Alabama Education Association, 162
Alabama Equal Suffrage Association, 164
Alabama Extension Service, 162
Alabama Federation of Colored Women's Clubs, 15–16
Alabama Federation of Women's Clubs (AFWC), 15, 16–17, 75, 165, 168, 171, 174–175, 181–182, 185
Alabama Food Administration, 158, 162
Alabama Fuel Administration, 158
Alabama Historical Commission, 65
Alabama History Commission, 208
Alabama Illiteracy Commission, 165–166
Alabama Machinery and Supply Company, 178
Alabama Marketing and Canning Company, 172
Alabama Medical Association, 185, 189
Alabama Memorial Commission (AMC), 201–202, 207, 210–218
Alabama Mother's Circle, 174
Alabama National Bank, 174
Alabama National Guard, 19, 24, 25–26, 27, 32, 34, 37–38, 40–42, 47, 50, 51
Alabama Polytechnic Institute (API), 7, 154–155
Alabama Power Company, 26–27, 52, 64
Alabama Public Utility Commission, 155
Alabama Railroad Commission, 14, 155, 191
Alabama River, 63
Alabama State Harbor Commission, 126–127, 139
Alabama State Normal School for Negroes, 172
Alabama Women's Christian Temperance Union, 185
Alabama World War Memorial, 202–203, 219. *See also* War memorial
Alcohol, sale of, 26, 35, 47, 60, 135. *See also* Prohibition
Alexander City Outlook, 160
Algernon Blair Company, 45, 63
Almon, Ed B., 105
American City, 204
American Federation of Arts, 205–207
American Federation of Labor, 11
American Legion, 218
American Missionary Association, 106, 112
American Protective League, 96
Andrews, Lt. Col. Frank M., 63
Andrews, J. W., 114
Anniston, Alabama, 10, 14, 19, 26, 30, 40, 50–53, 55, 59, 61–63, 155
Anniston Star, 54, 64
Arlington Pier Project (Mobile), 126–127, 129, 139–140
Army Air Service, 57, 63, 65
Attucks, Crispus, 70
Attwell, Ernest T., 91–92
Auburn, Alabama, 153, 155
Austin, Pvt. John C., 32
Autauga County, 88, 174, 213, 216
Automobiles, 34–35, 44
Auxiliary Remount Depot No. 312 (Montgomery), 48–49
Aviation Repair Depot No. 3 (Montgomery), 57–58, 63–65

Baer, Frank, 135
Baird, Lt. Ollie Josephine, 53
Baker, Mrs. Joseph, 180
Baker, Newton D., 48, 95
Baldwin, Katherine, 45
Banago (ship), 128
Bankhead, John D., 103, 219
Bankhead, John H., 123, 208, 217
Bankhead, Tallulah, 208
Bankhead, William, 219
Banks, S. T., 49
Barbour County, 165
Bashinsky, L. M., 153
Battle, Mrs. Maude, 62
Battle, Willie Maude, 62
Battle Abbey, 216
Bay Minette, Alabama, 28
Bedsole, T. J., 207, 214
Bell, Charles F., 172–173
Belsaw, Dr. E. T., 89, 132
Benton, Judge H. T., 155

Bessemer, Alabama, 10, 74–75
Beverley, John W., 72, 88–89
Bienville Square (Mobile), 125, 131, 136
Big Mules, 4, 6, 15, 18
Bilbo, Theodore, 131
Birmingham, Alabama, 2, 12, 26, 30, 40, 41, 50, 53, 68, 74, 78, 84, 92, 119, 123, 128, 153, 154, 160, 172, 174, 193, 207, 210, 212; Four Minute Men in, 73; Four Minute Women in, 163–164; history of, 10; labor agents in, 82, 87; NAACP branch, 79; Progressivism in, 14–18; racial segregation in, 76–77, 114; war work in, 75
Birmingham Age-Herald, 193
Birmingham Ledger, 82–83, 85
Birmingham News, 94
Birmingham Railway, Light, and Power Company, 76
Birmingham Reporter, 73, 164
Birmingham Trust and Savings Company, 154
Birmingham Weekly Voice, 83
Birth of a Nation, 81
Blackmon, Fred L., 50, 64–65
Blacks. *See* African Americans
Black Warrior River, 123, 128
Blair, Algernon, 203
Blake, W. H., 217
Blakely Island (Mobile Bay), 124
Blocton, Alabama, 82
Boll weevil, 6, 85, 103–104
Boothe, Charles O., 78
Boyd, Richard, 70
Boyd, W. L., 73
Boykin, Frank, 128–129, 131, 136
Bradley, R. L., 210
Brandon, William W., 192
Brannon, Peter, 203
Brewton, Alabama, 213
Bridges, guarded by Alabama National Guard, 26, 28, 30–33, 42
Briggs, Cyril, 97
Bromberg, Charles E., Jr., 135
Brookings Institution, 218
Brotherhood of Sleeping Car Porters, 71
Brown v. Board of Education, 1954, 79, 102
Bryce Hospital, 197–198
Buchanan, Walter S., 88, 117
Buford, G. T., 83, 86–87, 92–93, 95, 100
Bulger, T. L., 155
Bullock County, 213
Bureau of Investigation (BI), 82, 87, 92
Bureau of Negro Economics. *See* Division of Negro Economics
Burrell Normal School (Florence), 106, 112
Bush, Albert P., 153
Bush, Loraine Bedsole. *See* Tunstall, Loraine Bedsole (Bush)
Buttenheim, Harold S., 204, 206
Byrd, William, 118–120

Cadden, Helen, 177, 179
Cadets, U.S. Army Air Corps, 56–57, 64
Cahaba River, 27
Caldwell, Dr. W. A., 89, 132
Calhoun County, 50, 52
Camp Albert L. Mills, New York, 39, 47, 63, 94
Campbell, Pvt. Fred, 32
Camp Dodge, Iowa, 73–74, 91, 97
Camp Joseph Wheeler, Georgia, 38, 47
Camp Logan, Texas, 93
Camp McClellan, 20, 30, 56, 59, 61; becomes cantonment, 64–65; construction, 50–53; training at, 54–55, 62, 63
Camp Sheridan, 19, 22, 26, 27, 39, 47, 48, 52, 53, 54, 55, 56, 59, 64, 65, 182; camp life, 33–37, 49; construction, 42–46; Spanish influenza at, 62–63; training at, 50–51; and vice, 60–61
Camp Stuart, Virginia, 54
Canaan, Alabama, 106
Canning procedures, 75, 172–173, 177
Cantonment, 45, 64–65
Carbon Hill, Alabama, 30
Carollton, Alabama, 160
Carre, Mrs. H. B., 46
Carroll, Leigh, 166
Cary, Dr. Charles A., 154
Cary, R. L., Jr., 47
Cashin, N. E., 83
Cassel, J. H., 126

Central Committee of Colored Montgomery Citizens, 72
Chamber of Commerce (Montgomery), 174
Chastang, Leo, 135
Chattahoochee River, 26
Chattanooga, Tennessee, 176
Chicago Defender, 86
Chickasaw, Alabama, 128, 130, 138–139
Child welfare programs, 186, 188, 196
Chile, 103
Chilton County, 26
Christian Methodist Episcopal Church of Florence, 106
Churches, African American, 66–88
City of Chattanooga (ship), 138
Civil rights movement. *See* African Americans: civil rights
Clanton, Alabama, 26
Clarke County, 73, 157, 214
Clayton, Judge Henry D., 60
Clemmons, Rafe, 133
Cobb, Ned ("Nate Shaw"), 92, 100
Colbert County, 103–104, 214, 217
Colored Comfort Committee, 72
Comer, Braxton Bragg, 11, 14
Committee for Relief of Belgium, 170
Committee on Public Information, 73, 156, 161–162
Communism, 77–78
Community Buildings As War Memorials, 205
Conecuh County, 165–166
Confederate Memorial Day, 161
Congress, 1, 2, 3, 118, 119, 129, 152, 161, 170, 208
Connor, R. D. W., 201, 219
Convict lease, 11–12, 105, 193, 196, 198
Cordova, Alabama, 30
Corona Industrial and Normal School, 89
Corpier, Mary, 106
Council of National Defense, 2, 21, 152–153
County agents, 7
Covington County, 165
Craighead, Erwin, 85, 89, 100
Craighead, Lula Harris, 17, 134
Cravath, Paul D., 204
Crawford, George Gordon, 12, 128, 137, 139
Creel, George, 161–163
Creel, Pvt. John, 28
Crittenden, Thomas, 163
Crockett, W. B., 176
Cruikshank, George M., 85
Crumpton, Dr. W. R., 211–212
Cullman County, 157, 161, 166
Cumming v. County Board of Education, 1899, 104

Dadeville, Alabama, 155, 161, 167
Dale, E. M., 88
Dallas County, 73, 213
Daphne, Alabama, 86
D-Day (World War II), 54
DeBardeleben, Henry, 2, 11
Decatur, Alabama, 16, 40, 83
Decker, Maj. Stiles M., 57
Demopolis, Alabama, 83
Dent, Stanley, Jr., 42, 50, 55, 57, 63
DeWinter, Pvt. Ellis, 28
Dexter Avenue Baptist Church, 72–73
Disfranchisement. *See* African Americans: disfranchisement of
Division of Negro Economics, 86, 116, 118–119
Dixie Park (Mobile), 121, 132
Dock and harbor improvements, 123–124, 126–127
Dog River, 28
Doster, Mrs. Birdie, 173–174
Doster, J. J., 7
Douglass, J. Mason, 214–216
Dowell, Spright, 165, 211
Dryer, Captain, 88–89
DuBois, W. E. B., 71, 87, 95, 97
Duggar, J. F., 153
Dulin, Maj. Charles L., 51–52
Dunbar, Paul Lawrence, 74

Eason, James H., 69–70, 75–76
East St. Louis, Ilinois, race riot, 93

Education, 17, 68, 78, 79, 87, 97, 112, 119, 186, 188, 194, 196; chronic underfunding of, 4–5, 105–107, 195–196; increased funding under Governor Kilby, 198, 199
Egypt, in liberation theology, 70
Eisenhower, Capt. Dwight D., 61
Emancipation Day, 75–76
Emergency Fleet Corporation (EFC), 127–128, 137–138
Escambia County, 213
Ethiopianism, 70
Europe, James R., 94, 135–136
Exchange Hotel (Montgomery), 173

F. T. Ley Company, 129, 139
Fairfax, Alabama, 167
Farmers National Bank of Opelika, 156
Farnsworth, Maj. Gen. Charles S., 59
Feagan, Judge N. B., 17
Federal Council of Churches, 71
Federal Trade Commission, 177–178
Fields, James, 105
Fifteenth New York Infantry, 94, 135
First African Baptist Church (Tuscaloosa), 74
First National Bank of Dothan, 156
First National Bank of Tuscaloosa, 156
Fischesser, J. C., 178
Fisher, Charles L., 71, 78
Fisk University, 106, 116
Fitzgerald, F. Scott, 61, 63, 182
Fitzpatrick, C. T., 160
Flomaton, Alabama, 29
Florence, Alabama, 101, 103, 105–106, 113, 115
Florence Times, 104–105, 107, 111–112, 212
Food and Fuel Control Act, 1917, 170
Food conservation, 72–73, 89, 95, 163
Fore and Aft, 133
Fort McClellan, 65
Forty-second Infantry Division "Rainbow," 38, 213. *See also* 167th Infantry Regiment
Foster, Richard C., 174
Four Minute Men, 73, 158, 163–164, 168; choral division, 164; "Colored" division, 164; junior division, 164; women's division, 164
Franklin County, 214–216, 218
Frisco Railroad, 30, 31

Gabriel, L. A., 114
Gadsden, Alabama, 10, 26, 32, 40, 160
Gardner, Henrietta, 174
Garrow's Bend (Mobile River), 124–125
Garth, Col. W. F., 84
Georgia Tech, 56
German Relief Society (Mobile), 132
Gilbert, William, 68
Glanton, G. L., 73
Goodgame, John, 73, 76, 79
Gormley, Fred H., 162, 211–212
Government's role in society, 186, 190, 192, 194, 197, 199
Graves, Bibb, 219
Gray, C. G., 106
Gray, Sallie, 106
Great Migration, 20, 84–85, 86–87, 91, 97, 101, 107, 108, 117
Greene, Frances Nimmo, 174
Griffith, D. W., 81
Grove Hill, Alabama, 214
Gulf of Mexico, 124, 140

Hale County, 73
Hall, R. N., 76
Hall-Scott biplane trainer, 58–59
Hamell, James, 105
Handy, Josephine, 106
Harney, Mrs. A. W., 164
Hart, Dr. Hastings H., 17, 191–194, 196–198, 209
Hartwell, Harry, 126
Hatch Act, 1887, 7
Hatcher, E. L., 88
Hatcher, James, 105
Haynes, George E., 86, 116, 119
Head, Mrs. R. L., 176
Henderson, Charles M., 83–84, 88, 118, 131, 177; and Alabama Council of Defense, 153–159; conservative policies, 191, 196;

fear of African American troops, 96; reaction to Hart report, 196; and Selective Service, 91–92; and war memorial, 210
Henderson, William E., 153
Henderson Shipbuilding Company, 138–139
Henry County, 166
Hill, Amelia, 45
Hill, Lister, 64
Hines, Walter, 2
History of Alabama and Dictionary of Alabama Biography, 217
Hobbie, Richard M., 153, 175
Hoffman, Maj. E. L., 58–59
Hollinsworth, Will, 105
Home demonstration agents, 172–177
Hookworm, 22, 35, 187, 189
Hooper, Lloyd M., 153, 157
Hoover, Herbert, 153, 170–171, 173
Houghton, Mary, 174
House Committee on Expenditures in the War Department, 112, 114, 118
Housing, 107, 108, 110, 128; shortage, 51, 111, 117, 136, 140; surplus, 124
Houston County, 156
Howard University, 72
Hubbard, Gen. G. J., 24, 155
Hudson, R. F., 175
Hundley, Mrs. Bossie, 163
Hunt, W. H., 87
Huntsville, Alabama, 84
Hurley, Edward N., 127, 137
Hurricane, 1916, 124–125

Illiteracy Campaign, 165–166, 181
Illiteracy rates, 5, 17
Industrialism, 8–12, 13
Industrial Workers of the World, 52
Interdenominational Alliance, 76
Ionian Club (Montgomery), 171

J. G. White Engineering Company, 107, 114, 116
J. O. Chisholm and Company, 51
Jackson Freewill Baptist Church (Florence), 106
Jacksonville, Alabama, 51, 53, 62
James Alexander Construction Company, 56
Jasper, Alabama, 30
Jeffers Brothers Company (Montgomery), 46
Jefferson County, 75, 85, 165–166, 200, 207–208
Jefferson County Medical Society, 212
Jemison, David V., 69–71, 73, 76, 78–79
John F. Slater School (Florence), 106
Johnson, C. First, 70, 89, 132
Johnston, Elizabeth, 17
Johnston, Joseph, 17
Jones, Annie May Dimmick, 174, 179, 181
Jones, Pvt. Avner, 32
Jones, Laura, 45
Jones, Reese, 55
Jones, Thomas Goode, 11, 14, 175
Jordan, Capt. Mortimer H., 200
Judson College, 175

Kelly-Atkinson Corporation, 127, 129
Kennedy, Samuel P., 155
Kilby, Anne, 53
Kilby, Thomas E., 193, 197–198, 207, 210, 213–215; progressive agenda, 192, 196
Kirby, Rollin, 126
Kopp, Mrs. William A. J., 53
Ku Klux Klan, 76–77, 79, 115, 133

Labor agents, 84, 87, 104
Labor Efficiency Rally (Mobile), 131
Lacoaker, Cadet George H., 58
Lanett, Alabama, 167
Lanett Cotton Mills, 167
Langdale, Alabama, 167
Lauderdale County, 103–104
Lauderdale County Farmers and Merchants' Cooperative Association, 103
Law, Ruth, 55
LeBarre and Edwin Company (Anniston), 64
Leppert, W. J., 166
Liberation theology, 69, 80

Liberty Buildings. *See* War memorial: building
Liberty Loan, 73–75, 80, 95, 130, 132, 160–161, 163, 164, 194
Liberty Loan Organization, 158
Limestone County, 157
Livingston, Alabama, 212
Louisville and Nashville Railroad, 28, 29, 175
Lusitania (ship), 69
Lynching. *See* African Americans: lynching
Lyons, Pat, 126, 130, 133

MacLeish, Archibald, 220
Macon County, 16, 93
Maddox, Col. F. M., 25, 28–29
Madison, Marshall, 133
Madison County, 165
Magazine Club (Montgomery), 171, 183
Malaria, 36, 187
Marengo County, 73, 83, 156
Marion, Alabama, 160
Martin, Pvt. John T., 32
Mathews, Henry J., 28, 33
Maxwell Air Force Base, 64–65
Mayesville School (Mobile), 134
McAdoo, William, 2, 130, 155, 160
McAlpine, William, 78
McCall, James E., 90–91, 100
McCord, Charles E., 216
McCormick, Dr. J. H., 188–189, 194
Medical care, military, 25, 35–36, 59, 63
Meertief, Emmanuel, 61
Memphis, Tennessee, 30, 33
Merritt, Henry P., 207
Mexico, 125
Military Intelligence Division, 82
Military police, 35, 53, 57
Miller, Benjamin M., 218
Miller, Kelley, 72
Mills, Cadet George O., 58
Mississippi, 90, 107, 108, 115, 117, 123, 131
Mississippi River, 30
Mobile, Alabama, 10, 21, 25, 26, 33, 36, 40, 50, 74, 75, 86, 87, 89, 92, 94, 153, 160; home of the First Infantry Regiment, 24–25, 27–29, 41; NAACP in, 79; streetcar boycott by African Americans, 67–68; and the war, 121–140
Mobile and Ohio Railroad, 28
Mobile Bay, 121, 124, 139
Mobile County, 84
Mobile Loyalty League, 131
Mobile Register, 85, 100, 122–123, 125–126, 128–135, 137
Mobile Relief Hall, 137
Mobile River, 126, 129, 138–139
Mobile Shipbuilding Company, 129, 137, 139
Moffat, John, 157
Mohr, Dr. Charles, 137
Mon Louis Island (Mobile Bay), 121
Monroe Park (Mobile), 29, 121, 125
Montevallo, Alabama, 175
Montgomery, Alabama, 9, 10, 16, 18, 19, 26, 30, 33, 37, 40, 50, 51, 52, 53, 55, 62, 88, 89, 119, 153, 155, 160, 162, 193, 211, 215; accommodates African American soldiers, 72; accommodates Camp Sheridan, 72; headquarters for Army Air Service bases, 63; mobilization camp in, 24, 27, 35–36, 41–42; NAACP in, 79; Red Cross in, 166–167; secures Camp Sheridan, 42–43; streetcar boycott by African Americans, 67–68; and Taylor Field, 55–56; vice in, 59–61; war memorial in, 202–203, 205, 219; war work in, 172–184
Montgomery Advertiser, 43–45, 47, 55, 57, 60, 82, 91, 154–155, 173–175, 177–180, 182, 202, 217, 219
Montgomery Children's Home, 182
Montgomery City Federation of Women's Clubs, 173, 181
Montgomery Cooperative Canning Club, 171–184
Montgomery County, 166
Montgomery Emancipator, 90, 96
Montgomery Times, 176, 179
Montgomery Traction and Light Company, 44

Moody, Frank S., 156, 203–204, 212
Moore, Albert Burton, 99
Moore, Charles, 206
Morton, Maj. Gen. Charles G., 53–54
Mothers' Army and Navy League, 130, 134, 137, 140
Mother's Circle of Montgomery, 171–173, 183
Moton, Robert R., 71, 74, 77, 83, 87–88, 92, 98; investigates troop disturbances, 95–97
Mt. Meigs, Alabama, 16
Mt. Olive Baptist Church (Anniston), 74
Mt. Pilgrim Missionary Baptist Association, 68, 87
Murnan Corporation, 127
Muscle Shoals, Alabama, 21
Muscle Shoals Project, 101–120

National Association for the Advancement of Colored People (NAACP), 21, 71, 79–80, 95, 98, 114–115, 118–119, 134
National Association of Colored Women, 16
National Baptist Publishing Board, 70
National Child Labor Committee, 188, 198
National Commission of Fine Arts, 206
National Committee on Memorial Buildings (NCMB), 204–205
National Council of Jewish Women (Montgomery), 171, 182
National Defense Act, 3, 103
National Defense Conference, 153
National Emergency Labor Program, 116
National Urban League, 116, 119
Neal, W. T., 213
Negro Betterment Association, 79
Nelson, Alice Dunbar, 74–75
New Hope Association, 68
New Orleans, Louisiana, 124, 133, 136
Ninety-second Infantry Division, 95–96
Ninety-third Infantry Division, 55
Ninth Infantry Division, 61, 63
Nitrates, 101, 103
Nixon, Herman C., 99
No-Name Club (Montgomery), 171, 183
Nunn, Billy, 178–179

Official U.S. Bulletin, 162
Old Ship Church (Montgomery), 88
O'Neal, Emmet, 14
Opelika, Alabama, 74
Our Southern Home, 212
Owen, Marie Bankhead, 8, 18, 23, 208; becomes director of ADAH, 1920, 217; and the War Memorial Building, 218–219
Owen, Thomas M., 23, 174, 203, 211, 212, 213, 216, 219; biography and war service, 207–210; death of, 203, 217; founded ADAH, 201; as State War Historian, 204
Owens, A. F., 74, 78
Owsley, Frank L., 99
Oxford, Alabama, 53

Panama Canal, 125
Parades and rallies, 73–74, 88–89, 124, 130–131, 136–137
Parrish, A. G., 154
Partlow Home for Children, 175
Patton, Jesse, 104
Pellagra, 22, 187, 189
Pell City, Alabama, 160
Perdido River, 26
Perry County, 73
Pershing, Gen. John, 55, 96, 136, 204
Peters, Charles, 89
Peterson, James T., 89
Petrie, George, 99
Pettiford, William R., 78
Phillips, J. W., 72
Piggly Wiggly, 180–181, 183
Pike County, 191
Pillans, Harry, 124, 126–127, 133
Pinedale, Alabama, 172
Pitts, Alexander D., 83
Pizitz, Louis, 154, 160
Plessy v. Ferguson, 1896, 104
Police, 78, 114, 115, 119
Pollard, Dr. R. T., 77–79

Porter, George, 153–154
Post, Louis, 117
Powell, Prof. M. R., 62
Prattville, Alabama, 26, 88
Prattville Commercial Club, 172–173
Prattville Sanitary Canning Company, 172
Progressivism, description of, 13–18, 185–186
Prohibition, 15, 36, 43, 66, 123, 186. *See also* Alcohol: sale of
Prostitution, 35–36, 59–61, 65, 134–135
Public health, 21, 75–76, 80, 112–113, 117, 153, 155, 186, 188–190, 192–194, 196
Public Service Reserve, 158

Quinn, Vera, 175–178, 182
Quisenberry, Ralph, 178, 180

Randolph, A. Phillip, 71
Recreation, 45–46, 49, 75, 80, 113, 117, 119
Red Cross, 21, 45, 53, 55, 75, 77, 130, 134, 137, 157, 158, 161, 162, 164–165, 168, 183, 214; county chapters, 166–167; Negro Auxiliary of Montgomery, 167
Red Scare, 77
Regular Army, 54, 61, 72
Renfroe, N. P., 154
Rich, Joseph C., 133
Richardson, R. H., 157
Riverview, Alabama, 167
Roberson, T. H., 218
Roberts, Pvt. Marion, 32
Robinson, Uriah J., 74
Rodgers, Julian P., 88
Root, Elihu, 206
Rose, Pink, 105
Rosensthil, Henry J., 213
Royal Canner Company, 176
Rush, J. O., 135
Rushton, Ray, 153
Russell Sage Foundation, 17, 191, 197, 209
Russellville, Alabama, 214
Ryerson, Donald, 163

Salvation Army, 214
Sammies, 134
San Diego Plan, 82
Sanitation, 35, 37, 43, 45, 48, 53, 107, 113, 117, 155, 194–195
Sayre, Zelda, 61, 63, 182
Schumann, Maj. Carl J., 48
Scott, Emmett J., 95, 98, 160; counsels African American troops, 96–97; investigates troop disturbances, 93–94
Scott, H. C., 72
Screws, Col. William P., 39–40
Seale, Alabama, 155
Seals, Maj. Carl H., 30–31
Segregation, 10, 43, 66, 67–68, 77, 79, 81, 93, 97, 103, 104–106, 119, 121, 123, 132, 140, 163, 164; in health care, 113; in housing, 110–111, 112; in the military, 49, 54–55, 62, 97–98, 135–136
Selective Service Act, 1917, 54, 91, 135
Selectmen, 54, 91, 93, 94, 130, 132–133, 165, 187
Selma, Alabama, 16, 73–75, 153–154
Selma Fire and Marine Insurance Company, 154
Selma Gas Light Company, 154
Selma University (Alabama Baptist Normal and Theological School), 67–68, 71, 74, 77–78
Sesame Club (Montgomery), 171, 183
Sharecroppers and sharecropping, 8, 68, 103, 104
Shaw, W. H., 214
Shawmut, Alabama, 167
Sheehan, Capt. William T., 60, 155
Sheffield, Alabama, 101, 103
Shiloh Baptist Church (Birmingham), 75
Shipbuilding, 123–124, 126–128, 138
Shipyards, 131, 136–139
Shoals City, Alabama, 111
Simms, Harry, 172
Sipsey, Alabama, 89
Sipsey Resolutions, 89–90
Sixteenth Street Baptist Church (Birmingham), 73, 78
Sixth Infantry Division, 63
Smallpox, 187, 189
Smith, Pvt. Ferrall, 62
Smith, J. Q., 207

Smith, Tom, 154, 156
Smith, Brig. Gen. W. R., 59
Smith-Hughes Act, 1917, 7
Smith-Lever Act, 1914, 7
Smith-Lever Act, 1917, 172
Social Problems of Alabama, 191, 194–197
Society of American Archivists, 201
Southern Commercial Congress, 125
Southern Syrup Company, 178
Spanish influenza, 45, 62, 65, 98, 112, 134–136
St. Anthony Church, 74
St. Clair County, 156, 166
Stallings, W. S., 210, 214
State Street Zion Church (Mobile), 125, 132
Steiner, Brig. Gen. Robert Eugene, 26, 33–34, 36–37, 42
Stevens, Daniel, 133
Strassburger, Capt. Julien M., 62
Streetcars and trolleys, 34, 44, 52, 76–77, 107, 121, 125, 129, 131

Tabernacle Baptist Church (Selma), 73
Talladega National Bank, 156
Tallapoosa River, 31, 49
Taylor, Capt. Ralph L., 55
Taylor Field, 19, 55–56, 58, 61, 63–65, 182
Tennessee, 106, 108, 109, 110, 158
Tennessee Coal, Iron, and Railroad Company (TCI), 128
Tennessee River, 21, 101, 103
Tenth United States Cavalry, 88–89
Thirty-first Infantry Division "Dixie," 19, 38
Thirty-seventh Infantry Division "Buckeye," 43, 47–48, 59, 61–62, 182
Thomas, C. E., 213
Thompson, F. I., 122, 125–126, 138
Thorington, Jack, 60
Tilton, McClane, Jr., 156
Timber industry, 8, 9
Tintagil Club, 171, 181, 183
Tombigbee River, 27
Trade, 122, 124, 125
Training: flight, 56–57; military, 25, 37, 49, 50–51, 53–54, 56, 61, 93
Treat, Maj. Gen. Charles G., 47, 49, 59
Tri-Cities, 101, 102, 104–107, 110, 112–113, 115, 118–119
Trinity Baptist Church (Birmingham), 73
Troy, Alabama, 26, 153, 155, 160, 191
Troy Farmers and Merchants National Bank, 153
Troy Normal School, 174
Tuberculosis, 25, 187
Tulane, Victor Hugo, 72
Tunstall, Loraine Bedsole (Bush), 188, 190, 192, 198
Tuscaloosa, Alabama, 16, 32, 74, 175, 197, 203
Tuscaloosa County, 33
Tuscumbia, Alabama, 101, 103
Tuscumbia Dispatch, 105
Tuskegee, Alabama, 96, 102
Tuskegee Institute, 7, 16, 71, 77, 91, 94–95, 97, 117
Tuskegee Machine, 94–95
Twentieth Century Club (Montgomery), 171, 183
Twenty-fourth Infantry Regiment, 93
Twenty-ninth Infantry Division "Blue-Gray," 50, 53–54, 61–62
Twenty-third Street Baptist Church (Birmingham), 73
Tyler Realty Company (Florence), 110–111
Typhoid, 35, 52, 187, 189

U.S. Army Corps of Engineers, 140
U.S. Army Medical Corps, 134
U.S. Steel, 128–129, 139
Underwood, Oscar W., 103
United Daughters of the Confederacy, 164
United Mine Workers, 11, 90
United Mine Workers of Alabama, 11
United Service Organization (USO), 175
United States Department of Labor, 116, 119
United States Employment Service, 117
United States Food Administration, 2, 153, 170, 173, 183
United States Public Health Service, 53, 107, 188–190
United States Railroad Administration, 2
United States Shipping Board, 127, 138

United War Work, 161
University of Alabama, 7, 174–175, 188, 207

Vandiver Park (Montgomery), 41–42, 44, 47, 50, 58, 62, 64
Van Tassell, Howard P., 62
Veneral disease, 25, 36, 45, 59–60
Vote, right to, 15, 66, 79, 87, 134, 140. *See also* African Americans: disfranchisement of; Women's suffrage
Vrendenburg Saw Mill Company, 32

Wade, James, 154
Walker County, 89
Wallace, Y. A., 106
War Camp Community Service (WCCS), 46, 53, 59–60, 204–205
War Gardeners, 178
War Kitchen, 179–180
War memorial, 140, 201–220; building, 205, 207, 211, 217; fund raising for, 213–216; hospital for veterans, 211–212; "living memorial," 204–205; Memorial Building Day, 211, 213; nature of, 206–207, 215, 219; to the "Unknown Soldier," 206
War Relics Train, 161
War Savings Committee, 158
War Stamps, 73, 75, 95, 130–132, 160
Warren, Knight, and Davis (architects), 203, 212
Warrior River, 32
Washington, Booker T., 16, 69, 70, 71, 75, 78, 79, 81–82, 83, 88, 93–94, 95, 97, 160
Washington, Margaret Murray, 16, 75
Waterman, John, 138
Waterman Steamship Company, 138
Watkins, W. F., 72, 88
Weadock, J. F., 59
Webb, John C., 83
Weil, Adele, 46, 174, 180, 183
Welch, Dr. Samuel W., 155, 189–190, 192, 194, 197
Welfare capitalism, 11–12
Wells, Oscar, 153
Western of Alabama Railway, 31
Westminster Abbey, 216
West Point Manufacturing Company, 167
Wetumpka, Alabama, 160
Whistler, Alabama, 28
White, G. N., 113
White, John, 32–33
Whiteside, Henry, 118, 120
Williams, A. C., 73, 76
Williams, John Sharp, 90
Williams, Dr. Roger, 132
Williamson, Lillie, 134
Williams v. Mississippi, 1898, 104
Wilson, J. A., 83
Wilson, Woodrow, 1, 2, 21, 68, 71, 81, 87, 89, 92, 95, 96, 100, 101, 122, 123, 125, 131, 138, 161–162, 170, 173
Wilson Dam, 21, 103, 108, 118
Windham, Cpl. C. C., 28
Women, 43, 52–53, 97, 106, 108, 131, 140, 168; French, raped by American troops, 95; as laborers, 128; and progressivism, 15–18; socializing with soldiers, 60–61, 62, 134–135; war work, 46–47, 55, 74–75, 80, 132, 134–135, 163–164, 165, 166–167, 171–184. *See also* individual names
Women's Clubs, 15–18, 171–172
Women's Committee of the Council of National Defense, 2, 74–75, 80, 134, 158, 163, 171, 183
Women's League for Service, 173, 182
Women's suffrage, 18, 134, 140
Workers and laborers, 48, 51–52, 84–85, 89–90, 103–104, 108–110, 113–114, 128–129, 131, 133, 137–138, 139, 173, 176, 179
Work-or-Fight Laws, 115–117, 119
Wright, Orville, 57
Wright Field (Montgomery), 57
Wynn, Cpl. Pearson, 62

York, Alabama, 82
Young, J. W., 112
Young Men's Christian Association (YMCA), 37, 45, 46, 49, 53, 56, 62, 113, 157, 162

Ziegler, Miss Leo, 177
Zimmermann telegram, 82, 125